COMPLETE EDITION GUITAR

FINGERSTYLE

Beginning • Intermediate • Mastering

LOU MANZI
NATHANIEL GUNOD
STEVE ECKELS

CONTENTS

Alfred Music
P.O. Box 10003
Van Nuys, CA 91410-0003
alfred.com

ISBN-10: 0-7390-7525-X (Book & CD)
ISBN-13: 978-0-7390-7525-8 (Book & CD)

Cover Photo: Karen Miller

FINGERSTYLE

LOU MANZI

Audio tracks recorded and engineered at High Heels Studios, Baltimore, MD
Performed by Nathaniel Gunod

ABOUT THE AUTHOR

Lou Manzi began his career in music in 1974. He has performed in various styles in the New York area and teaches at the National Guitar Summer Workshop. He is the author of *The Complete Acoustic Blues Method*, also published by Alfred and the National Guitar Workshop. Lou lives in Stonington, Connecticut where he teaches and helps administrate the National Music Workshop's lesson programs throughout New England.

ACKNOWLEDGMENTS

Thanks to: Barbara Smolover, Michael Allain and the people at Alfred Music for helping with this book; to David Smolover for the opportunities he has given me; and special thanks to Nat Gunod, my editor, for the chance to put this book into print.

DEDICATION

Beginning Fingerstyle Guitar is dedicated to Dorothy Chaplaski for the countless ways she has helped me over the years.

00

Track I

An MP3 CD is included with this book to make learning easier and more enjoyable. The symbol shown at bottom left appears next to every example in the book that features an MP3 track. Use the MP3s to ensure you're capturing the feel of the examples and interpreting the rhythms correctly. The track number below the symbol corresponds directly to the example you want to hear (example numbers are above the icon). All the track numbers are unique to each "book" within this volume, meaning every book has its own Track 1, Track 2, and so on. (For example, *Beginning Fingerstyle Guitar* starts with Track 1, as does *Intermediate Fingerstyle Guitar* and *Mastering Fingerstyle Guitar*.) Track 1 for each book will help you tune to the CD.

The disc is playable on any CD player equipped to play MP3 CDs. To access the MP3s on your computer, place the CD in your CD-ROM drive. In Windows, double-click on My Computer, then right-click on the CD icon labeled "MP3 Files" and select Explore to view the files and copy them to your hard drive. For Mac, double-click on the CD icon on your desktop labeled "MP3 Files" to view the files and copy them to your hard drive.

CONTENTS

INTRODUCTION

Welcome to *The Complete Fingerstyle Guitar Method,* a comprehensive series of books designed specifically for the aspiring fingerstyle guitarist. This method consists of three separate volumes now available in this complete edition. Each of the three volumes (*Beginning Fingerstyle Guitar, Intermediate Fingerstyle Guitar* and *Mastering Fingerstyle Guitar*) is an important step along the way to mastering fingerstyle guitar.

INTRODUCTION TO *BEGINNING FINGERSTYLE GUITAR*

I can trace it all back to one moment. Way back in the early '70s, I had borrowed an album from the local library. I had never heard of the artist, a guy named Ry Cooder, but the cover looked interesting so I checked it out. When I got home I was spinning this vinyl disc and enjoying the music very much.

But then something big happened. One of the tunes threw me for a loop. Ry was singing and playing *Police Dog Blues* as a soloist. One voice, one guitar and an unbelievable sound that affected me so strongly I can still feel the impact it made over 25 years later.

Here was a great player fingerpicking his version of a classic blues tune originally done by the important early blues/ragtime artist, Blind Blake. Now, I have to admit I knew nothing about Ry Cooder or Blind Blake. I eventually learned that the tune was played in open D tuning, but at the time I had no knowledge of alternate tunings for guitar other than the tunings I may have been coming up with while trying to get my guitar into standard tuning.

I was only a beginning player who was lucky to get from a G to a C chord without a pause. I was happy to strum my way through a few Bob Dylan or Woody Guthrie songs. As a novice flatpicker, I couldn't play fingerstyle if my life depended on it. But when I heard Ry picking away on *Police Dog Blues* I was as hooked as a fish on a line. I was going to have to become a fingerstyle guitar player.

It was the intricate sound of the independent bass lines blending with the simultaneous melodic riffs on the upper strings that captivated me. I found the fact that one person, playing one guitar, could do so much and make such a full and complete sound very intriguing. It was this inspiration that motivated me to become a fingerstyle guitar player.

Presumably, you've already been inspired to become a fingerstyle player. This book will help you reach your goal. In the *Beginning* section, we will cover the essentials of technique and take you through the first steps of playing in this exciting style.

I hope you will go through this section slowly and thoroughly, mastering all of the techniques, exercises and pieces that are included. You'll be introduced to some of the most common styles that are played in fingerstyle, such as folk, blues, contemporary acoustic and others. With devotion, perseverance and enough practice time, you'll be able to take your playing to whatever level you can imagine. And the better your playing gets the more fun you'll have with it. I hope you enjoy all the steps along the way.

CHAPTER 1

Getting Started

THE OPEN STRINGS

Holding your guitar in playing position, the strings are numbered from 6th to 1st with the 6th or lowest string being the one closest to the ceiling. Many beginning players don't know which end is up when it comes to the guitar. Since we are playing musical sounds, we refer to high and low depending upon the height and depth of our notes. The first string may be closest to the floor, but it is called the highest string because it is tuned to a higher *note* than the other strings. Music is made up of *notes*. A note is a musical sound, or *pitch*, of a specific degree of highness or lowness. Each note is given one of seven alphabetical names: A, B, C, D, E, F or G.

The following diagram shows that the strings are named E, A, D, G, B, E from 6th to 1st. The sentence "Ernie's Ant Does Get Big Eventually" may help you memorize these notes.

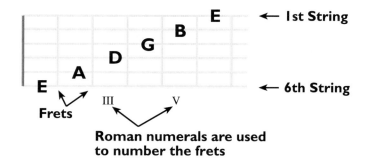

ROMAN NUMERALS

Here is a review of Roman numerals and their Arabic equivalents.

I.....i......1	IV..iv....4	VII.....vii..7	X........x....10	XIII.....xiii...13	XVI.....xvi.....16
II....ii.....2	V....v.....5	VIII....viii.8	XI......xi...11	XIV....xiv...14	XVII....xvii....17
III...iii....3	VI..vi....6	IX......ix...9	XII.....xii..12	XV.....xv.....15	XVIII...xviii...18

Guitars need to be tuned frequently. Tuning your guitar may be difficult or easy depending upon the level of your musical ear. You may have problems at first, but as you work with the guitar your ear will develop and it will become easier. There are many ways to tune. Here are two practical tuning methods to get you started.

RELATIVE TUNING

In this standard tuning method we match open strings to fretted notes on other strings. It is called *relative* tuning because we are tuning one string relative to another. Follow the steps below and listen very carefully to the pitches. This method should get your strings tuned properly. Even if you don't succeed the first time you'll improve with a little practice.

Step 1. Play the 6th String, 5th fret to sound A. Match the 5th string open to this A.

Step 2. Play the 5th String, 5th fret to sound D. Match the 4th string open to this D.

Step 3. Play the 4th String, 5th fret to sound G. Match the 3rd string open to this G.

Step 4. Play the 3rd string, 4th fret to sound B. Match the 2nd string open to this B.

Step 5. Play the 2nd string, 5th fret to sound E. Match the 1st string open to this E.

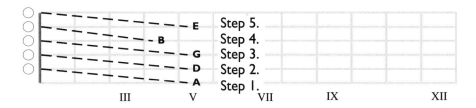

To get your strings truly in tune with this method, first you've got to be sure that your starting note (the 6th string) is in tune. You can match it to a piano, another guitar, tuning fork or a pitch pipe. Of course, you can also use an electronic tuner.

ELECTRONIC TUNERS

There are two main types of electronic tuners: the "guitar tuner," which will limit you to only tuning your six strings to standard tuning; and the "chromatic tuner," which will tune any string to any pitch. This will enable you to easily tune to any of the many alternate tunings that are popular for fingerstyle guitar.

Most professional guitarists use electronic tuners for speed and accuracy. When less experienced players use them, they can be sure they are tuned and can get their ears used to hearing the strings tuned correctly. Of course, you must not depend on the electronic tuner as your only method. Be sure to learn how to tune without it.

To help you get started, the CD has tuning notes on Track 1.

Track 1

FINGERBOARD BLACKOUT
AND HOW TO PREVENT IT

If you've already been playing for awhile, the chances are you probably suffer or have suffered with Fingerboard Blackout. Play any note on the neck at random. Can you name that note? If the answer is no, then you too suffer from Fingerboard Blackout. Of course, if you are just getting started, you can easily relate to this feeling. You should address this issue now, before it becomes a gap in your knowledge.

This strange syndrome of playing music and having no clue as to what notes we are hitting seems to mainly strike guitarists, leaving most other instrumentalists immune. Yes, the average pianist, woodwind player, brass player, etc. can name each note on their respective instruments. This does not make them better than us; after all we can play *Smoke on the Water* and *Stairway to Heaven*. But this gap in our knowledge will cost you gigs. What are you going to do when a club owner says, "Yeah, I liked your audition, but B♭ is my favorite note. Why don't you play a few while we sign these contracts for your extended booking?"

I confess that when I first started to play, I too had Fingerboard Blackout syndrome. But I can testify that when I learned the note names, my playing improved. I could see the relationships among the chords, scales and notes I was playing. You too can master the note names, but first you need to know the *chromatic* scale.

THE TWELVE HALF-STEP PROGRAM TO CHROMATIC ENLIGHTENMENT
Like most fretted instruments, the guitar is fretted in *half steps*, or *chromatically*. A half step is the distance from any fret to any adjacent fret. For instance, from the 1st fret to the 2nd fret is a distance of one half step. The term *chromatic* is derived from the word "chroma," which means color. A *scale* is a series of notes arranged in a specific pattern. The chromatic scale is the scale that contains all twelve notes we use in music: the seven *natural notes* (A, B, C, D, E, F and G) and the *accidentals*. Accidentals, often called chromatic tones, are either sharps ♯, which indicate that a natural note should be raised one half step (played one fret higher), or flats ♭, which indicate that a natural note should be lowered one half step (played one fret lower).

The top line of this diagram shows the natural notes. As you will see in the diagram at the top of page 10, they correspond to the white notes on the piano keyboard. Notice that there are gaps between some of these notes.

The gaps are filled by the accidentals. They can be called either sharp or flat depending upon the musical situation. When two notes have different names but sound the same, such as A♯ and B♭, they are called *enharmonic equivalents*.

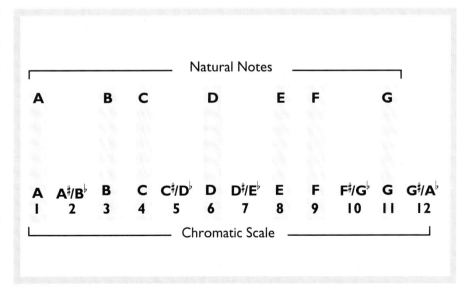

The accidentals correspond to the black notes on the piano keyboard. The bottom line in the diagram above contains the names of all twelve notes in our chromatic scale.

The *interval*, or musical distance, between each note and the next note in the chromatic scale is a half step. We call B-C and E-F natural half steps because there are no sharps or flats between them. Another interval you must know is the whole step, which is equal to two half steps (A-B, B-C#, etc.). Since a half step is the distance from any fret to any adjacent fret on the guitar, a whole step is equal to two frets.

It is easy to see the pattern of naturals and sharps and flats on the piano keyboard because of the white and black keys.

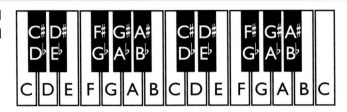

We do not have this visual advantage on the neck of the guitar, but the fingerboard is fretted in half steps and contains all twelve chromatic notes on each of our strings. The following fingerboard chart illustrates the names of the notes on the guitar, from the open strings to the 17th fret.

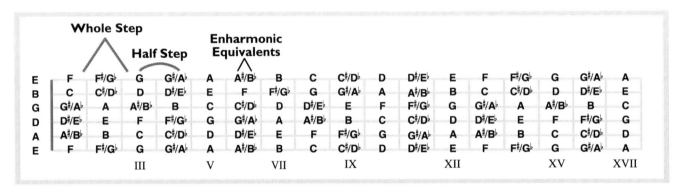

This chart shows us that although we have many more than twelve notes on the neck, the only note names we have are our twelve chromatic tones.

Because of the nature of stringed instruments, we have the same exact pitches in two, three or four locations. For example, the 1st string open E is also found on the 2nd string 5th fret, 3rd string 9th fret and 4th string 14th fret.

We also have the same note names in different *octaves*. An octave is the distance of twelve half steps, or the distance from any note to the next note with the same name. For instance, the distance from the E on the open 1st string to the E on the 12th fret of the 1st string is an octave. Octaves are higher and lower frequencies of the same note names Acoustically speaking, the note A, 1st string, 5th fret, vibrates 440 times per second. The A on the 3rd string second fret vibrates at 220 vibrations per second. We get different octaves whenever the frequencies of a note are doubled or halved.

The frequencies double and we get into higher octaves once we pass the twelfth note in the chromatic scale. If we start on A, this occurs when we hit the G#/A♭ pitch. Our next note is A an octave higher than our starting A. Then we would continue with A#/B♭, B, C, etc, as before. Our 12th fret notes are all one octave higher than our open strings and, of course, the scale continues up the neck from there until we run out of frets.

An influential fingerstyle and slide player for decades,
Ry Cooder *(b. 1947) also makes extensive use of*
alternate tunings.

MUSIC NOTATION

Learning to read music on guitar is easy if you apply yourself and have some patience. You may not be able to rip through the Bach lute suites right away, but you'll get the basics covered quickly and, if you stick with it, you'll eventually be reading through more difficult pieces.

PITCH
Pitch is the aspect of standard music notation that indicates the degree of highness or lowness of a musical tone.

Notes
Music is written by placing *notes* on a *staff*. Notes appear in various ways.

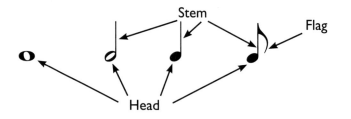

The Staff and Clef
The staff has five lines and four spaces which are read from left to right. At the beginning of the staff is a *clef*. The clef dictates what notes correspond to a particular line or space on the staff. Guitar music is written in *treble clef* 𝄞 which is sometimes called the *G clef*. The ending curl of the clef circles the G line on the staff.

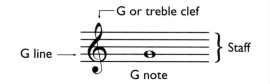

Here are the notes on the staff using the G clef.

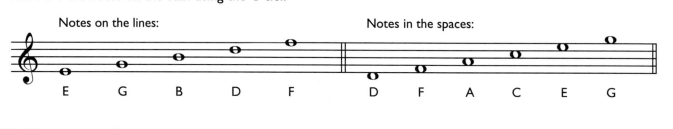

Ledger Lines
The higher a note appears on the staff, the higher it sounds. When a note is too high or too low to be written on the staff, *ledger lines* are used.

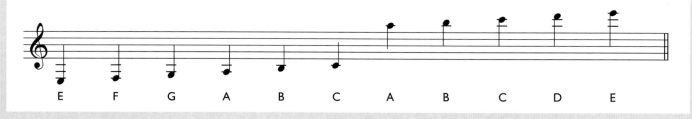

Guitar music is traditionally written one octave higher than it actually sounds. This allows us to write and read music on one clef, instead of using two clefs as with keyboard instruments.

TIME

Musical time is measured in *beats*. Beats are the steady pulse of the music on which we build *rhythms*. Rhythm is a pattern of long and short sounds and silences and is represented by *note* and *rest values*. Value indicates duration.

Measures and Bar Lines

The staff is divided by vertical lines called *bar lines*. The space between two bar lines is a *measure* or *bar*. Measures divide music into groups of beats. A *double bar* marks the end of a section or example.

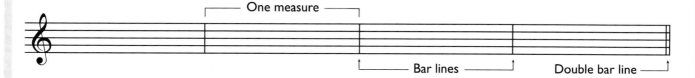

Note Values

The duration of a note—its value—is indicated by the note's appearance or shape.

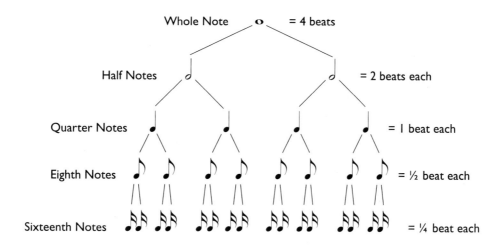

Whole Note		= 4 beats
Half Notes		= 2 beats each
Quarter Notes		= 1 beat each
Eighth Notes		= ½ beat each
Sixteenth Notes		= ¼ beat each

Time Signatures

A *time signature* appears at the beginning of a piece of music. The number on top indicates the number of beats per measure. The number on the bottom indicates the type of note that gets one beat.

$\frac{4}{4}$ = 4 beats per measure
Quarter note ♩ = one beat

$\frac{3}{4}$ = 3 beats per measure
Quarter note ♩ = one beat

$\frac{6}{8}$ = 6 beats per measure
Eighth note ♪ = one beat

Sometimes a **C** is used in place of $\frac{4}{4}$.
This is called *common time*.

Rest Values

Every note value has a corresponding *rest* value. A rest indicates silence in music. A *whole rest* indicates four beats of silence, a *half rest* is two beats of silence, etc.

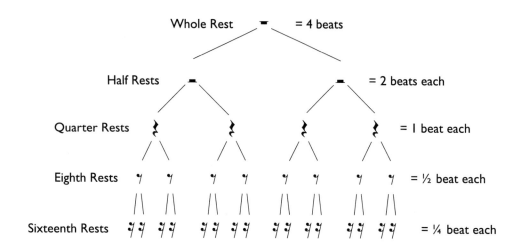

Ties and Counting

A *tie* is a curved line that joins two or more notes of the same pitch that last the duration of the combined note values. For example, when a half note (two beats) is tied to a quarter note (one beat), the combined notes are held for three beats (2 + 1 = 3).

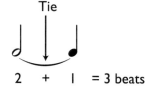

Notice the numbers under the staff in the examples below. These indicate how to count while playing. Both of these examples are in $\frac{4}{4}$ time, so we count four beats in each measure. *Eighth-note* rhythms are counted "1–&, 2–&, 3–&," etc. The numbers are the *onbeats* and the "&"s (pronounced "and") are the *offbeats*.

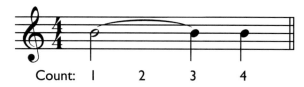

Dots

A *dot* increases the length of a note or rest by one half of its original value. For instance, a half note lasts for two beats. Half of its value is one beat (a quarter note). So a *dotted half note* equals three beats (2 + 1 = 3), which is the same as a half note tied to a quarter note. The same logic applies for all dotted notes.

Dotted notes are especially important when the time signature is $\frac{3}{4}$, because the longest note value that will fit in a measure is a dotted half note. Also, dotted notes are very important in $\frac{6}{8}$ time, because not only is a dotted half note the longest possible note value, but a dotted quarter note is exactly half of a measure (counted: 1–&–ah, 2–&–ah).

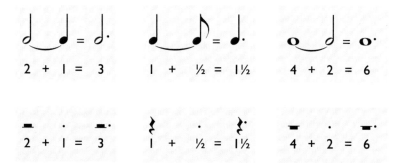

Triplets

A *triplet* is a group of three notes that divides a beat (or beats) into three equal parts.

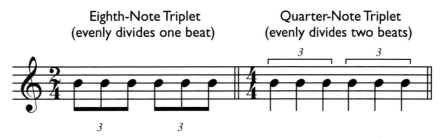

Beaming

Notes that are less than one beat in duration are often *beamed* together. Sometimes they are grouped in twos and sometimes they are grouped in fours.

Swing Eighths

In the blues and jazz styles, eighth notes are usually not played exactly as notated. Rather, they are interpreted in a "swing" style. This makes a pair of eighth notes sound like the first and last notes of a triplet. Swing eighths:

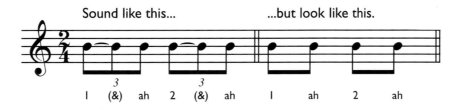

Repeat Signs

Repeat signs are used to indicate music that should be repeated.

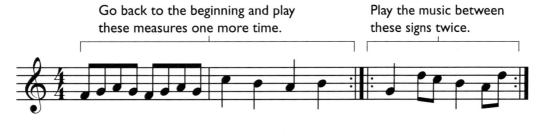

This sign 𝄍 tells us to repeat the previous measure.

Playing by the Numbers, or Understanding Tablature

Tablature is an alternative method of notation used for guitar and other fretted instruments. Forms of it have been in use since before the Renaissance period. When reading tablature we read fret numbers which tell us exactly where to place our fingers on the neck. Tablature, when combined with standard notation, provides the most complete system for communicating the many possibilities in guitar playing.

In this TAB system, as in most, **rhythm** is not notated. For that, you will have to refer to the standard notation. Six lines are used to indicate the six strings of the guitar. The **top line** is the high E string (the string closest to the floor) and the **bottom line** is the low E string. **Numbers** are placed on the strings to indicate **frets**. If there is a "0," play that string open.

Fingerings are sometimes included in TAB. You will find them just under the bottom line. A "1" indicates your left index finger. A "4" indicates your left pinkie.

In the following example, the first note is played with the first finger on the first fret. The next note is played with the second finger on the second fret, the third finger plays the third fret, and the fourth finger plays the fourth fret.

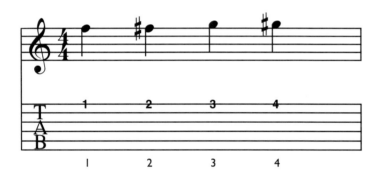

A **tie** in the music is indicated in TAB by placing the tied note in parentheses.

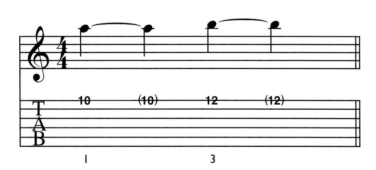

Fingerstyle Notation

The standard rule in notation is that notes on the middle line of the staff or higher have their stems descending, and lower notes have their stems ascending. This won't work in lots of fingerstyle music, since it often involves playing more than one line at a time. In order to clearly separate the bass line when there is more than one line, we must borrow from classical guitar notation: we use descending stems for all notes played by the thumb, and ascending stems for all other pitches. This is an easy way to show two or more simultaneous melodic lines.

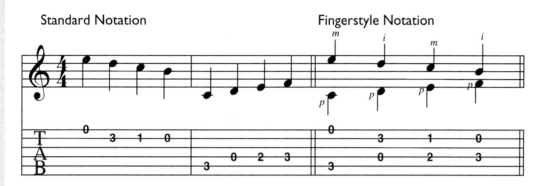

Scale Diagrams

The top line of a scale diagram represents the 1st (highest) string of the guitar, and the bottom line the 6th. The vertical lines represent frets, which are numbered with Roman numerals.

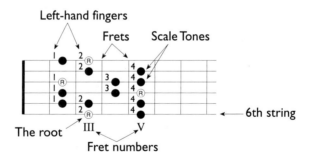

Chord Diagrams

Chord diagrams are similar to scale diagrams, except they are oriented vertically instead of horizontally. Vertical lines represent strings, and horizontal lines represent frets. Roman numerals are used to number the frets.

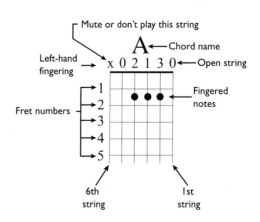

CHAPTER 2

Technique

This book was written primarily for the beginning, or less experienced fingerstyle player. If this describes you, don't skip over the material in this first chapter. You may be very tempted to jump ahead to the musical selections and patterns that are in the following chapters, but it's best to resist this temptation. Even if you have been playing for a while, it would be a good idea to check over this material as a review.

The ideas in this chapter are important because they will help you develop good habits and correct playing techniques. Playing with the proper technique will enable you to take your playing to more advanced levels without having to correct bad habits. To express yourself through a good control of dynamics and tone you'll need to have a firm foundation in the basic mechanics of how to play your instrument. This book, and this chapter, will help you build that foundation. Have fun!

PLAYING POSITION

Many people start playing without giving much thought to how to hold their instrument. For example, many people sit with the guitar resting on the right leg with the neck horizontal to the floor. This forces a severe bend in the left wrist and a bad angle for the right hand.

Since I've seen many players suffering from guitar-related stress injuries, I advise you to try the following positions which are more "user friendly." It is important to play in a manner that is comfortable and offers easy access to the guitar. Move the guitar until it fits you, don't stretch awkwardly to try and reach the guitar.

SITTING
The position I recommend is the standard for classical guitarists, and is used by lots of fingerstyle players, too (see the drawing on page 19). It provides good access to the instrument for both hands. Although many non-classical players would not think of sitting with the neck of the guitar elevated, as classical players do, it is interesting to notice that when the same players stand with straps attached to their guitars, they tend to end up in that position.

Elevating the neck of the guitar is particularly helpful for the left hand. This provides much easier access to the entire fingerboard. Also, both the left and right should be in comfortable and stress-free angles for playing. Sitting this way will help you do this, too.

Here are some helpful guides to find this position:

1. Rest the left foot on some kind of footstool. You can buy an adjustable guitar footstool at most music stores. Don't raise the left foot too high. The idea is to have the guitar resting on your chest about one hand's width from the base of your neck. The left thigh provides good support for the guitar, and the right thigh and chest provide stability.
2. Angle the guitar at a 45 degree angle.
3. The right forearm rests lightly on the outer rim of the body, just to the right of the bridge, and helps to keep the guitar stable.
4. The left hand should not support the neck.

Sitting in this fashion, your right and left hands will be in optimum positions, with the left thumb centered on the neck and the left wrist straight. The knuckles and most of the left hand should be in front of the fingerboard. The right hand will be slightly bent but not severely.

STANDING

Perhaps the best way to play is standing with a strap. In this position you can easily angle the neck up, giving your left hand good access to the fingerboard. It also allows a good position for the right hand. You can have the instrument in a "classical" style position while still keeping both feet on the floor. Many musicians feel that standing while performing gives them added stage presence. This is an added benefit of this way of playing.

No matter what position you play in, keep in mind the following guidelines:

1. Avoid any severe angles for the right or left wrists.
2. Your playing position should allow you to be relaxed yet still able to hold the guitar securely.
3. Both hands should have easy access to the guitar in a comfortable, stress free and natural manner.
4. You should move the instrument to fit your position, and not stretch awkwardly to reach the guitar.
5. If your playing position looks pleasing to your audience, they will feel that you are in control of your performance. If you look like you are struggling to play—you probably are.

THE LEFT HAND

The fingerings for the left hand are 1, 2, 3 and 4 for the index finger through the ring finger.

The thumb should rest in the center of the neck in a relaxed manner. It should be curved outward slightly in a natural way, and the first joint should never be bent towards the first finger.

The left hand fingers should be slightly curved. They should meet the fingerboard on their tips at a slight angle that is almost perpendicular to the fingerboard.

Do not over press! You don't need much pressure to fret the strings. Press firmly, but remember, the neck is not a baseball bat! Keep it light and minimize tension in the hand or arm.

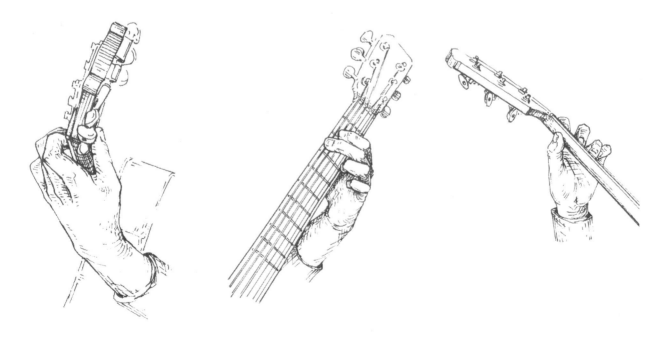

It is essential that you adopt a comfortable yet effective right-hand technique. This hand is largely responsible for the tone and dynamic variation you will achieve. Having a good technique will give you a strong sound and help you avoid stress-related muscle problems in the future.

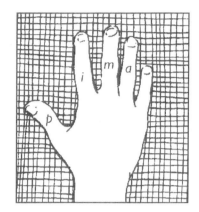

In labeling right-hand fingerings I have borrowed from the classical guitar tradition of using the Spanish terms: *p* for pulgar (thumb), *i* for indice (index), *m* for medio (middle) and *a* for anular (ring).

Stay relaxed and don't tense up your fingers, wrist or arm. The strings are easy to sound and you don't need much power from the right hand.

Keep your fingers and thumb in a naturally curved position. Pretend you are loosely holding a ball that is roughly two inches in diameter.

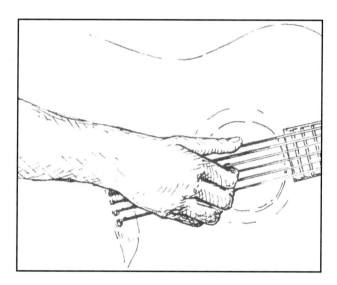

Your right hand should be comfortably aligned with your arm. The fingers will now strike the strings at about a 45 degree angle, and should make contact with the strings where the left side of the nail meets the flesh. A combination of nail and flesh will provide a big, clearly articulated sound.

When sounding the strings, the fingers are drawn firmly in without actually touching the palm. This is called follow-through. They strike the string, move smoothly upward toward the right hand palm, clearing the other strings, and quickly return to playing position. The fingers should move with minimal palm or hand movement.

In making your stroke, it is best if there is movement in all three finger joints. Your volume will depend on the amount of follow-through you use.

The thumb should remain loose and strike the string downward, towards the floor, with a slight movement in both joints. The point of contact should be the left side of the thumb near the nail. It should strike and quickly return to playing position.

Don't bring the thumb deep into the palm; its follow-through should bring it towards the *i* finger.

*Throughout his long and distinguished career, **James Taylor** (b. 1948) has used his refined fingerstyle technique to support his songs. It was his work in the 1960s, along with several other pivotal singer/songwriter/guitarists, that sparked a whole generation's interest in fingerstyle guitar as an accompanimental instrument.*

CHAPTER 3

Basic Fingerstyle Patterns

Fingerstyle (or finger-picking) patterns are based on *chords*. A chord is any group of three or more notes (usually harmonious) played together. In fingerstyle guitar, we often play chords as *arpeggios*. In an arpeggio, the notes of a chord are played individually, rather than together. In this chapter you will be introduced to some basic right hand fingerstyle patterns. Although these easy arpeggios are often used for song accompaniments, creative composers also use them as the basis for their original instrumental pieces.

Practice these examples slowly at first. When you feel comfortable with them, you should increase speed gradually. Be sure to keep the *tempo* (speed) steady and make the notes ring out evenly. Your right-hand fingers should strike the strings firmly, with an even volume on every note. Hold each left-hand finger down as long as you can to allow the notes to sustain.

Notice the use of fingerstyle notation in these examples. The bass notes, played by the thumb of the right hand (*p*), are stemmed down, and the other notes are stemmed up. This makes it easier to find the bass line, and makes its independent identity as a separate part clear. Notice how many of the bass notes have two stems: one going up and one going down. This shows the bass line as distinct from the other notes, but also shows how it fits into the overall rhythm, usually as the first in a group of eighth notes.

PATTERN #1

This is our easiest and simplest arpeggio. When playing this *p-i-m-a* arpeggio, drop *i*, *m* and *a* back out toward the strings as *p* plays. Then let the fingers follow one another into your palm as they play, re-extending *p* for the next stroke.

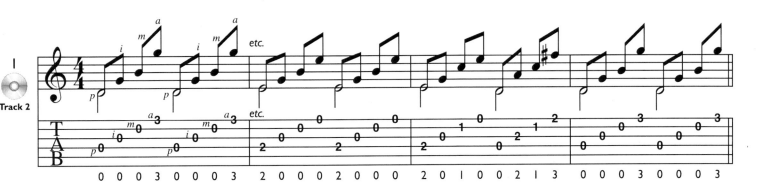

Example 2, in the style of Jimmy Page, will give you more practice with this pattern.

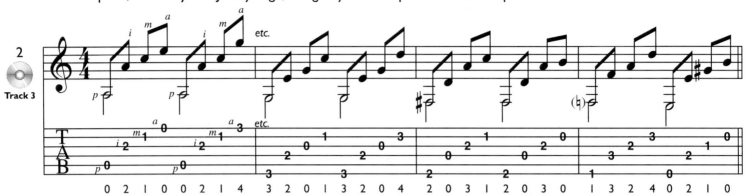

PATTERN #2

Pattern #2 is similar in concept to Pattern #1, but the order of the 1st, 2nd and 3rd strings have been reversed. When playing this *p-a-m-i* arpeggio, drop *a*, *m* and *i* back out toward the strings as *p* plays. Then let the fingers follow one another into your palm as they play, re-extending *p* for the next stroke.

Notice that Example 3 uses exactly the same notes as Example 1. All you have to do is apply the new fingerstyle pattern.

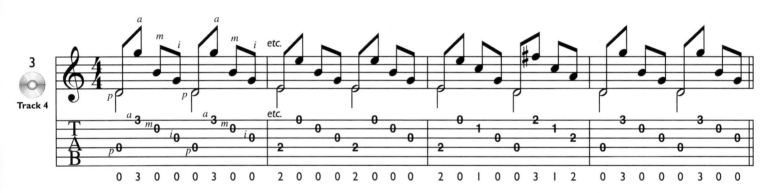

In Example 4, notice how the notes of the arpeggio on the treble strings (the upper three) remain constant as the *bass part*, on the lower strings, is moving.

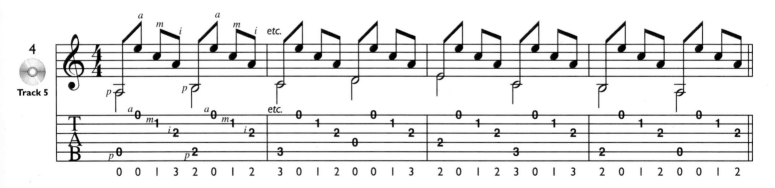

Pattern #3 alternates the two previous arpeggios to create a new one: *p-i-m-a-p-a-m-i*. Notice how Pattern #1 is followed by Pattern #2 in the same measure. Example 5 has the same notes as Examples 1 and 3. Just put the new pattern to use.

5

Track 6

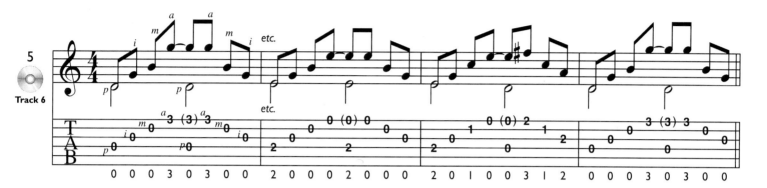

0 0 0 3 0 3 0 0   2 0 0 0 2 0 0 0   2 0 1 0 0 3 1 2   0 0 0 3 0 3 0 0

Example 6 will give you some additional practice with this pattern.

6

Track 7

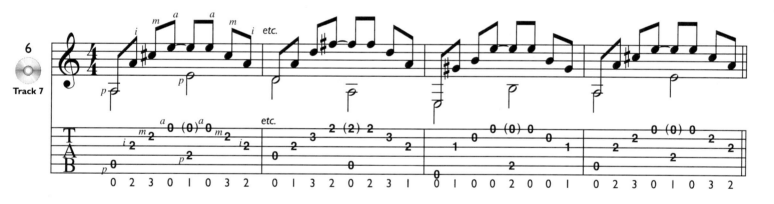

0 2 3 0 1 0 3 2   0 1 3 2 0 2 3 1   0 1 0 0 2 0 0 1   0 2 3 0 1 0 3 2

Pattern #4 combines Patterns #1 and #2 again to create another variation. This time we start with Pattern #2, and Pattern #1 follows.

Example 7 uses the, by now, familiar notes from Examples 1, 3 and 5.

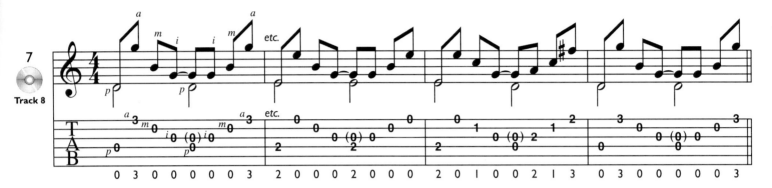

Here is another example using Pattern #4.

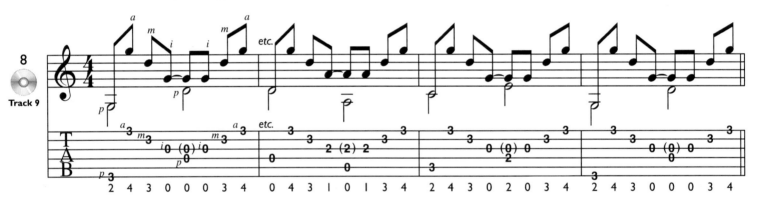

CHAPTER 4

Playing Two Lines

Before beginning this chapter, you should review the material on pages 21 and 22 concerning right-hand technique. As you go through this material, pay close attention to the position of your right hand and how the fingers are working.

OPEN POSITION EXERCISES

To be a good fingerstyle player, you will need to have good control with your right hand fingers. The following open string exercises will enable you to concentrate on getting a good sound without worrying about fretting notes on the strings. Listen to your sound and try to get the best *tone* possible. Tone refers to the quality of your sound. It should be strong (but not forced), warm (but not muddy) and clear.

In Example 9 you'll only be using the thumb (*p*) on the lower three strings.

9

Track 10

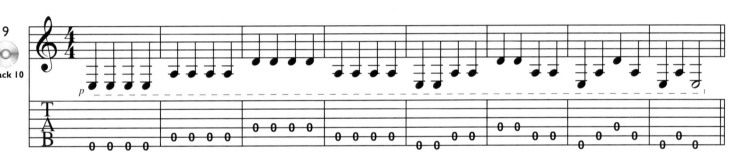

Example 10 is on the first three strings and requires you to alternate between your index (*i*) and middle (*m*) fingers. This is a common approach to playing melodies on the upper three strings.

10

Track 11

This exercises is played entirely on the open strings. It's a very basic *twelve-bar blues* in the key of A. No, it doesn't sound like Robert Johnson, but it's a start. You'll be playing lower and upper strings together. Be sure to observe the right hand fingerings. The *p* finger will play the 4th, 5th and 6th strings, and *i* and *m* will handle the 1st and 2nd strings.

OPEN STRING BLUES

Track 12

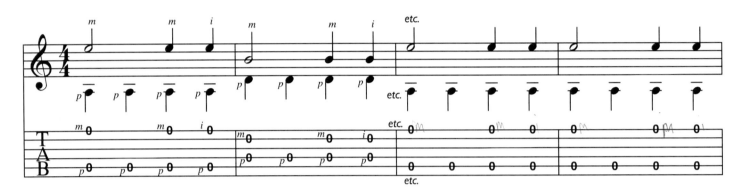

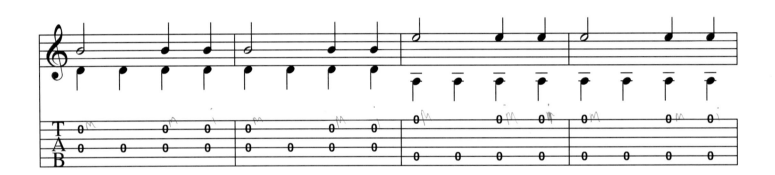

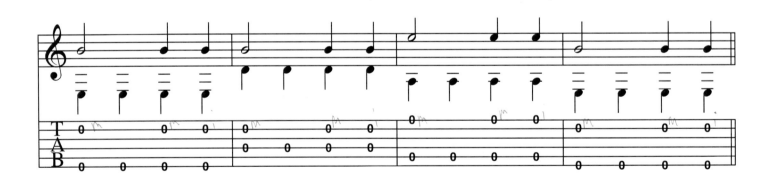

COMBINING OPEN AND FRETTED NOTES

The next two examples combine fretted notes on the lower strings, played by *p*, with the open upper strings. It's a good idea to look over these, and all of the following examples, before you try to play them. Name each note aloud and review the string and fret locations. Then practice each example until you can play it effortlessly.

MOVING BETWEEN THE LOWER STRINGS

MOVING ON THE 6TH STRING

In Example 14, *i* and *m* play the melody on the upper strings while *p* plays open bass notes on the lower strings.

MOVING ON THE UPPER STRINGS

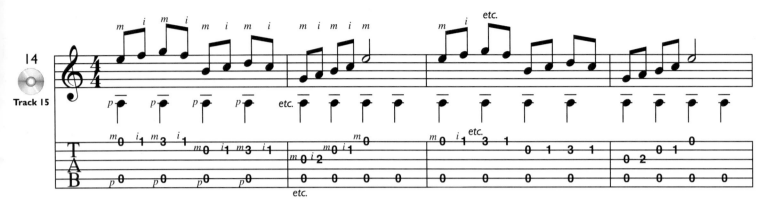

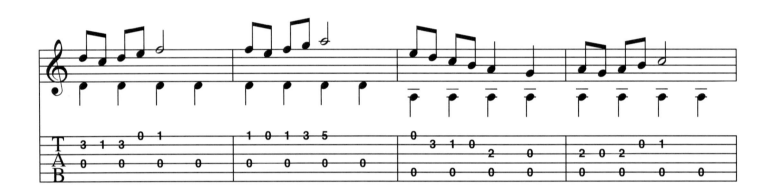

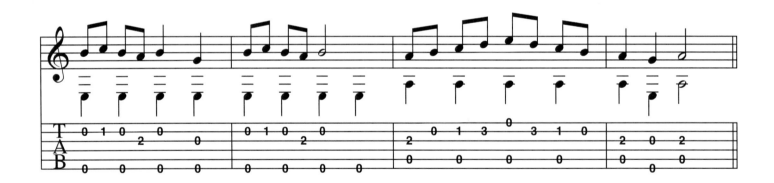

Examples 15 and 16 are the first with fretted notes on both upper and lower strings. Be sure to watch the fingerings for both hands and keep your tempo steady.

BOTH PARTS MOVING

Martin Simpson (b. 1953), one of the few fingerstyle players to be influential in more than one style, is known for both his blues and Celtic-inspired compositions.

Example 17 also has fretted notes on all the strings. It's a little more difficult because of the eight notes in the upper part. Start with a very slow *tempo* (speed), and increase it gradually as you gain confidence.

BOTH PARTS MOVING, ADDING EIGHTH NOTES

CHAPTER 5

Basic Theory

Maybe you've heard this old musicians joke:
"What's the difference between a trombone player and a chicken crossing the road?"
"The chicken is going to a gig!"
If it's got a gig, the chicken probably understands music theory.

Most professional players, be they human or poultry, have had a good grasp of theoretical knowledge.

Music is the organization of sounds in time. Music theory is the study of the relationships among these sounds. Each melody, chord, phrase, or any other musical element, can be analyzed, identified and understood if we know the rules of music theory. Learning theory is the fastest way to improve your composing, improvisation, note reading and music memorization.

THE MAJOR SCALE

The standard approach to theory is to use the major scale as a starting point for understanding all of our other scales and chords. This common scale can begin on any pitch and is made up of a series of whole and half steps. The *formula* of whole steps and half steps is:

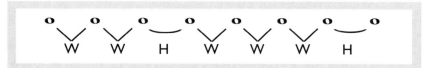

∨ and W = Whole step
⌣ and H = Half step

The phrase, "Wendy Witch Has Wild, Wonderful, Wavy Hair" will help you memorize the major scale pattern.

18

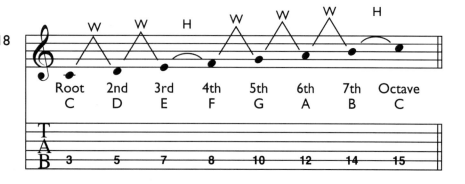

Root	2nd	3rd	4th	5th	6th	7th	Octave
C	D	E	F	G	A	B	C

If we build a major scale starting on C, our formula gives us the notes C, D, E, F, G, A, B and C. Playing this scale horizontally up the fifth string, starting with the C on the 3rd fret, enables us to clearly see the pattern of whole and half steps on the neck.

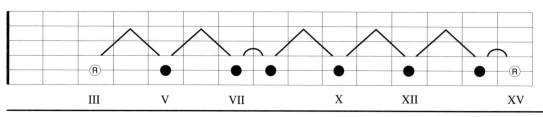

III   V   VII   X   XII   XV

We can also play the same notes in different locations by going vertically across the neck:

ROOT ON THE 5TH STRING

19

C Major Scale

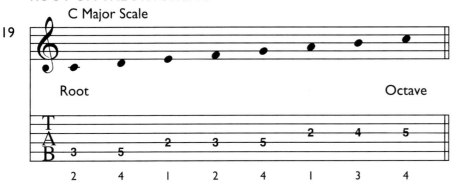

Root

Octave

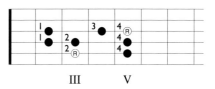

III   V

2 4 1 2 4 1 3 4

The C major scale is the only one without sharps or flats. If we start on any other *root*, or starting pitch, we will need sharps or flats to fill out the formula.

When our root is G we will need an F♯ to get our whole step between our 6th and 7th notes, since E-F is a natural half step.

ROOT ON THE 4TH STRING

20

G Major Scale

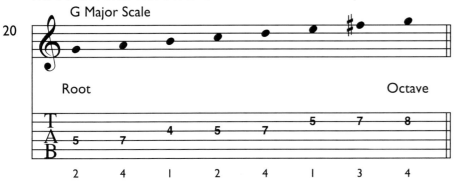

Root

Octave

V   VII

2 4 1 2 4 1 3 4

Starting on F will give us a B♭ for our 4th scale degree.

ROOT ON THE 4TH STRING

21

F Major Scale

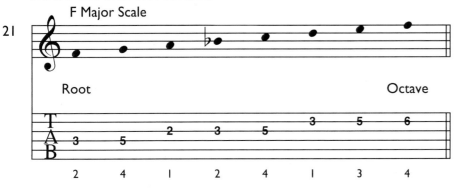

Root

Octave

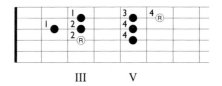

III   V

2 4 1 2 4 1 3 4

There is a musical rule that no letter names can be skipped when writing a scale. This rule helps us to name notes correctly. For example, in the F Major scale, we must name the 4th note B♭. You will recall that B♭ and A♯ are enharmonic equivalents (see page 9). Even though B♭ and A♯ sound alike, we can not go from A to A♯ in the F Major scale because we must move alphabetically, and the letter B must be represented. So, we must go from A to B♭.

A MINOR DIVERSION: THE NATURAL MINOR SCALE

There are many different types of minor scales. The most basic one is the natural minor. Its formula of whole and half steps is as follows:

> *Music's power to affect our feelings is deep and complex, and it is often said that major sounds are bright and happy, and that minor sounds are darker, sadder and moodier.*

The phrase, "When Harry Was Wet He Went Wild" will help you remember this formula. Like any scale, the natural minor can begin with any note. If we start with the note A our formula will give us all of the other natural notes.

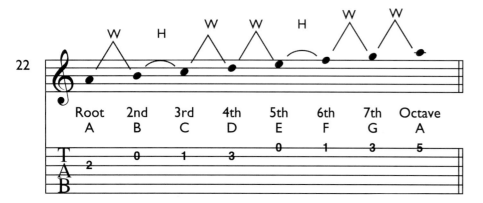

22

	Root	2nd	3rd	4th	5th	6th	7th	Octave
	A	B	C	D	E	F	G	A

MEETING THE RELATIVES: THE RELATIVE MINOR

Each major scale has a relative minor, and the root of this minor is always the 6th note, or *6th degree*, of the major scale. Notice that the C Major scale and A Minor scale have the same notes, but with different roots.

	R	2	3	4	5	6	7	8					
C Major C	D	E	F	G	A	B	C						
A Natural Minor ....A	B	C	D	E	F	G	A						
					R	2	3	4	5	6	7	8	

Notice the numbers in the relative minor diagram on page **36**. It is important to remember that the notes of a scale can be given *scale degree* numbers. We use these numbers to create numerical formulas for scales and chords. In this approach, we are looking at *parallel* relationships instead of relative. For instance, the scale formula for the natural minor scale is:

1   2   ♭3   4   5   ♭6   ♭7   8

This tells us that if we take a major scale from any root, and lower the 3rd, 6th and 7th degrees by a half step each, we will have created a natural minor scale from that root. For instance, the parallel natural minor scale to the C Major scale is C Natural Minor:

C   D   E♭   F   G   A♭   B♭   C

C Major Scale

C Natural Minor Scale

Here is a common fingering for the natural minor scale.

C NATURAL MINOR

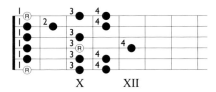

KEY SIGNATURES

Before we can properly notate a piece of music, we must be able to determine what major or minor scale it is based on. We need to list the sharps or flats that are characteristic to this scale right after the clef on every staff in our composition. This list is called the *key signature*. Remember, C Major and A Minor have no sharps or flats.

SHARP KEYS   **FLAT KEYS**

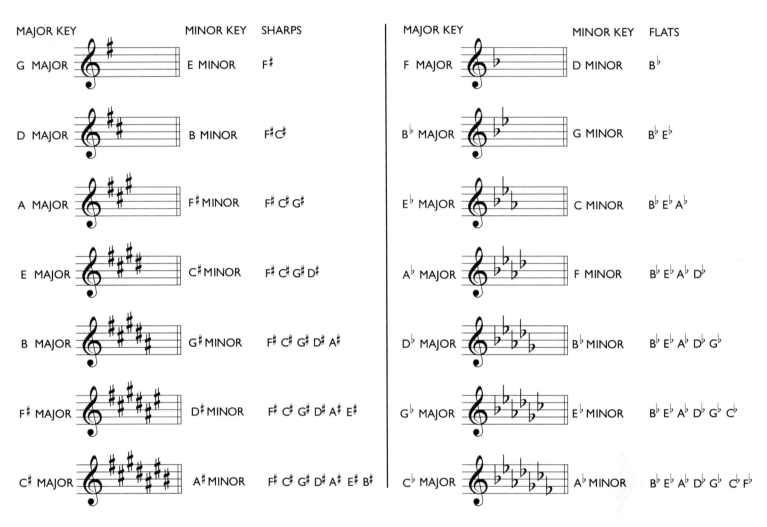

The key signature helps our note reading by letting us know what sharps or flats to expect. Even when playing by ear, or "faking it," knowing the key signature gives us clues as to the chords and notes used in the piece.

CHAPTER 6

Basic Chords

Do you want to know how to make a guitar teacher twitch? Just ask, "How many chords are there anyway?" This is a question that seems impossible to answer.

A chord can be based on any of our twelve chromatic scale notes. We can have major, minor, diminished, augmented, dominant 7th, major 7th, minor 7th, 9th chords, 13th chords, etc. And the fact that really gets us twitching is that each one of these chords can be played in various versions in multiple locations on the neck.

Learning chords and chord theory does not need to be overwhelming. Just go slowly and make sure you get the basics ingrained first. That is our goal for this section.

PHOTO BY DEBORAH FEINGOLD/COURTESY OF COLUMBIA RECORDS

Country fingerstylist Chet Atkins (1924–2001) is unsurpassed as an arranger for solo guitar and is respected by guitarists of all styles.

The concept of a chord is simple. Sit at a piano keyboard, select any three notes, play them together (they don't have to sound good together) and that's a chord. Try the same thing on guitar, play any three notes on three different strings, play them together and that's a chord. Get two friends, on the count of three you each sing random notes and that's a chord. So, a chord is a combination of any three (or more) tones.

Most chords are constructed by stacking notes that are an *interval of a 3rd* apart. For example, C to E is a 3rd (C_1 - D_2 - E_3), and E to G is a 3rd (E_1 - F_2 - G_3), so C - E - G is a three-note chord. We call these basic three-note chords *triads*. The most common types of triads are *major*, *minor* and *diminished* triads.

We can understand any chord or scale by knowing it's numerical formula—comparing it to the major scale with the same root as we did the parallel natural minor scale on page 37. Here are the formulas for the most common basic chords. We will use the C Major scale for all of our examples.

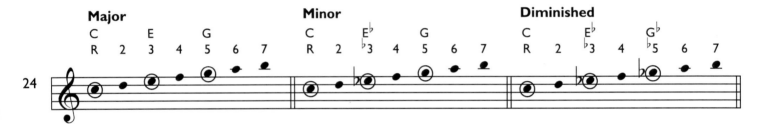

A major triad contains the root, 3rd and 5th degrees of the major scale. The C Major triad is: C-E-G.

The minor triad is 1-♭3-5. We must lower the 3rd, E, a half step to E♭. The C Minor triad is: C-E♭-G.

The diminished triad is 1-♭3-♭5. We must lower the 3rd, E, a half step to E♭, and the 5th, G, one half step to G♭. The C Diminished triad is: C-E♭-G♭.

DIATONIC HARMONY

Now that we've covered the formulas for the most basic chords we need to see how they are related within one major key. The word *diatonic* means "within the key." For each of the seven different notes in the major scale, we can build a corresponding triad. These are the diatonic triads for that key. There will be a particular pattern of major and minor triads, with a diminished chord at the end, that is the same in any major key. The following are the diatonic chords in the key of C Major:

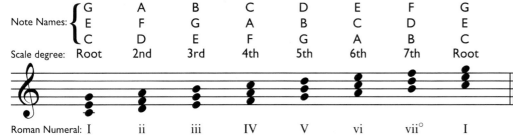

The preferred way to refer to chords is with a number that represents their diatonic position in the key. We use Roman numerals to write these numbers, upper case for major chords (I, IV and V), and lower case for minor (ii, iii and vi). For the diminished chord that occurs on the 7th degree, we add a small circle (○) to a lower-case Roman numeral (vii○). For a quick review of Roman numerals, see page 7.

Here is a summary of the diatonic chords for any major key:

> **I, IV and V**.....**are always**.....**major**
> **ii, iii and vi**.....**are always**.....**minor**
> **vii○**...................**is always**........**diminished**

THE DOMINANT 7TH CHORD

Frequently, the V chord has another tone added a *minor 3rd* (a distance of three half steps) above the 5th, which is a ♭7 above the root (1 - 3 - 5 - ♭7). This is called a *dominant 7th* chord (V7). The example on the right shows the V7 chord in the key of E, which is B7.

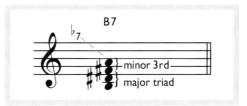

Don't worry about the thousands of chord possibilities on the neck, they will only keep you awake at night. That's why some guitarists look so tired. Let's face it, even Elvis probably couldn't play fourteen different versions of B♭7♭5♯9, but he did OK with the chords he did know.

You'll do fine with chords if you learn these basic ones first. Don't move on until they are mastered. Strum across the correct strings with your right hand thumb, or the backs of your fingernails. It is a good idea to review the section on page 17 about reading chord diagrams before continuing.

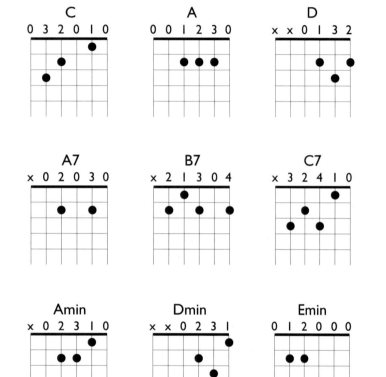

*This sign ⌒ indicates a barre. A barre is when one finger (usually the 1st finger) plays more than one string. For this F Major chord, lay the left side of your first finger down across the 1st and 2nd strings, directly next to the fret. Be patient, it takes time for this chord to become comfortable.

Tips for learning these chords:
- Learn to place your fingers down all at once. Be patient. Move slowly.
- Press your fingertips in as close to the correct frets as possible.
- Avoid touching other strings. Curving your first joints (the ones nearest your fingernails) will help.
- Keep your left-hand fingernails very short.
- Don't press too hard. A clear sound is the result of good placement next to the frets, rather than strength.
- Memorize each chord.
- Strum and listen to the sound of each note in every chord, staying with it until you get them all to ring clearly.
- Create original *progressions* (a *progression* is a sequence of chords) by changing from each chord to all the other chords.
- Don't get frustrated. Elvis did it, so can you!

PRACTICING OPEN CHORDS

Here are some progressions for you to strum through. Learning these will familiarize you with the open position chords and give your left-hand fingers a workout. Pay attention to the Roman numerals above the chord names. This will help you begin to understand how diatonic chords relate to each other. Also, notice the four "slashes" in each measure. This is a common way of showing that the specified harmonies should be strummed throughout each measure, but it does not imply any specific rhythm. You can strum straight quarter notes (once per beat), or make up rhythms of your own.

CHAPTER 7

More Fingerstyle Patterns

If you are feeling completely comfortable with the patterns you learned in Chapter 3, its time to add some more to your arsenal. This chapter will introduce Patterns #5, #6 and #7. Enjoy!

PATTERN #5

This common arpeggio adds two more notes to Pattern #1 (*p-i-m-a*, page 23). The resulting arpeggio, *p-i-m-a-m-i*, is done by extending *i*, *m* and *a* to the strings when *p* plays. Then, as *a* plays, re-extend *m* and *i*. Then, be sure to let the *i* finger follow *m* into the palm. As *i* plays, re-extend *p*. The six-note pattern that emerges from this finger combination fits into the time signature $\frac{3}{4}$. You will recognize the notes in Example 33 from several examples in Chapter 3.

33
Track 26

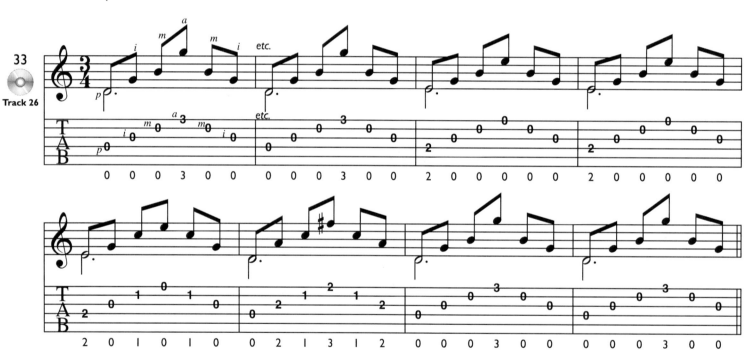

Example 34 will give you some more practice with Pattern #5.

34
Track 27

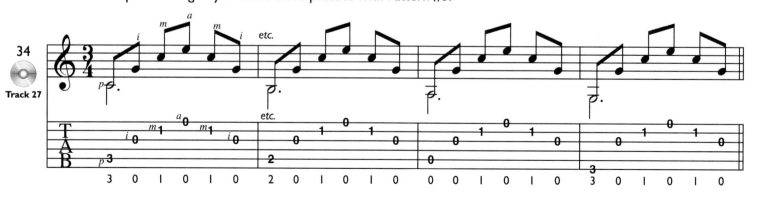

PATTERN #6

In Pattern #6 we have Pattern #5 with an extra beat added. This brings us back to $\frac{4}{4}$ time and gives us an additional bass note played by *p* on the first half of the fourth beat. This arpeggio is performed the same as Pattern #5, but there is an additional exchange between *p* and *i* at the end of the measure. As you play that final *i* stroke, re-extend *p* to begin the whole pattern again.

Since the notes in Example 35 are the same as those in Example 33, you can concentrate on the new right hand pattern.

Representative of the new breed of fingerstyle guitarists,
Preston Reed *(b. 1955) is known for his show-stopping percussive guitar playing.*

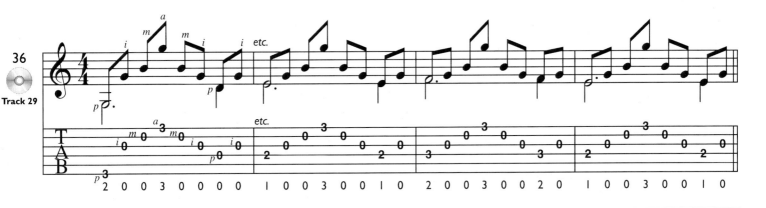

Like Pattern #6, Pattern #7 has two bass notes. In all of the previous patterns, the bass notes were played directly on the downbeats, or on the 1, 2, 3 or 4 of each measure. This pattern is different in that the second bass note falls on an upbeat, between the second and third downbeats. This gives us a feeling of *syncopation*, or rhythmic displacement.

To perform this arpeggio, drop out *i* and *m* as *p* plays. Let *i* follow *m* into the hand as *p* re-extends. Then, as *p* plays again, drop out all three fingers and play *a*. Let *i* and *m* follow *a* into the palm, but re-extend *i* to play once more as *m* plays. As *i* plays its final note, re-extend *p* to begin the pattern again.

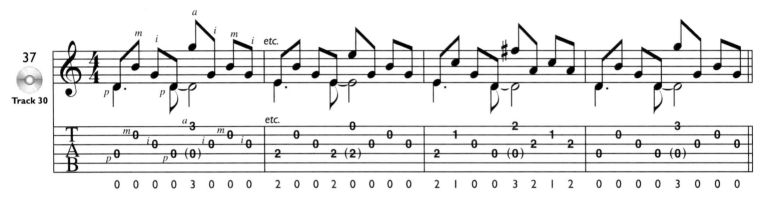

In Chapter 6 you learned about chords. By now, you may have noticed that many of the left-hand finger combinations required to play the examples in this book resemble some of the chord forms introduced on page 42. In Example 38, it is especially helpful to think of the left hand in terms of chord forms. You will find them marked above the music. This kind of notation is standard practice. It will be used in many examples as this book continues, to give you an idea of what chord forms most closely relate to the notes being played. Even if a few of the notes played are not part of the chords suggested, seeing and playing groups of notes as chord fingerings will make your playing sound better.

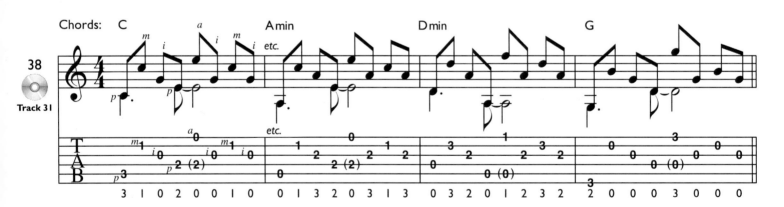

CHAPTER 8

Alternating Bass

When bass players make up parts for the songs they play, they need to come up with patterns that fit the chords in the chord progressions. In many styles it is standard practice for them to alternate among the roots, 3rds and 5ths of these chords. This works well, of course, because the chords themselves are composed of these notes.

In fingerstyle music, alternating bass patterns are played by moving *p* from string to string with a steady quarter note rhythm. They are common and important, especially in folk, blues and country styles. The steady thumping beat that alternating bass patterns create give pieces drive, strength and interest.

BASIC ALTERNATING BASS PATTERNS

The following examples demonstrate typical alternating bass choices for many common chords. Be sure to use *p* exclusively, and learn to move from the spot where your thumb joins the hand. Try not to move your hand or wrist. Hold your left-hand fingers down on the notes of each chord for the entire measure, thus allowing them to sustain.

ALTERNATING BASS IN G

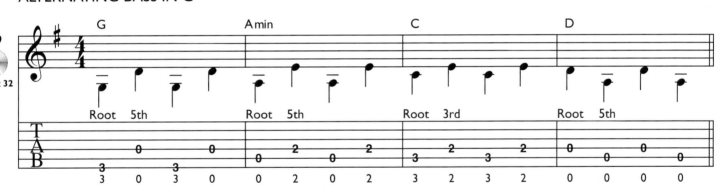

ALTERNATING BASS IN C

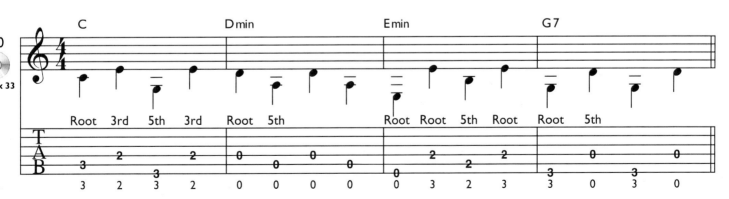

In Examples 41 and 42 we find the alternating bass patterns from Examples 39 and 40, but now with added notes on the upper strings. Patterns like these are very effective as song accompaniments.

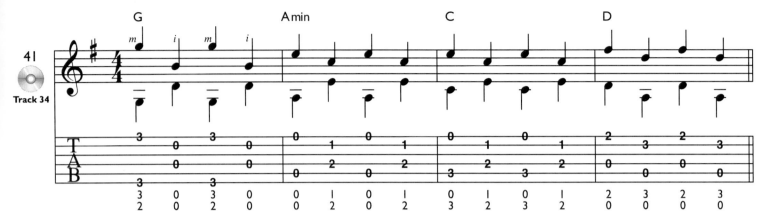

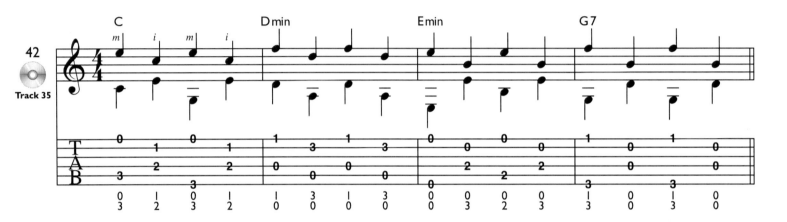

Country fingerpicker Merle Travis (1917–1983) is famous for his signature alternating bass pattern.

In Chapters 3 and 7 we covered seven useful arpeggio patterns. Now that we've begun to play alternating bass lines, we can cover three very common picking patterns that include this approach.

Each pattern may be used for accompaniment or, with a little more melodic variation, can form the basis of an instrumental composition.

SLASH CHORDS

In the examples that follow you will notice chord symbols that include a *slash* mark, such as D/F♯. These are called slash chords, and they indicate that a note other than the root of the chord is played in the bass. In some cases, as in the Bmin/A in *Picking on Travis*, the note in the bass may not even be part of the chord. The tablature will tell you all you need to know in order to finger these attractive sounding chords, so there's no need to learn lots of new chord shapes (yet!).

Shadow Boxing uses a pattern similar to the one in *The Boxer* by Simon and Garfunkel.

 SHADOW BOXING

Track 36

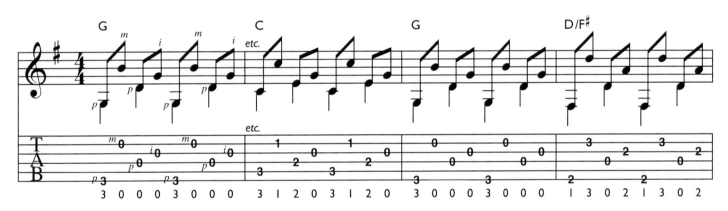

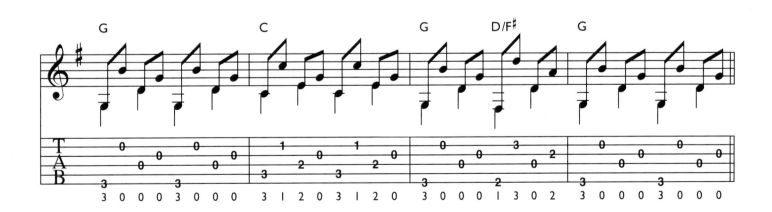

Travis picking is perhaps the most common of all picking patterns. It is named for the influential country picker, Merle Travis, but it would be hard to find a fingerstyle artist who has not used it in one way or another. It involves an alternating bass part, and an exchange between *p* and the other fingers.

Picking On Travis combines Travis picking with a common chord progression. Notice that the first bass notes in the first four bars form a descending pattern (C, B, A, G).

 PICKING ON TRAVIS

Track 37

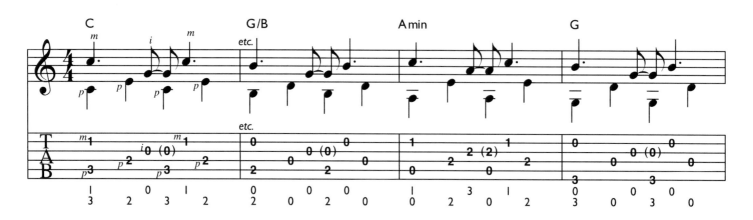

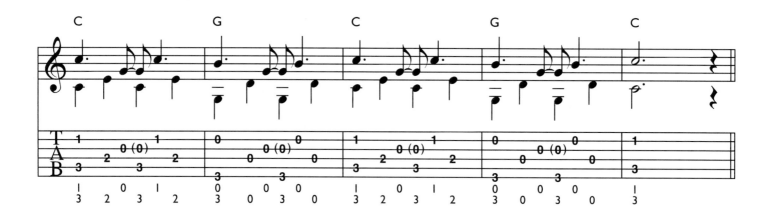

This next example is in the key of D. The pattern is sometimes called the *backwards roll*.

THE BACKWARDS ROLL

Track 38

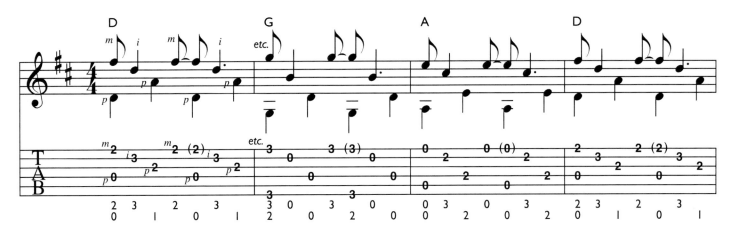

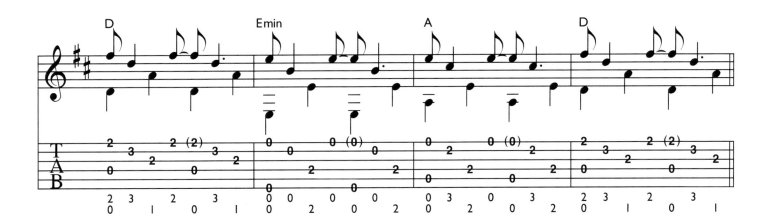

When you master the alternating bass picking patterns in *Shadow Boxing*, *Picking on Travis* and the *Backwards Roll*, try to incorporate them into songs and pieces. For variety you can switch among them within the same composition. You should also try making up your own patterns.

The next three *etudes* (an *etude* is a piece designed for the study of a particular technique or concept) demonstrate how our three alternating bass picking patterns can be used with melodic variations on the upper strings.

ALTERNATING BASS ETUDE #1

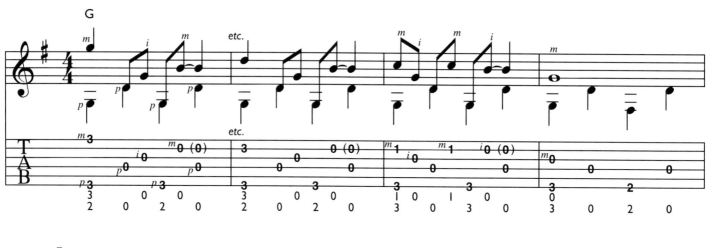

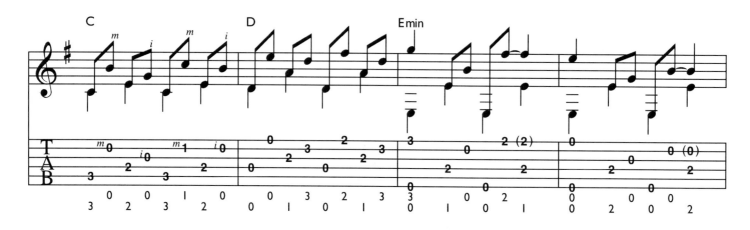

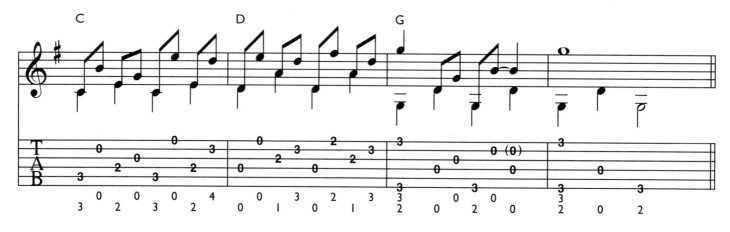

ALTERNATING BASS ETUDE #2

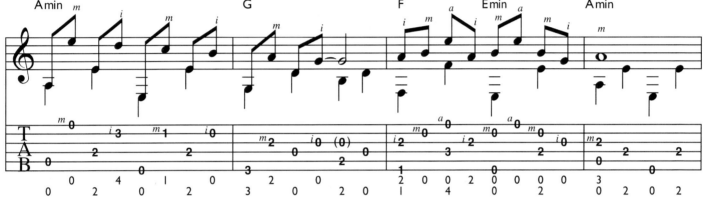

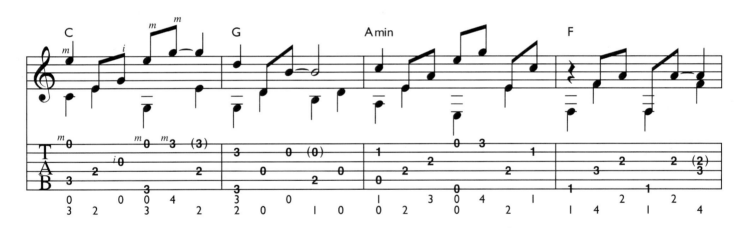

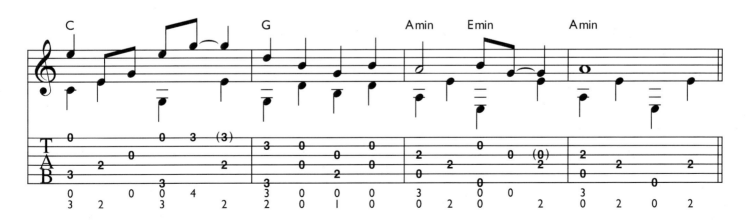

ALTERNATING BASS ETUDE #3

Track 41

CHAPTER 9

Some More Fingerstyle Patterns

PATTERN #8

This interesting pattern has a *Latin* feel because of the placement of the bass notes. *Latin* refers to music that uses rhythms found in South American music. The bass notes fall on the first beats, between the second and third, and on the fourth beats. Example 43 shows how this arrangement of bass notes groups the eighth notes in each measure into two groups of three followed by a group of two.

You will recognize the sequence of notes in this example from previous chapters about fingerstyle patterns (Chapters 3 and 7). The familiarity of the notes will help you concentrate on the right hand pattern.

Pattern #8 is performed by executing two *p-i-m* arpeggios followed by an exchange between *p* and *i*. A *p-i-m* arpeggio is done by releasing *i* and *m* as *p* plays, and then re-extending *p* as *m* plays. After the end of the second *p-i-m* arpeggio, re-extend *p* to play once again. As *p* plays, release *i*, and as *i* plays the final note, re-extend *p* to begin the pattern again.

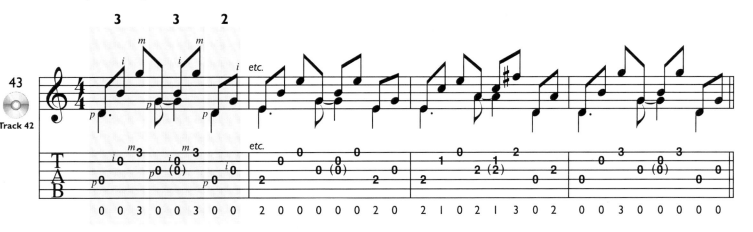

Note the minor 7 chord (Amin7) in the third measure of Example 44. A minor 7 chord is a minor triad with an added ♭7.

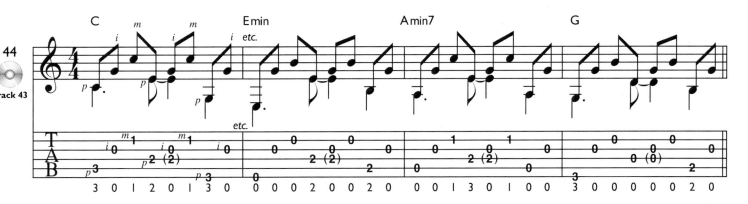

With Pattern #9 we go back to one bass note per measure falling on the first beat. In this arpeggio the third string is repeated after each of the other strings is played. Make sure you strike it strongly and try to keep it ringing throughout.

To perform Pattern #9, release *i* and *m* together when *p* plays. Let *m* follow *i* into the hand, and return *i* to its string as *m* plays. As *i* plays for the second time, release *a* to the 1st string. As *a* plays, release *i* and *m* together and repeat the sequence of movements from the beginning of the pattern. As *i* plays the final note in the measure, re-extend *p* to begin the pattern again. One way of looking at this arpeggio is to think of the *a* finger as a substitute for *p*: it's *p-i-m-i-p-i-m-i*, but *a* substitutes for the *p* stroke in the middle of the measure.

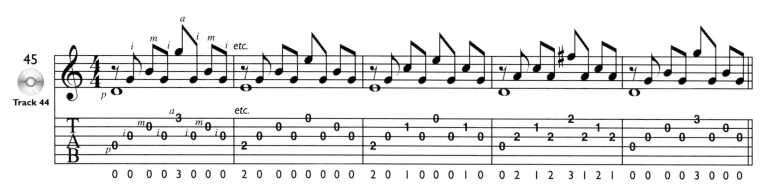

Note the add9 chord in the third measure of Example 46. An add9 chord is a major triad with an added 9. A 9 is the same as the 2nd scale degree, but an octave (twelve half steps) higher. For instance, in the third measure, the D is the 9 of the Cadd9 chord, because the D is the same as the 2nd scale degree above C (C_1-D_2-E_3-F_4-G_5-A_6-B_7-C_8-D_9).

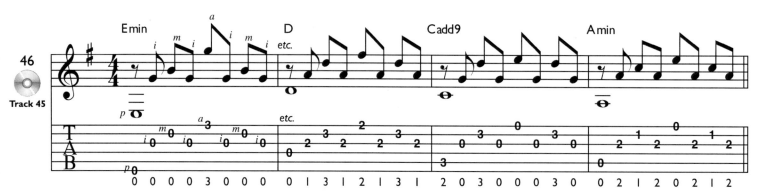

This pattern has *double stops* (two notes played at the same time). Be sure to pluck the first and second strings evenly, both notes should ring out at the same volume.

This arpeggio is performed just like Pattern #1 (page 23), except that *m* and *a* play together, instead of separately. As *p* plays, release *i*, *m* and *a* to the strings. Let *m* and *a* follow *i* into the hand to play the double stop. As *m* and *a* play, re-extend *p* to begin the pattern again.

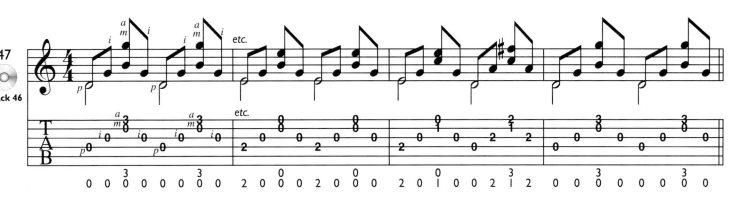

The chord sequence in Example 48 is based on a common descending chromatic bass line.

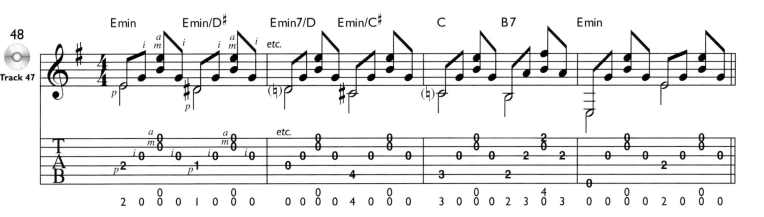

This arpeggio also has double stops. It is really a combination of the first half of Pattern #9 and the first half of Pattern #1, with an additional note on the first string added above the bass notes.

To perform this arpeggio, work *a* and *p* together as a unit, playing and releasing them together. As *a* and *p* play, release *i* and *m* together to alternate on the 3rd and 2nd strings respectively. As *i* plays for the second time, re-extend *a* and *p*. As *a* and *p* play for the second time, release *i* and *m*. Let *m* follow *i* into the hand, simultaneously releasing *a*. After *a* plays the final note, re-extend *a* and *p* to begin the pattern again.

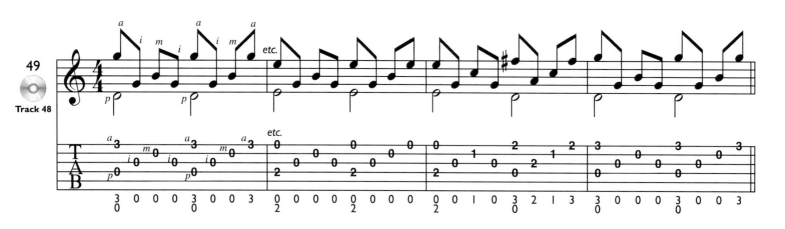

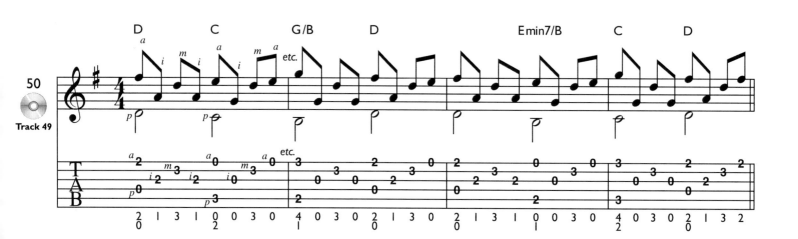

Practice all fingerstyle pattern exercises until you can play them smoothly. Then you can use these arpeggios to accompany your singing or to make up your own pieces or songs. Try to be creative by combining patterns, adding notes or inventing your own new arpeggios.

CHAPTER 10

Other Fingerstyle Basics

MELODY IN THE BASS

In this section we will work with a melody on the lower or bass strings. The melody in Example 51 will be arranged with chords and arpeggio patterns on the upper strings. First, here is the tune (be sure you play all notes with *p*):

51

Track 50

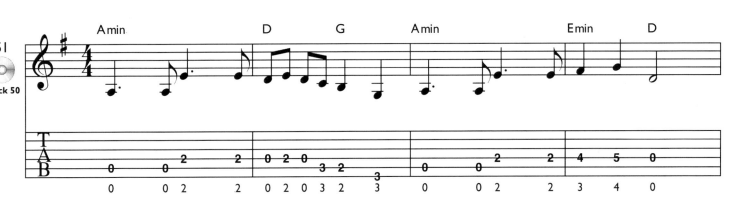

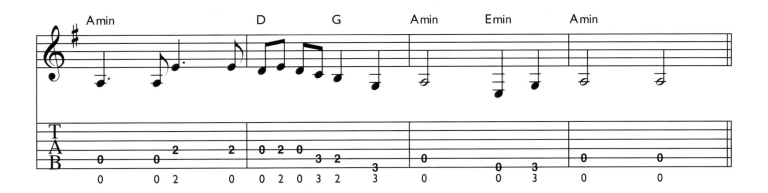

Example 52 (next page) has the same melody as Example 51. Arpeggios or chord tones have been added to fill in the spaces between the notes. When you play arrangements like this, be sure you play the melody strongly and make it stand out from the chords. You can create an entire composition with the melody in the bass, or use this technique as a variation section in a piece.

Notice the three-note *block chord* (three or more notes played simultaneously) on the first beat of the second measure. You may want to practice this out of context before digging in to this example.

Adrian Legg (b. 1948) is not only a prominent fingerstyle guitarist, but an extraordinary storyteller and a fine photographer. Known for his remarkable technique and eclectic compositional style, he is one of today's most popular players.

SYNCOPATION

Rhythms that are unexpected, or off the beat, are considered *syncopated*. Syncopation is achieved by shifting notes to the upbeats, or between the beats, rather than placing them on downbeats. This creates a rhythmic feel that is an essential aspect of blues, jazz, rock and many other contemporary styles. In fingerstyle music, syncopation goes hand in hand with the alternating bass. The steady quarter note bass notes provide a perfect setting against which syncopated lines on the upper strings can be played.

To understand how syncopation works, lets start with a basic $\frac{4}{4}$ pattern without any upbeat rhythms. The chords chosen are dominant sevenths that would be used in a typical blues song in the key of A.

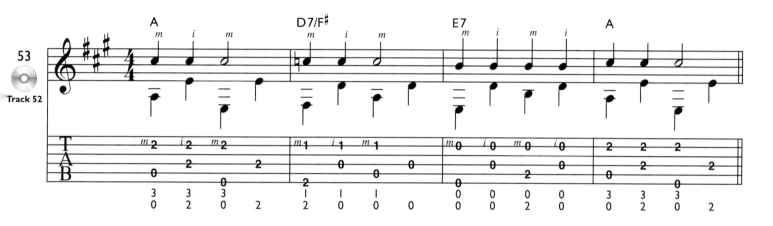

In Example 54 we have the same chords, notes and bass patterns as in Example 53, but the second string notes have been shifted. They do not fall on the quarter note pulse, as before, but are played on the "ands," or between the quarter pulses. They are now syncopated.

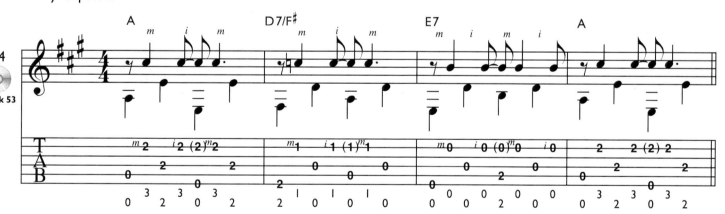

The *Syncopated Etude* is in the ragtime/blues style. This type of music is very syncopated. Notice that the B at the very end of measure five is part of the G chord that appears in measure six, and the C that ends measure six belongs to the C chord in measure seven. These notes are syncopated ahead of the beat and anticipate their chords. They are called *anticipations*.

SYNCOPATED ETUDE

Track 54

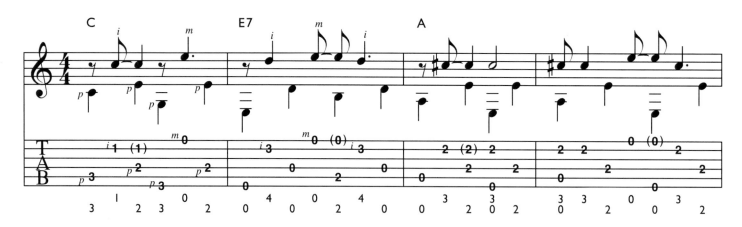

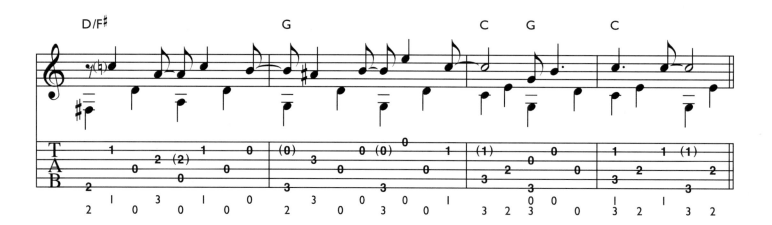

Walking bass lines are scale passages played by *p* on the lower strings. In some pieces, these bass lines are so distinctive they make the chords, and even the melody, seem secondary. The chord pattern and melody can be created to fit the bass, rather than the other way around. The following example is a common descending bass line in the key of C.

55
Track 55

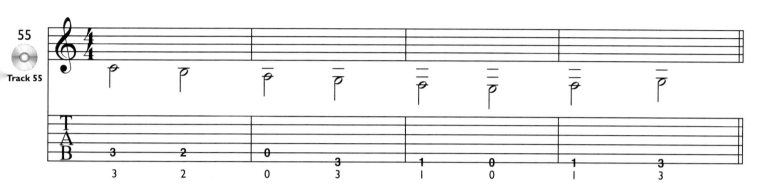

Example 56 adds chords to the walking bass line in Example 55. This creates an accompaniment pattern that is often heard in folk, pop or country music.

56
Track 56

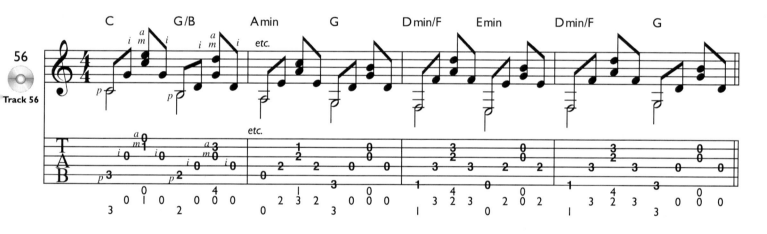

Example 57 (next page) adds a syncopated blues/jazz style melody to a walking bass line in E Minor. Notice the slide indications ( ) on the first bass notes in measures 9, 11 and 13. These notes are all E on the 5th string, 7th fret. Slide your 3rd finger up to this note from the 5th fret D. Slides are a common expressive device in all styles of guitar playing.

Swing the eighths (see page 15).

In fingerstyle guitar, melodies are often *harmonized* with added notes. To harmonize is to add agreeable sounds. The word *interval* refers to the distance between notes. Any two notes can be named by the interval, or distance, between them. Although you may just be getting started on fingerstyle guitar, you already know about lots of intervals. For instance, you know that a major triad is comprised of 1, 3 and 5 of the major scale. These numbers represent intervals. For instance, the distance from 1 to 3 is an interval of a 3rd. The distance from 1 to 5 is the interval of a 5th. To make a 7 chord, you add a 7th above the root of the chord.

Harmonizing with intervals adds interest and color to a tune. 3rds and 6ths are considered the most pleasant, or sweet sounding, intervals and are a common choice for harmonizations. Harmoniziations are almost always done with notes that are diatonic (in the key—see page 41).

Example 58A shows an A Major scale in single notes. Notice that the key of A Major has three sharps: F♯, C♯ and G♯. Example 58B shows the same scale harmonized in 3rds. Every note in the scale has an added note that is three scale steps higher. For instance, C♯ is three scale steps higher than A in the A Major scale, so A is harmonized with C♯.

A) A MAJOR SCALE

58
Track 58

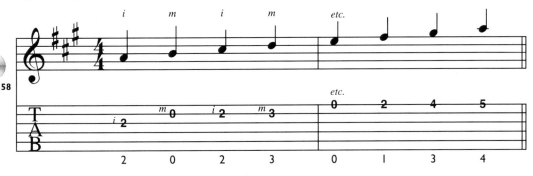

B) A MAJOR SCALE HARMONIZED IN 3RDS

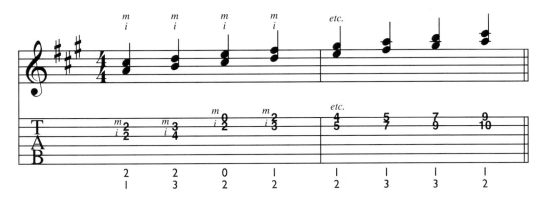

When we harmonize in 6ths we add a note six steps lower than the original note. This gives us a wider, or fuller sound than that of the 3rds. But 3rds and 6ths are closely related. In the key of A Major, when we start with A and count up three steps we find C#. If we count six steps backward from A, we also wind up with C#. Because of this, we say that 3rds and 6ths are *inversions* of each other. If you *invert* (turn upside-down) a 3rd, you create a 6th.

Play the following A Major scale in 6ths and compare the sound to the A Major scale in 3rds in Example 58B.

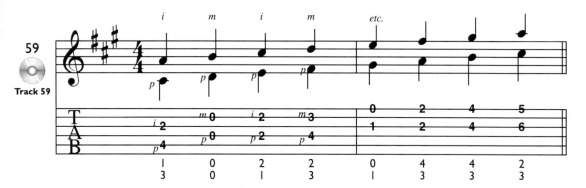

We know that in an A Major scale, the third note from A is a C#. Because all major scales can repeat into the next octave, we can count up ten steps from A and once again find a C# for an interval of a 10th. This C# is eight steps, or an octave, higher than the first C# above A. 3rds and 10ths have the same letter names, and similar sounds, but the 10th is fuller and richer due to it's wider range.

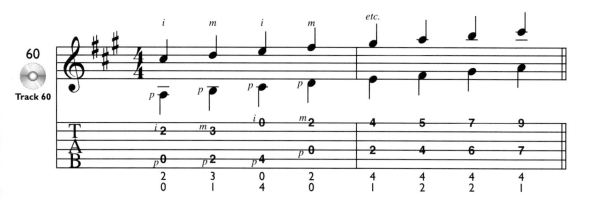

3rds, 6ths and 10ths are important intervals in fingerstyle music. Writing them out and practicing them in the common keys of C, G, D, E, A Minor and E Minor (see page 36 to review minor keys) will help you learn new pieces, and will provide inspiration for you to create your own music.

There are two interval etudes on the following pages. The first, *Interval Etude in G*, focuses on 10ths. The next, *Interval Etude in A*, explores 3rds and 6ths.

Track 61

INTERVAL ETUDE IN G

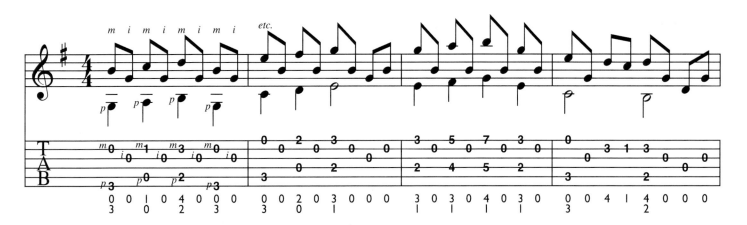

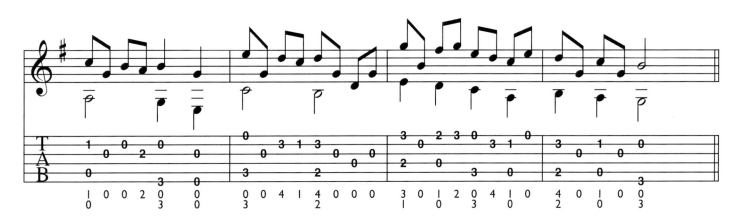

Bluesman/guitarist **Mississippi John Hurt**
(1893–1966) has influenced a whole new
generation of blues musicians, especially
among fingerstyle guitarists.

INTERVAL ETUDE IN A

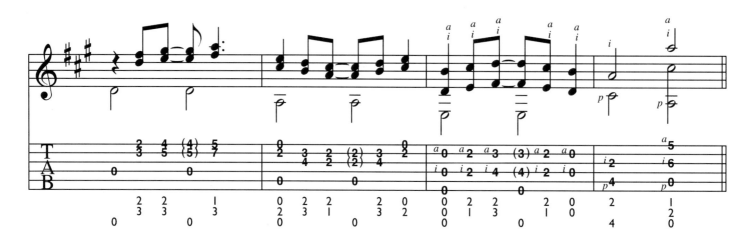

CHAPTER 11

Special Techniques

HAMMER-ONS AND PULL-OFFS

Hammer-ons and pull-offs, otherwise known as *slurs*, are the most commonly used devices for creating *legato* (smooth) connections between notes on the guitar. In both techniques, the right hand plucks the first note and subsequent notes are played by the left hand. Slurs are notated with a slur sign ⌒ and an H for hammer-ons, or a P for pull-offs.

HAMMER-ONS

A hammer-on is a slur from a lower to a higher note. There are two steps to performing a hammer-on. First, the right hand strikes the string. Then, a left hand finger strikes, or hammers, a higher note on the same string. The second note must be struck firmly and as close to the fret as possible. Example 61 will get you started using this technique.

61
Track 63

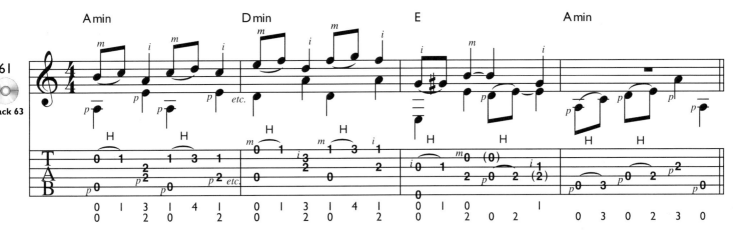

PULL-OFFS

A pull-off is a descending slur, from a higher to a lower note on the same string. To perform a pull-off, pluck the first note then lift the left-hand finger off the note in such a way as to cause the lower note to sound. Moving the finger downward (towards the floor) and away from yourself in slight curve will cleanly snap the note and help your finger clear any other strings. Practice the pull-offs in Example 62.

H = Hammer-on
P = Pull-off

62
Track 64

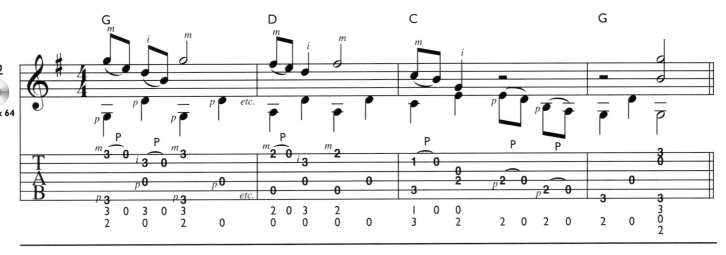

This *Slur Etude* incorporates many of the most common hammer-ons and pull-offs used in fingerstyle guitar. Notice how they decorate and add melodic interest to basic chord forms. Notice the major 7 chord (GMaj7). A major 7 chord is a major triad with an added 7. Have fun playing this piece, and be sure to practice it slowly at first.

SLUR ETUDE

Track 65

On the harp, it is easy to keep notes sustaining while other notes are played. Each note will ring out until it dies a natural death, or until the player stops the vibration. It is possible to get many notes overlapping and ringing at the same time. We can get a similar effect on guitar by holding notes down as long as possible. But we run into a problem: when we go from one fretted note to another fretted note, higher or lower on the same string, the original note stops vibrating. Of course, a digital delay unit will solve this problem if you play an electric, or acoustic-electric, but there is a natural approach you can also use.

Try the phrase on the first three strings in Example 63A in the conventional manner, as indicated in the TAB. You can hold down the A while you play the other notes, and let the E ring once it is hit. But since we have three notes, B, C and D, on the 2nd string, we do not get much sustain. Now try Example 63B, which has the same notes, but fingered higher up on the neck.

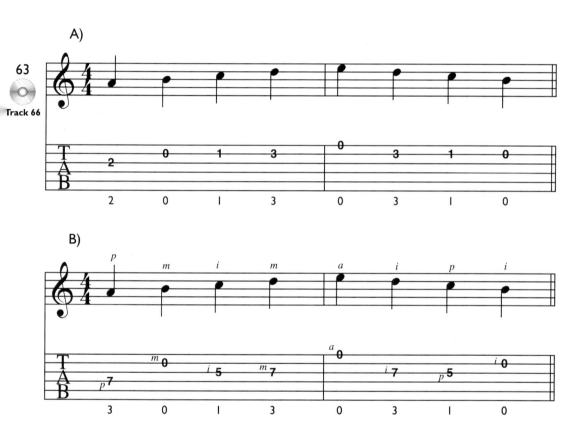

63
Track 66

The fingering in 63B has the same notes as 63A, but adds one more string to the phrase. If you hold down the notes, as you should in this style, you get much more sustain. This is because almost every note has its own string, like a harp, and also because some of the notes have been relocated on lower strings, which have more sustain. This style of playing is called harp style, or cross picking. The goal is to arrange or create phrases where each note, or almost every note, has it's own string. Of course, to really get the sustain needed notes must be held as long as possible. Back in the 16th, 17th and 18th centuries (yes, there were fingerstyle guitarists back then!) guitarists called this *compeñella* fingering. *Compeñella* means "little bells" in Spanish.

Have fun with these "harp style" examples. Be creative and use them to make up your own pieces. Then try the next piece which is an etude on this approach.

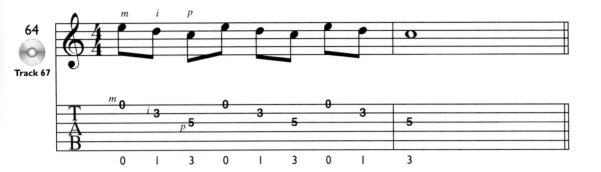

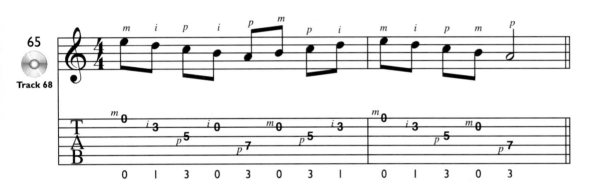

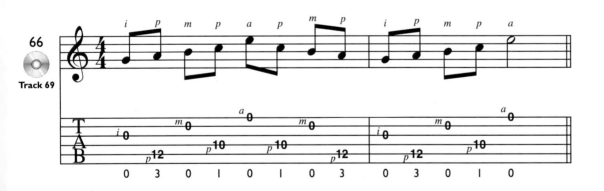

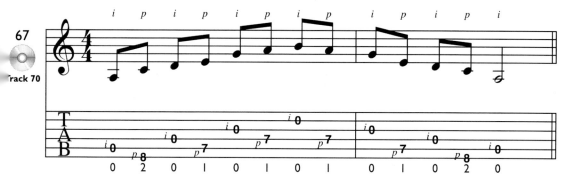

*Fingerstyle genius **Pierre Bensusan** (b. 1957)*
makes extensive use of harp-style playing.

The following etude was inspired by the playing of Seth Austen. This is our first piece that features sixteenth-notes, which are counted: "1-e-&-ah, 2-e-&-ah, 3-e-&-ah, 4-e-&-ah," etc.

 HARP-STYLE ETUDE

Track 71

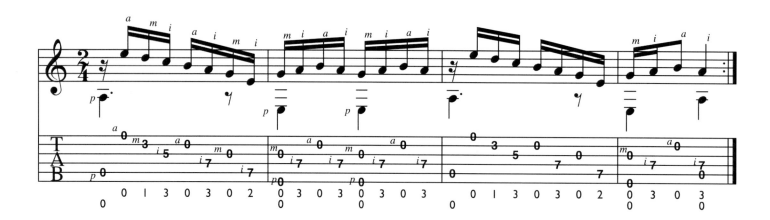

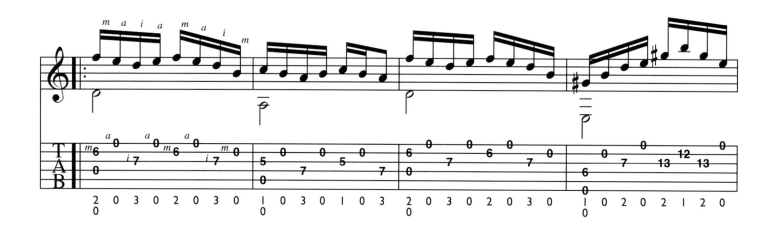

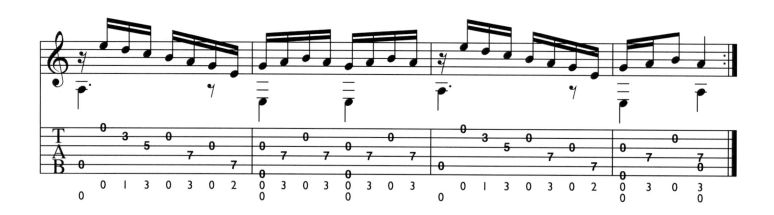

NATURAL HARMONICS

If you've listened to much guitar music, you may have noticed occasional high chiming notes that have a bell like tone. These were probably *harmonics*. Every musical note, or *fundamental tone*, is accompanied by an array of *overtones*. We aren't usually aware of them—they are just there, the way that many colors of the spectrum are there when we perceive a single color. A harmonic is what happens when we touch the string in such a way as to isolate one of these overtones from the fundamental tone and most of the other overtones. These high, pure sounding tones are distinctive, and add a beautiful color to pieces. They can be very effective as highlights in the music. There are various ways to make harmonics on the guitar. In this book, we will cover *natural* harmonics.

Let's start with the easiest natural harmonics to play on the guitar. These are found in the 12th fret.

- **Lightly touch, do not depress, the 12th fret, 6th string directly over the 12th fret wire. Be sure you are right over the fret wire, not behind it where we usually play notes.**

- **Pluck the string with a right hand finger.**

- **Immediately upon striking the note, lift the finger that is touching the note off the string. This finger must be lifted quickly to let the harmonic ring out.**

Try this a few times. If you do it right you should hear a clear high, bell like tone. Now try the harmonics on each of the other strings at the 12th fret. You will also find strong harmonics at the 5th and 7th frets. All of these are notated below. Notice the diamond shaped note heads. The notes in Example 68 are open, like whole notes. But filled-in note heads, like quarter notes and eighth notes, can be diamond shaped to indicate harmonics, too (look at the *Harmonics Etude* on page 76). Also, written between the staff and the TAB, you will find indications to help you find the location of each harmonic. For instance, *Harm. 7* means to play the harmonic on the 7th fret.

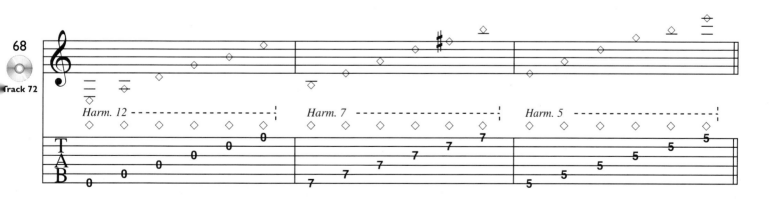

Harmonics sound one octave higher than they are written.

The melody in the *Harmonics Etude* is played entirely in harmonics. Emphasize these notes by playing them louder than the others. The circled numbers indicate which string to play.

HARMONICS ETUDE

Track 73

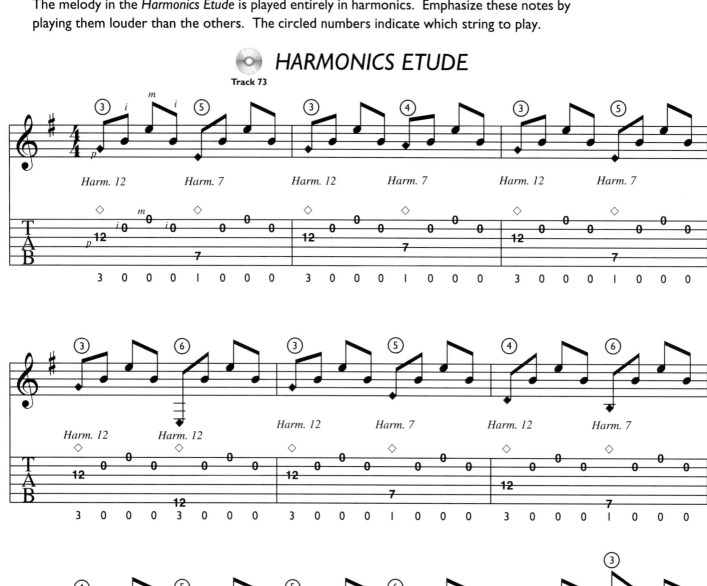

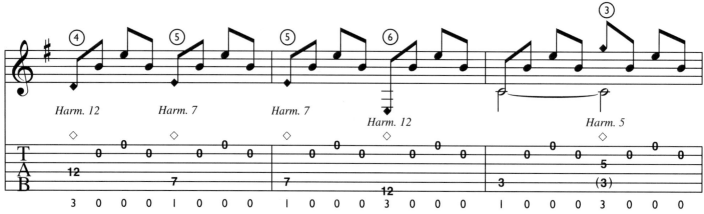

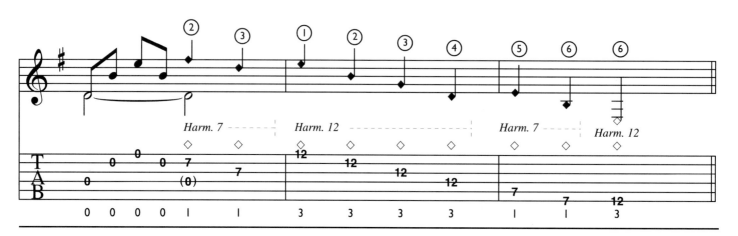

CHAPTER 12

Alternate Tunings

One of the most exciting and colorful things about fingerstyle guitar is the wealth of non-standard or "open" tunings available to players. Many leading artists work with these alternative tunings exclusively, but even those who play mainly in standard tuning will have a few alternate tuning pieces in their repertory. You'll hear alternate tunings in the work of Adrian Legg, Leo Kottke, Michael Hedges, Joni Mitchell, Ani DiFranco and almost any other major player.

This book introduce you to two of the most common alternate tunings. To learn more about this fascinating area check out *Alternate Tunings* by Mark Dziuba, also published by Alfred and the National Guitar Workshop.

DROP D TUNING

Track 74

In drop D tuning we lower the 6th string (E) down a whole step to D. You can do this by using an electric tuner, tuning to Track 74 on the CD that is available with this book, or by using either of the following two methods:

1) Play a harmonic at 12th fret of the 6th string and tune the 6th string down to match the open 4th string.
2) Play the 7th fret of the 6th string and tune the 6th string down to match the open A 5th string.

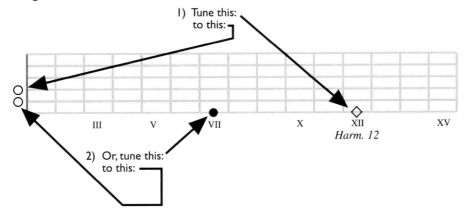

With the 6th string tuned to D, notice how much fuller a simple D chord sounds. Now we have a rich and resonant bass note for pieces in the key of D. The fingering for most chords don't not change, but we will need new versions of G, Emin and E and E7.

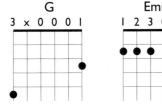
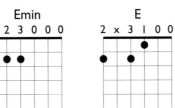
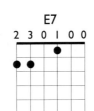

This blues style etude uses drop D tuning in the key of D. The octave D alternating bass provides a very strong sound. In the last two bars, 6ths are used to create a very common blues *turnaround*, or ending phrase.

 DROP D BLUES

Track 75

Swing the eighths.

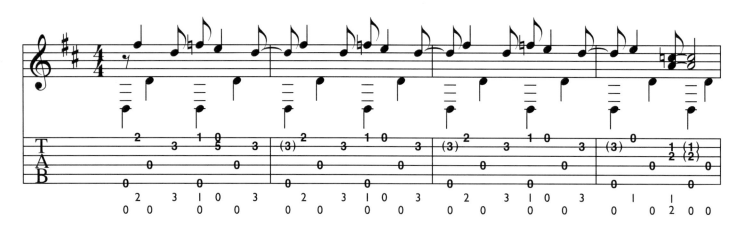

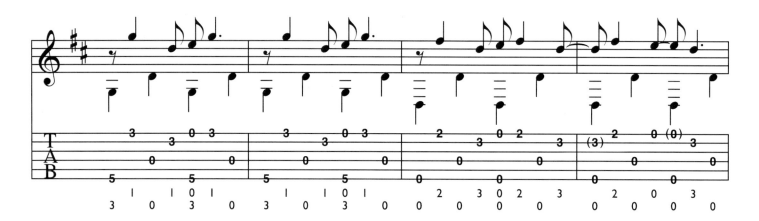

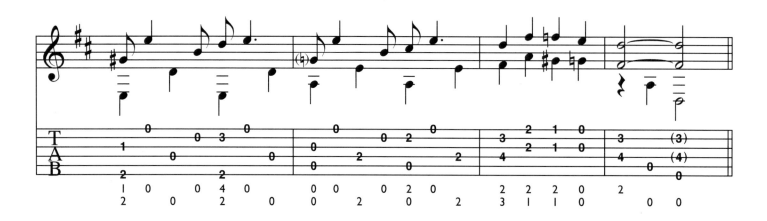

Although it is sometimes called "Spanish tuning," open G is not commonly used in standard Spanish guitar music. It is used by many instrumental fingerstyle soloists such as Leo Kottke, John Fahey and others, and was also used by blues players such as Robert Johnson and Muddy Waters. Joni Mitchell, one of the most influential singer/songwriters, also wrote most of her hits in open G.

In open G, the strings are tuned D, G, D, G, B, D, from the 6th string to the 1st. The 2nd, 3rd and 4th strings do not change, but the others are lowered to their new pitches. Since a G Major chord is made up of the notes G, B and D, this tuning gives us the sound of a G chord by simply strumming the open strings.

Track 76

To tune to G from standard tuning, use an electric tuner, tune to Track 76 on the CD, or follow these steps:

1. Play the 6th string, 7th fret and lower it until it matches the 5th string open.
2. Play the open 5th string and lower it until it matches the 6th string, 5th fret.
3. Play the 1st string and lower it until it matches the 2nd string, 3rd fret.

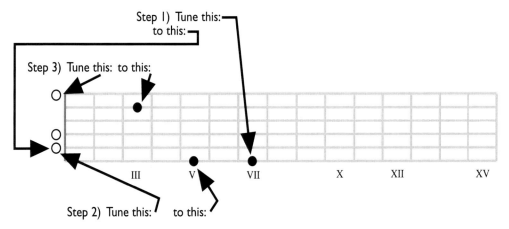

In this tuning you will need to learn new chord shapes. Note that since the open strings automatically give us a G Major chord, we can play other major chords simply by *barring* all the strings at any fret. (A *barre* is done by laying the thumb side of your 1st finger straight across the strings as close to the fret as possible. Holding your left elbow in, close to your side, will give you additional leverage.) The note on the 5th string is the root. For instance, since the 5th fret of the 5th string is the note C in this tuning, barring the 5th fret will get you a C Major chord. This list shows the locations of the most common major barre chords:

G-12th fret, A-2nd fret, B-3rd fret, C-5th fret, D-7th fret, E-9th fret, F-10th fret.

= Barre

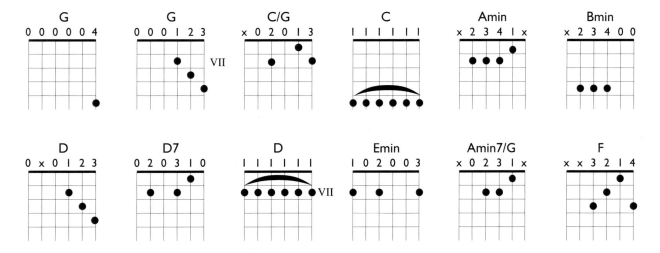

Compositions in open G are often based on phrases in 6ths and 10ths. These intervals allow open strings to ring through and sustain the G Major sound throughout the phrases. They also suggest chords without locking us into full chord fingerings.

Example 69 places the G Major scale on the 5th string, and harmonizes it with 10ths on the 2nd string.

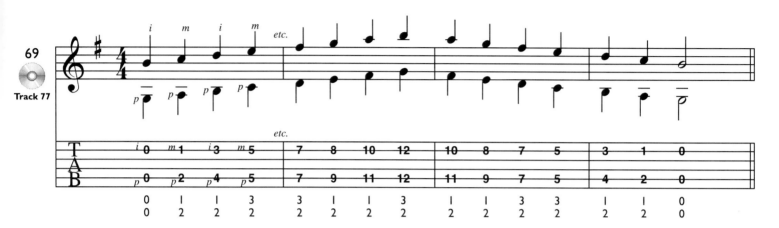

Now play this pattern of 6ths on the 2nd and 4th strings and notice how the added open 3rd and 5th strings ring out and sustain the sound of G.

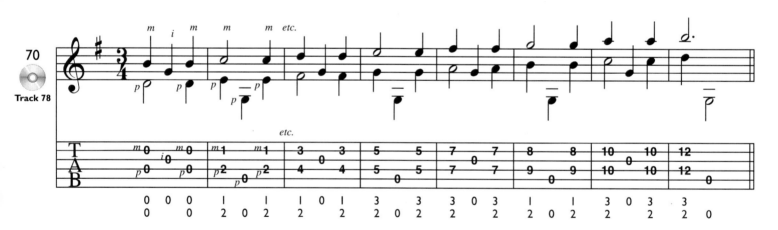

The next two works show how 6ths and 10ths can be used in open G. *Open G Blues* is a blues in $\frac{12}{8}$ time and follows a standard twelve-bar blues progression (I-IV-I-I-IV-IV-I-I-V-IV-I-V). It ends with a turnaround that is a favorite in open G. The pattern of 6ths from the previous page has been altered to include the ♭7 (F) and ♭3 (B♭), which are important notes for a "blues" sound.

In $\frac{12}{8}$ time, try to emphasis beats 1, 4, 7 and 10: **1**-2-3-**4**-5-6-**7**-8-9-**10**-11-12. Essentially, there are four beats in each measure, and each beat is divisible by three. The ♩. = 1 beat.

OPEN G BLUES

Track 79

Open Minded moves 10ths up and down the fingerboard along with a few of the chord fingerings we've covered. Notice the use of barre chords in the thirteenth and fourteenth measures.

OPEN MINDED

Track 80

CHAPTER 13

Fingerstyle Pieces

This collection of pieces incorporates many of the techniques and concepts covered in this book. They are etudes intended to teach you some of the common patterns and progressions in their styles. Once you learn these tunes, you can try to add or improvise other sections by using ideas from them, or create new pieces in these styles. Before you play each piece, study the appropriate tips provided below.

TIPS FOR PLAYING THE PIECES

This piece is based on Pattern #8 (see page 55). It is comprised of steady eighth notes, but they are grouped into two sets of three, followed by a set of two. This creates a popular rhythm that can be counted 1-2-3-1-2-3-1-2. Also notice the harp style phrases in measures twelve through fifteen.

The chord pattern in this piece is built on a descending bass pattern (A, G, F♯, E). It also includes hammer-ons and an alternating bass. The squiggly line before the chords in the second section tell us to slightly separate, or arpeggiate, the notes rather than pluck them all at the same time. This creates a fuller sound. Notice the *Da Capo al Fine* marking at the end. This tells us to play through the piece, start again, and end at the *Fine* in the last measure of the first section.

This piece has many of the typical moves found in ragtime/blues tunes in the key of C. Rev. Gary Davis was one of the greatest at this style of guitar playing. It includes popular turnarounds in the endings of each section. Play it with a swing eighth note feel (see page 15). Be sure to read the directions in regard to the form of the piece.

Blues in G follows the twelve-bar blues chord progression (I-IV-I-I-IV-IV-I-I-V-IV-I-I) and is based on the steady alternating bass style of Mississippi John Hurt. Here again, the eighth notes must swing.

The standard boogie-woogie bass, originally borrowed from piano music, contrasts with the syncopated melody. Of course, it's played with a swing feel, as is most blues based music.

Lightning Hopkins played in a style often called *Texas Blues*. He based his pieces on melodic licks played on the upper strings over repeated droning notes in the bass. Many of the licks contain slides, which are notated by a straight line leading up to the notes:

In $\frac{12}{8}$ time, try to emphasize beats 1, 4, 7 and 10: **1**-2-3-**4**-5-6-**7**-8-9-**10**-11-12. Essentially, there are four beats in each measure, and each beat is divisible by three. The ♩. = 1 beat.

You will recognize all the various picking patterns used in this piece. Bring out the melody on the first string. In the last five measures, the same melody appears in the bass, played by the thumb, with a different rhythm.

Lucy's Waltz is in drop D tuning and in $\frac{3}{4}$ time. Be sure to accent the first beat in each measure. The inspiration for this tune was the many traditional Irish tunes played in the same tuning and time signature. The really tiny notes in the notation are *grace notes*. These are hammer-on/pull-off combinations played as quickly as possible. The main melody notes should still fit into the rhythms notated—the grace notes are basically squeezed in between. This is an important decorative technique in this style.

Notice that this piece (and the next one, *The Light Through the Leaves*) begins with two eighth notes in a measure by themselves. These are called *pickup* notes. Since there is only one beat in that measure, the last measure in the piece is an *incomplete measure*. It has only two beats, thus accounting for the extra beat at the beginning.

This drop D piece was inspired by traditional Celtic or Irish fiddle music. The time signature is $\frac{6}{8}$. Try to accent the 1st and 4th beats in each measure: **1**-2-3-**4**-5-6. This can be thought of as two beats per measure, with each beat divisible by three, and the ♩. = 1 beat, as in $\frac{12}{8}$ time. Be careful with the hammer-on and double pull-off slur in the seventh measure.

THREE PLUS THREE PLUS TWO

SURFIN' IN THE SAND

Track 82

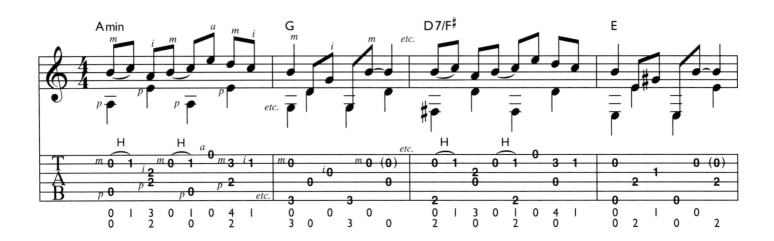

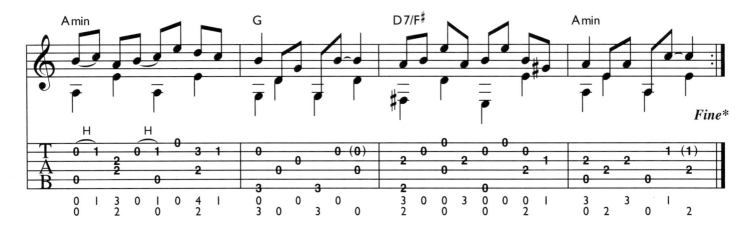

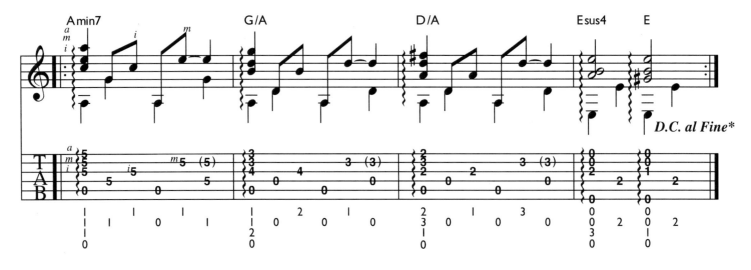

* See notes on page 83.

} = Arpeggiate, or "roll" chords with this symbol.

COFFEE TIME RAG

Track 83

Here's the form for this tune:

- Start at the beginning and play through the eighth measure. Notice the repeat and *first ending* sign.

- Go back to the beginning and play through the seventh measure, skip the first ending and jump to *second ending*. Continue through to next repeat sign in the middle of the third line on page 88.

- Go back to repeat sign facing to the left at the beginning of the second line on page 88. Play the first two measures of the section again, skip the first ending and jump to second ending. Notice the **D.C. al Coda** notation. This stands for *Da Capo al Coda*, which means go back to the beginning and play through to the *Coda* sign ⊕, which in this case is at the end of the seventh measure (*capo* means "head" and *Coda* means "ending" in Italian).

- When you hit the Coda sign this last time around, jump directly to the ending, marked ⊕ at the very end of the piece.

Right now, this may make programming your DVR seem easy! But all of these signs and directions are conventional and you will get to know them.

Swing the Eighths.

(Continued on next page)

= *Fermata.* To hold or pause. This sign tells us to hold the chord or note under it for longer than the written value. The performer decides the duration.

BLUES IN G

Track 84

Swing the Eighths!

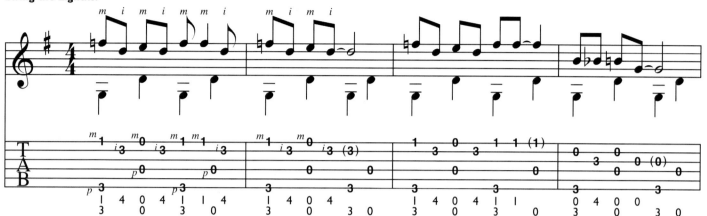

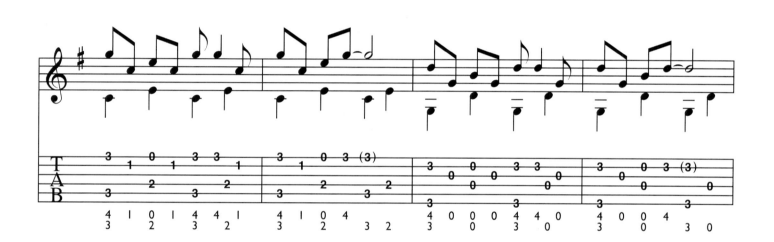

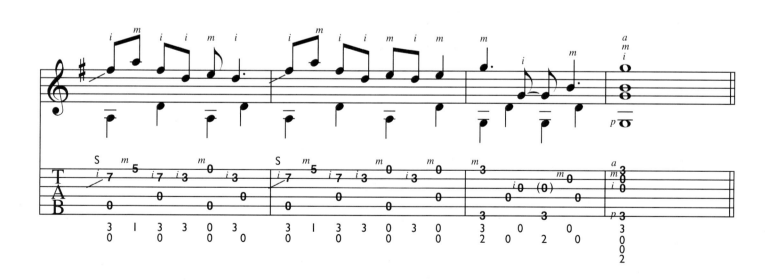

BOOGIE IN E

Track 85

Swing the Eighths!

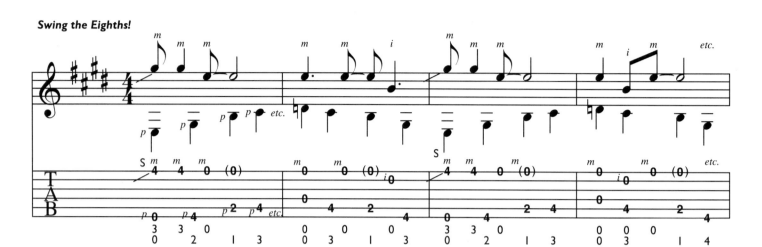

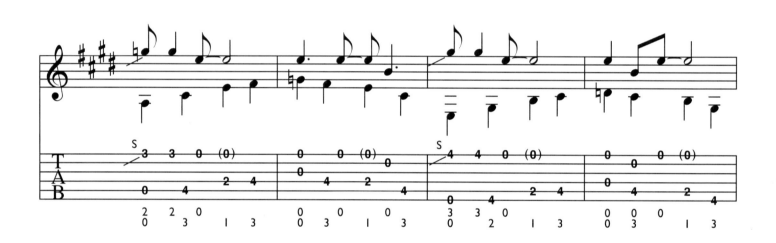

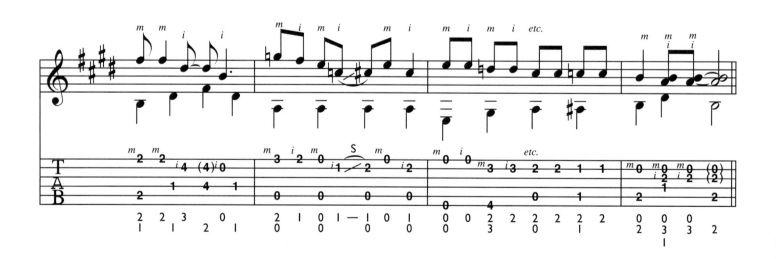

SOUNDS LIKE LIGHTNING

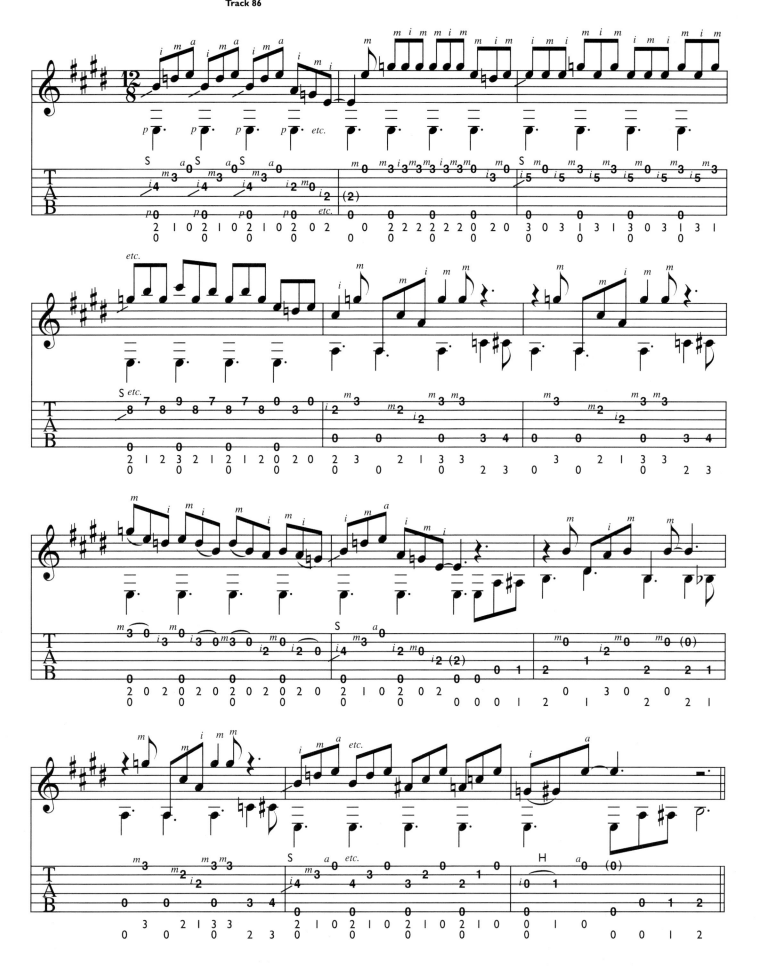

GARDEN SONG

Track 87

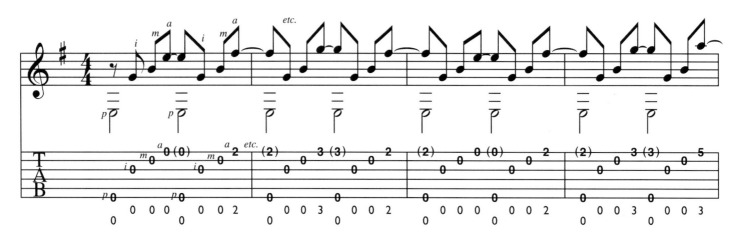

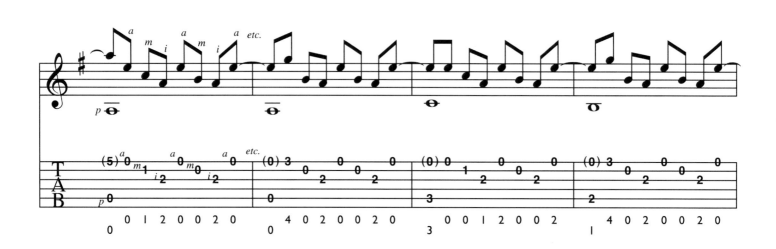

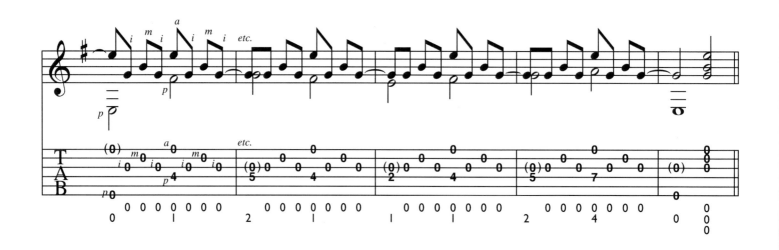

LUCY'S WALTZ

Track 88

Drop D Tuning

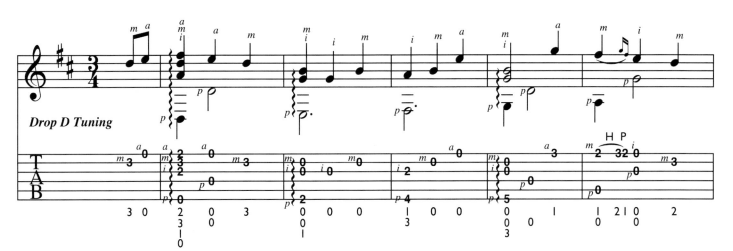

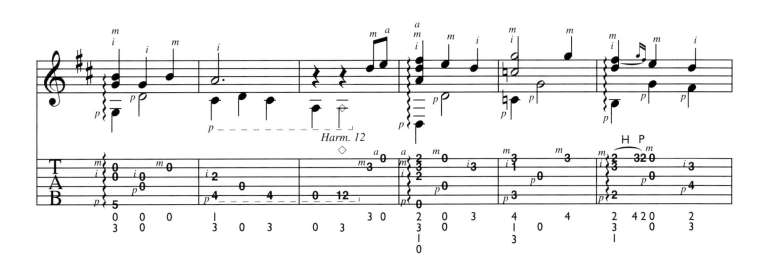

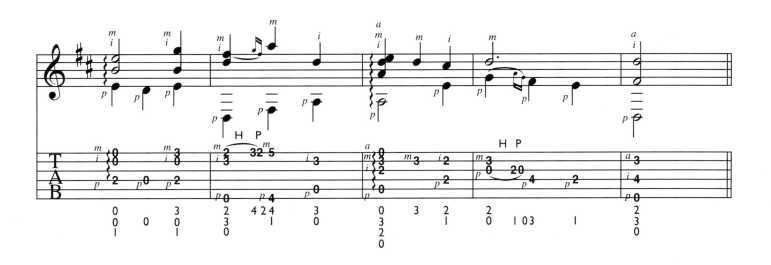

THE LIGHT THROUGH THE LEAVES

Track 89

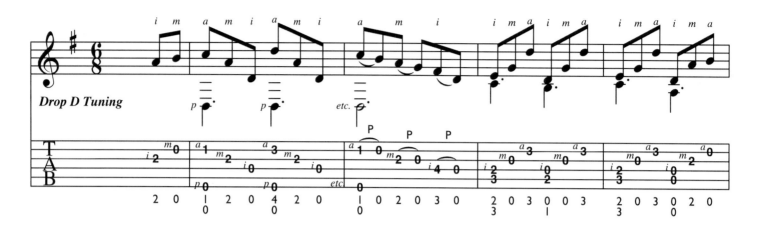

Drop D Tuning

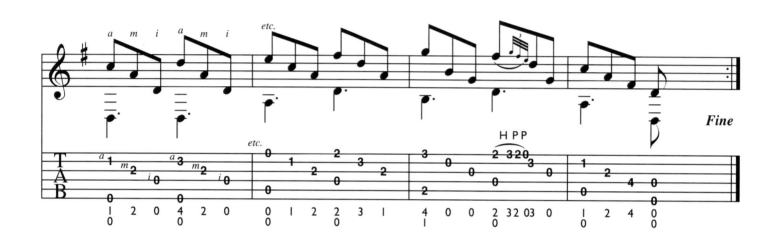

Fine

D.C. al Fine

AFTERWORDS

ON PRACTICING

Do you think "practice" is a dirty word? Does it remind you of something your mom used to make you do? If you feel this way you've got to lose your bad attitude. If you love playing the guitar, you should love the time you spend working on new and challenging material and techniques. This is what practicing is all about.

With a regular practice routine, you will see your playing improve and find yourself becoming more comfortable with the guitar. Because it is a physically challenging instrument, you may feel clumsy at first. But if you move at a good, slow and steady pace you will reach the point where your playing is natural. You will come to feel like you are at one with the instrument, and be able to play and improvise almost effortlessly.

Practice daily. A short amount of practice each day will be more effective than hours on the weekend. There is no way to "cram" for music. Start each day by playing things you play well. This will give you confidence and warm up your fingers. It will also get you in a good frame of mind for practice

After you've played some things that you are satisfied with, move on to things that need improvement. Have clear goals in mind. Don't say to yourself: "I'm going to practice some pieces for one hour." Instead, say: "Now I'm going to practice for one hour. I'll review some works I can play well, and then work on some hammer-on exercises. Next I'll work on a piece that contains hammer-ons, giving special attention to, and repeating, the phrases with hammer-ons. My goal for this part of my practice routine is to review my repertory and improve my hammer-ons."

Practicing with goals in mind will help you gauge the progress you are making. Of course, your goals must be realistic and specific. Getting better is not a good goal because it's too general. Playing a particular technique or pattern effectively is a good goal because it's more specific.

Be realistic, and don't let frustration get to you. It is easy to feel that you are not getting anywhere. You will not see much improvement from day to day, but think back to what you could play two weeks ago, last month—and how about last year? The guitar is a lifetime commitment and we should evaluate our improvement over the years, not over a few days or weeks.

EXPRESS YOURSELF

There are many reasons people play the guitar. Some may consider music as a career option. It is a difficult field in which to succeed. But there is an easy way to wind up with a million dollars if you're a guitarist—just start out with two million!

Another reason people learn to play is because they think it will impress prospective significant others. I must admit that although I began to play for more noble reasons (I figured I had a good shot at becoming the fifth Beatle if I worked on my English accent), I did meet my wife at a gig.

Whatever your reason was for beginning to play this instrument, you must be aware of what playing is all about. Music, like any art form, is a form of expression. To be a good musician, you will need to express yourself through the music, whether you play original compositions or the works of other writers. You must put your feelings and personality into the pieces you perform whether you are playing in your living room or Carnegie Hall.

Here are some tips for expressive playing on the guitar:

Tone - *Tone* (the quality of your sound) is affected by where and how you pluck the strings. Near the bridge the sound is clear and trebly. Over the fingerboard it is richer, with more bass. Repeat a phrase while slowly moving the picking hand between these spots. Tone is also affected by how notes are struck. Play one note with nail alone, flesh alone and a combination of flesh with nail. Experiment and learn to control these variations.

Volume - The area of expression that includes tone and volume is called *dynamics*. Try playing a phrase as quietly as you can, increase the volume until you reach top volume and decrease until notes fade to nothing.

Tempo - *Tempo* refers to speed. Practice phrases as slowly as possible, increase gradually until you reach your top speed. Then slowly decrease speed. Learning to make subtle tempo changes is important. Don't take tempo for granted. Try different speeds for each piece until you find one you feel is best.

> *Music can express things we can not put into words. Good technique and a creative approach will enable you to express these feelings. Like the Staples Singers said, "Express Yourself."*

LISTENING

There are too many great players to list here. You need to find your own musical role models to emulate. These are just a few players you should hear:

Will Ackerman	Leo Kottke	Lightning Hopkins	Preston Reed
Chet Atkins	Rev. Gary Davis	Mississippi John Hurt	John Renbourn
Seth Austen	Guy Van Duser	John Jackson	Dave Van Ronk
Duck Baker	Alex DeGrassi	Skip James	Martin Simpson
Pierre Bensusan	John Fahey	Bert Jansch	Joseph Spence
Blind Blake	Davey Graham	Blind Lemon Jefferson	Merle Travis
Ry Cooder	Stefan Grossman	Robert Johnson	
Elizabeth Cotten	Michael Hedges	Adrian Legg	

Of course, many singer/songwriters are known for their interesting accompaniment styles. James Taylor, Paul Simon and Joni Mitchell are well known for this.

Listen to all styles of music and try to incorporate them into your playing. Enjoy!

INTERMEDIATE

GUITAR

FINGERSTYLE

LOU MANZI
NATHANIEL GUNOD

Audio tracks recorded and engineered at Bar None Studio, Cheshire, CT
Performed by Lou Manzi

CONTENTS

ABOUT THE AUTHORS

PHOTO BY TIMOTHY PHELPS

Lou Manzi began his career in music in 1974. He has performed in various styles in the New York area and teaches at the National Guitar Summer Workshop. He is the author of *The Complete Acoustic Blues Method*, also published by Alfred and the National Guitar Workshop. Lou lives in Stonington, Connecticut where he teaches and helps administrate the National Music Workshop's lesson programs throughout New England.

Nat Gunod is the chief editor for Workshop Arts, the publishing arm of the National Guitar Workshop. As of this writing, he has edited over 70 books and directed 10 videos. He is the author of *Classical Guitar for Beginners, Renaissance Duets: Play Along Library* and *Progressive Classical Solos*. Nat is an Associate Director of the National Guitar Workshop (NGW) and directs the NGW Classical Guitar Seminar. He has performed all over the United States and taught students from all over the world at the Workshop and at various colleges, including the Peabody Conservatory of the Johns Hopkins University. He wrote all of the text for *Intermediate Fingerstyle Guitar*.

INTRODUCTION

Welcome to the *Intermediate* section. To get the most out of this section, you should have a good grasp on the material from the first section, or the following applies to you:

- You know how to read standard music notation and/or TAB

- You know the basic open chords and are ready to learn barre chords

- You have an understanding of basic theory (triads, major scale, diatonic harmony, key signatures, etc.) and are ready to learn 7th chord theory

- You play a number of different fingerpicking patterns, including Travis picking and are ready for more

- You know some basic altered tunings, such as Drop D and Open G and want to try more

- You are familiar with alternating bass lines and walking bass lines and want to learn about arpeggio bass lines

- You know techniques such as hammer-ons, pull-offs and natural harmonics and want to learn artificial harmonics, right hand slapping and right hand tapping.

- You want to begin learning how to arrange for fingerstyle guitar

- You want to study counterpoint

- You want to learn about the modes

- You want to play pieces in the styles of great fingerstyle players

A basic notation review starts on the next page. If you do not need this review, go ahead and skip to page 108. Just remember, to get the most out of this or any other instruction book, practice the pieces slowly—a section at a time. You can understand something intellectually almost immediately, but physically, it takes a lot longer. Be patient, keep an open mind, practice lots, and have fun!

00

Track 1

An MP3 CD is included with this book to make learning easier and more enjoyable. The symbol shown at bottom left appears next to every example in the book that features an MP3 track. Use the MP3s to ensure you're capturing the feel of the examples and interpreting the rhythms correctly. The track number below the symbol corresponds directly to the example you want to hear (example numbers are above the icon). All the track numbers are unique to each "book" within this volume, meaning every book has its own Track 1, Track 2, and so on. (For example, *Beginning Fingerstyle Guitar* starts with Track 1, as does *Intermediate Fingerstyle Guitar* and *Mastering Fingerstyle Guitar*.) Track 1 for each book will help you tune to the CD.

The disc is playable on any CD player equipped to play MP3 CDs. To access the MP3s on your computer, place the CD in your CD-ROM drive. In Windows, double-click on My Computer, then right-click on the CD icon labeled "MP3 Files" and select Explore to view the files and copy them to your hard drive. For Mac, double-click on the CD icon on your desktop labeled "MP3 Files" to view the files and copy them to your hard drive.

CHAPTER 1

Review of the Basics

THE OPEN STRINGS

Holding your guitar in playing position, the strings are numbered from 6th to 1st with the 6th or lowest string being the one closest to the ceiling. Many beginning players don't know which end is up when it comes to the guitar. Since we are playing musical sounds, we refer to high and low depending upon the height and depth of our notes. The first string may be closest to the floor, but it is called the highest string because it is tuned to a higher *note* than the other strings. Music is made up of *notes*. A note is a musical sound, or *pitch*, of a specific degree of highness or lowness. Each note is given one of seven alphabetical names: A, B, C, D, E, F or G.

The following diagram shows that the strings are named E, A, D, G, B, E from 6th to 1st. The sentence "Ernie's Ant Does Get Big Eventually" may help you memorize these notes.

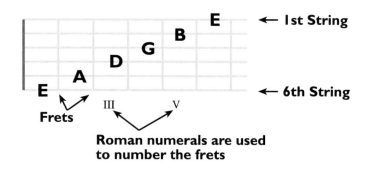

ROMAN NUMERALS

Here is a review of Roman numerals and their Arabic equivalents.

I.....i......1	IV..iv....4	VII.....vii..7	X........x.....10	XIII.....xiii...13	XVI.....xvi.....16
II....ii.....2	V....v.....5	VIII....viii.8	XI......xi...11	XIV....xiv...14	XVII....xvii....17
III...iii....3	VI..vi....6	IX......ix...9	XII.....xii..12	XV......xv.....15	XVIII...xviii...18

PITCH

Notes

Music is written by placing *notes* on a *staff*. Notes appear in various ways.

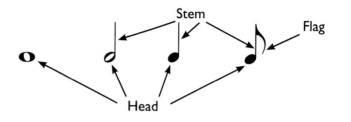

The Staff and Clef

The staff has five lines and four spaces which are read from left to right. At the beginning of the staff is a *clef*. The clef dictates what notes correspond to a particular line or space on the staff. Guitar music is written in *treble clef* 𝄞 which is sometimes called the *G clef*. The ending curl of the clef circles the G line on the staff.

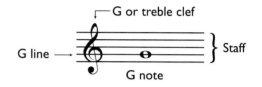

Here are the notes on the staff using the G clef.

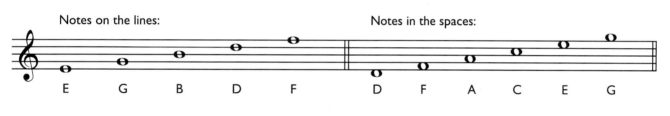

Notes on the lines:
E G B D F

Notes in the spaces:
D F A C E G

Ledger Lines

The higher a note appears on the staff, the higher it sounds. When a note is too high or too low to be written on the staff, *ledger lines* are used.

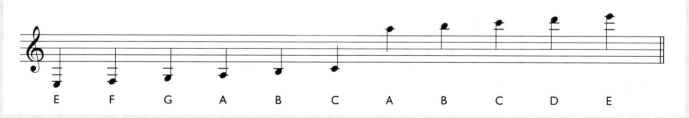

E F G A B C A B C D E

Guitar music is traditionally written one octave higher than it actually sounds. This allows us to write and read music on one clef, instead of using two clefs as with keyboard instruments.

TIME

Musical time is measured in *beats*. Beats are the steady pulse of the music on which we build *rhythms*. Rhythm is a pattern of long and short sounds and silences and is represented by *note* and *rest values*. Value indicates duration.

Measures and Bar Lines

The staff is divided by vertical lines called *bar lines*. The space between two bar lines is a *measure* or *bar*. Measures divide music into groups of beats. A *double bar* marks the end of a section or example.

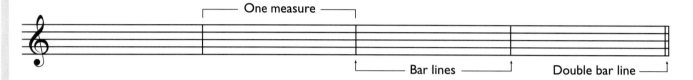

Note Values

The duration of a note—its value—is indicated by the note's appearance or shape.

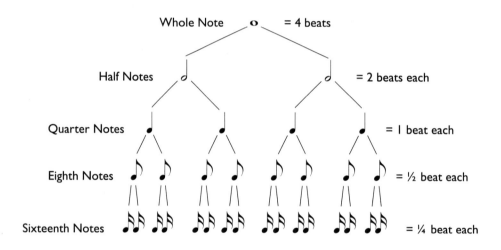

Time Signatures

A *time signature* appears at the beginning of a piece of music. The number on top indicates the number of beats per measure. The number on the bottom indicates the type of note that gets one beat.

$\frac{4}{4}$ = 4 beats per measure
Quarter note ♩ = one beat

$\frac{3}{4}$ = 3 beats per measure
Quarter note ♩ = one beat

$\frac{6}{8}$ = 6 beats per measure
Eighth note ♪ = one beat

Sometimes a **C** is used in place of $\frac{4}{4}$.
This is called *common time*.

Rest Values

Every note value has a corresponding *rest* value. A rest indicates silence in music. A *whole rest* indicates four beats of silence, a *half rest* is two beats of silence, etc.

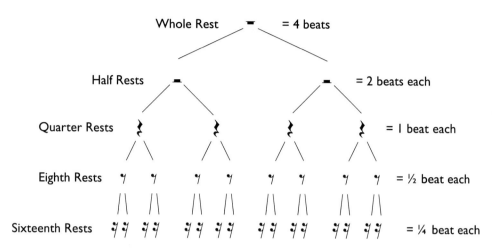

Ties and Counting

A *tie* is a curved line that joins two or more notes of the same pitch that last the duration of the combined note values. For example, when a half note (two beats) is tied to a quarter note (one beat), the combined notes are held for three beats (2 + 1 = 3).

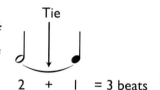

Notice the numbers under the staff in the examples below. These indicate how to count while playing. Both of these examples are in $\frac{4}{4}$ time, so we count four beats in each measure. *Eighth-note* rhythms are counted "1–&, 2–&, 3–&," etc. The numbers are the *onbeats* and the "&"s (pronounced "and") are the *offbeats*.

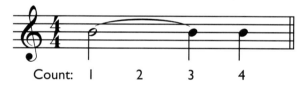

Dots

A *dot* increases the length of a note or rest by one half of its original value. For instance, a half note lasts for two beats. Half of its value is one beat (a quarter note). So a *dotted half note* equals three beats (2 + 1 = 3), which is the same as a half note tied to a quarter note. The same logic applies for all dotted notes.

Dotted notes are especially important when the time signature is $\frac{3}{4}$, because the longest note value that will fit in a measure is a dotted half note. Also, dotted notes are very important in $\frac{6}{8}$ time, because not only is a dotted half note the longest possible note value, but a dotted quarter note is exactly half of a measure (counted: 1–&–ah, 2–&–ah).

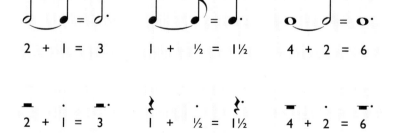

Triplets

A *triplet* is a group of three notes that divides a beat (or beats) into three equal parts.

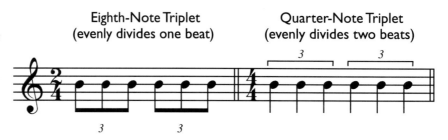

Eighth-Note Triplet
(evenly divides one beat)

Quarter-Note Triplet
(evenly divides two beats)

Beaming

Notes that are less than one beat in duration are often *beamed* together. Sometimes they are grouped in twos and sometimes they are grouped in fours.

Beamed eighth notes

Beamed sixteenth notes

Beams

Beams

Swing Eighths

In the blues and jazz styles, eighth notes are usually not played exactly as notated. Rather, they are interpreted in a "swing" style. This makes a pair of eighth notes sound like the first and last notes of a triplet. Swing eighths:

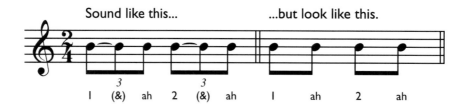

Sound like this...

...but look like this.

Repeat Signs

Repeat signs are used to indicate music that should be repeated.

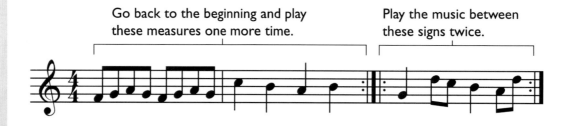

Go back to the beginning and play these measures one more time.

Play the music between these signs twice.

This sign ∕. tells us to repeat the previous measure.

Fingerstyle Notation

The standard rule in notation is that notes on the middle line of the staff or higher have their stems descending, and lower notes have their stems ascending. This won't work in lots of fingerstyle music, since it often involves playing more than one line at a time. In order to clearly separate the bass line when there is more than one line, we must borrow from classical guitar notation: we use descending stems for all notes played by the thumb, and ascending stems for all other pitches. This is an easy way to show two or more simultaneous melodic lines.

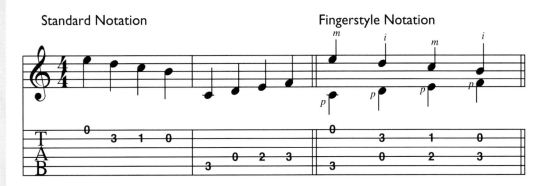

Scale Diagrams

The top line of a scale diagram represents the 1st (highest) string of the guitar, and the bottom line the 6th. The vertical lines represent frets, which are numbered with Roman numerals.

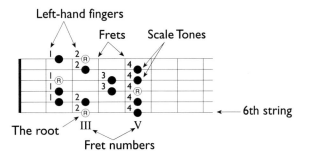

Chord Diagrams

Chord diagrams are similar to scale diagrams, except they are oriented vertically instead of horizontally. Vertical lines represent strings, and horizontal lines represent frets. Roman numerals are used to number the frets.

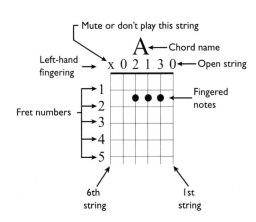

CHAPTER 2

Fingerstyle Patterns

REVIEW OF PATTERNS #1 – #11

Fingerstyle (or finger-picking) patterns are based on *chords*. A chord is any group of three or more notes (usually harmonious) played together. In fingerstyle guitar, we often play chords as *arpeggios*. In an arpeggio, the notes of a chord are played individually, rather than together. In this chapter you will be introduced to some basic right hand fingerstyle patterns. Although these easy arpeggios are often used for song accompaniments, creative composers also use them as the basis for their original instrumental pieces.

Notice the use of fingerstyle notation in these examples. The bass notes, played by the thumb of the right hand (*p*), are stemmed down, and the other notes are stemmed up. This makes it easier to find the bass line, and makes its independent identity as a separate part clear. Notice how many of the bass notes have two stems: one going up and one going down. This shows the bass line as distinct from the other notes, but also shows how it fits into the overall rhythm, usually as the first in a group of eighth notes.

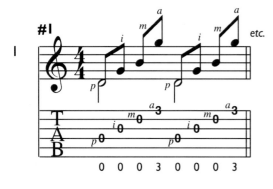

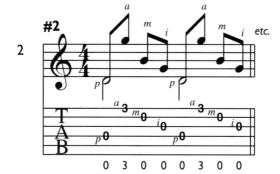

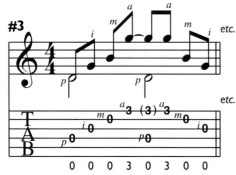

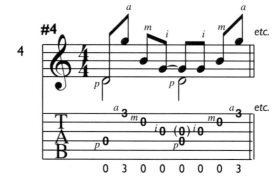

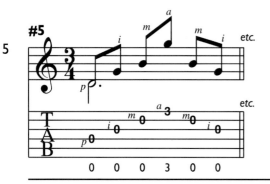

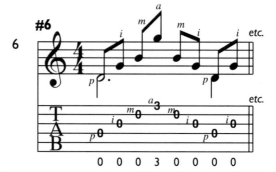

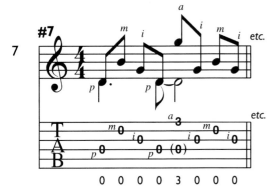

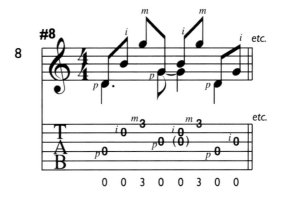

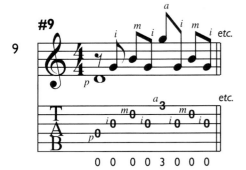

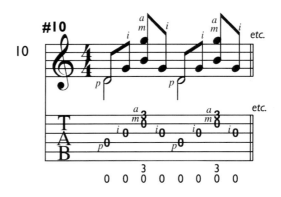

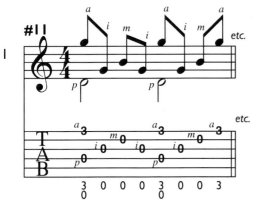

Pattern #12 creates a new pattern with a part of pattern #10: the double stop with *m* and *a* followed by a single note with the *i* finger. In this case, *p* is combined with the double stop. As *p*, *m* and *a* play, release *i* to its strings. As *i* plays, re-extend *p*, *m* and *a*. Continue alternating in this way.

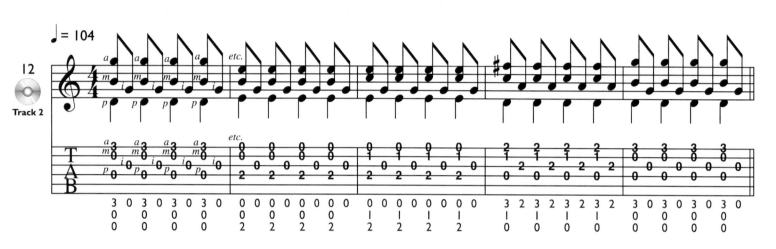

Example 13 will give you more practice with Pattern #12.

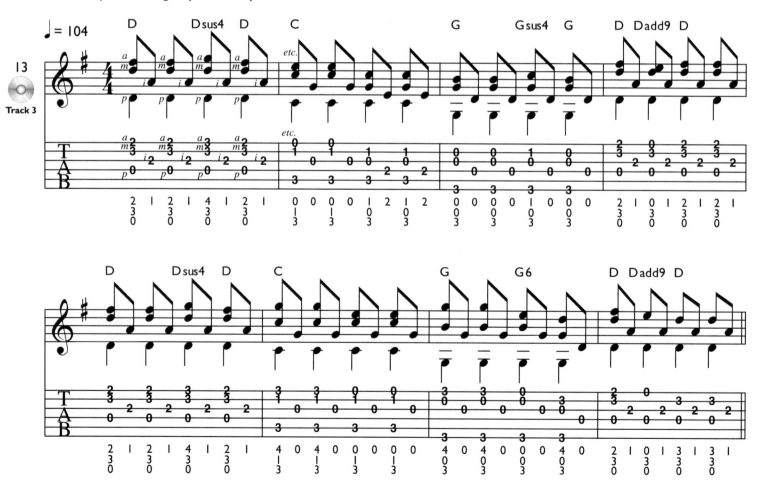

PATTERN #13

Pattern #13 is based on the same Latin (South American) rhythm as Pattern #8. This time, the rhythm is even more pronounced because *a* and *p* play together, further emphasizing the 1-2-3,1-2-3, 1-2 rhythm of the bass. Start with *a*, *m* and *i* all poised to play their respective strings. The fingers should follow each other into the hand, and as *i* plays *a* and *m* should release back their strings. Return *i* back to the 3rd string as *a* strokes the 1st. Always return *p* to its string as *a* returns to the 1st string. On the last eighth of each measure, return *a* to the 1st string as *m* plays.

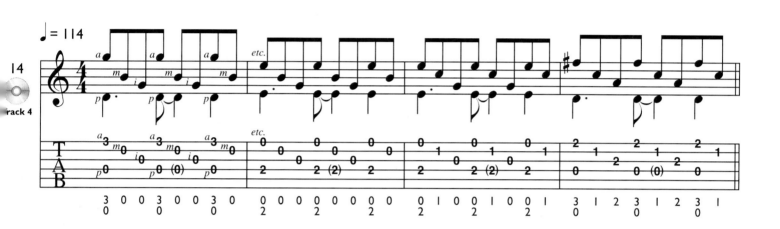

Enjoy playing this example based on Pattern #13.

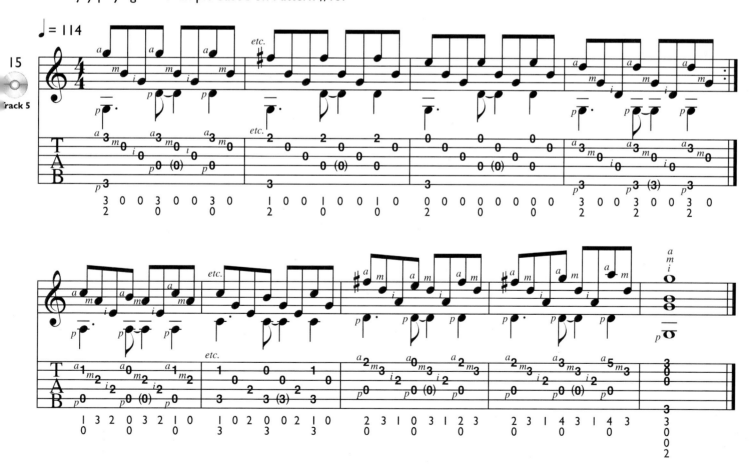

PATTERN #14

Pattern #14 is based on the alternating bass Travis picking introduced on page 50. The *p* finger alternates between the 6th and the 4th or the 5th and the 4th strings. Try to move *p* from the wrist joint, where the thumb connects to the wrist. Keep the hand still as you keep the steady quarter note rhythm of the bass going. There is plenty of time to prepare *m* on the 1st string before playing. This will give you added security and control of the tone.

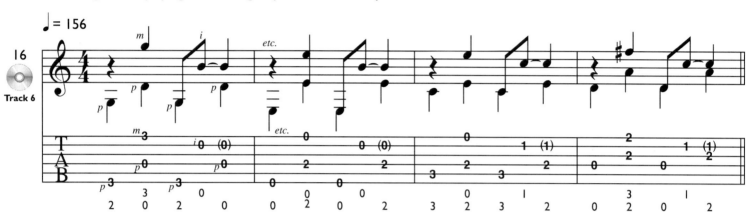

Remember, slash chords such as the D/F♯ in the second measure of Example 17 indicate the chord shown has a note other than the root in the bass. For instance, D/F♯ indicates a D Major chord with an F♯ in the bass.

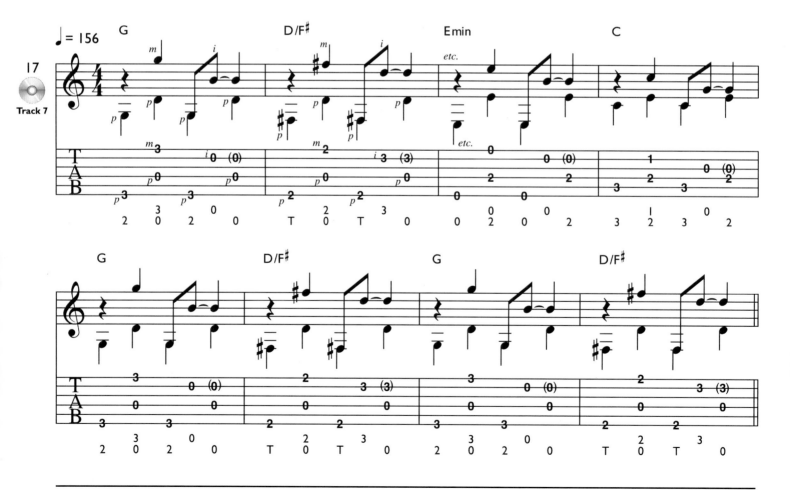

Another variation on Travis picking, Pattern #15 provides another opportunity to practice finger alternations (this time between *i* and *m*) against a steady, driving alternating bass. Remember to keep your hand as still as possible. Let your fingers do the work!

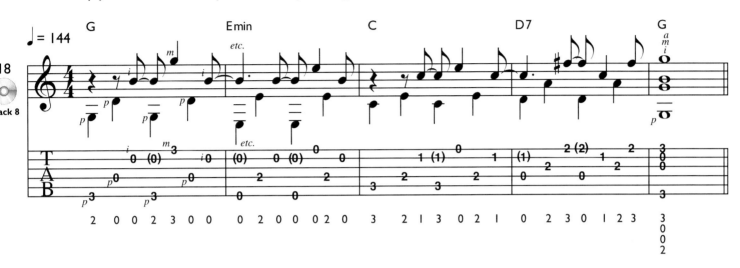

Example 19 is chock-full of new and interesting chords. Spend some time with each and get to know their sounds. Here they are:

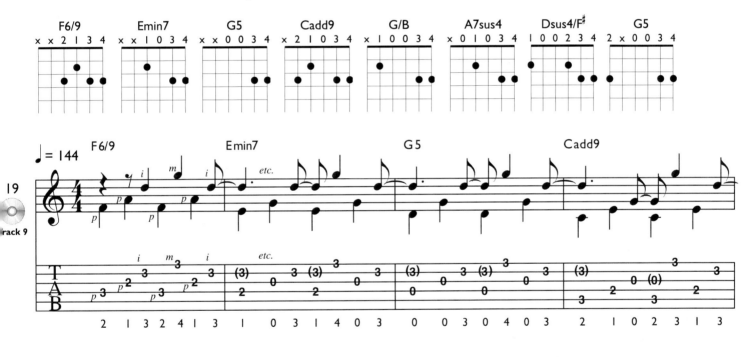

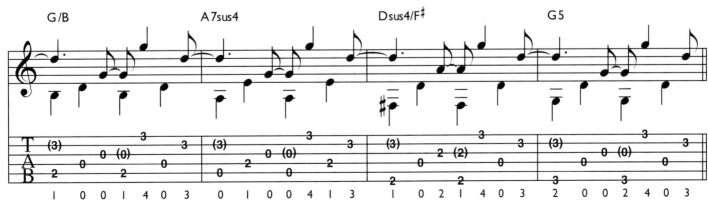

CHAPTER 3
Special Techniques

MULTIPLE HAMMER-ONS AND PULL-OFFS

By now, you are probably well acquainted with *hammer-ons* and *pull-offs*. If not, it would be a good idea to review pages 69 and 70.

Briefly, hammer-ons and pull-offs, otherwise known as *slurs*, are the most commonly used devices for creating *legato* (smooth) connections between notes on the guitar. In both techniques, then right hand plucks the first note and subsequent notes are played by the left hand. Slurs are notated with a slur sign ⌒ and an H for hammer-ons, or a P for pull-offs.

In this section, we will be expanding on these techniques connecting more than two notes with hammer-ons and pull-offs. That's right...you can play more than two notes with only one pluck. This is a great way to group notes together and play quickly. While it is very important to learn to pluck rapidly, there's no harm in getting a little speed with less effort. And, as long the notes involved can be played on a single string, hammer-ons and pull-offs can get you three or more very quick notes for the price of one!

As always, an important issue with these legato techniques is rhythm. It is challenging to build a technique that can perform rhythmically even hammer-ons and pull-offs. Beware of the tendency to rush into the second or third notes in, say, a three note group. Practice your eight-note slurs with a metronome set to eighth notes. This will help you acquire a feel for even legatos.

The next three pages contain examples and pieces using these techniques. Practice them all slowly at first, with a metronome. Have fun!

PHOTO COURTESY OF GAMI-SIMMONS

*One of the few classical guitarists to successfully cross over into the fingerstyle "acoustic music" world, **Benjamin Verdery** came to prominence in the 1980s. He has performed to delighted audiences in both fingerstyle and classical guitar festivals all over the world.*

Check it out! By measure three of Example 20, you'll be whippin' out those sixteenth note licks like butter. But work-up to playing them quickly. Practice slowly at first. You will find, however, that it is impractical to practice hammer-ons and pull-offs *too* slowly. At very slow speeds, rhythmic accuracy becomes unreasonable to expect.

Pay special attention to the last note in the first measure (D on the 2nd string). This note is played with a hammer-on, even though the string has yet to be struck by the right hand. In a way, this is really a *tap*. Make sure that the 2nd finger strikes the 3rd fret with sufficient force to make the D note sound clearly, but not so much that the note sounds percussive.

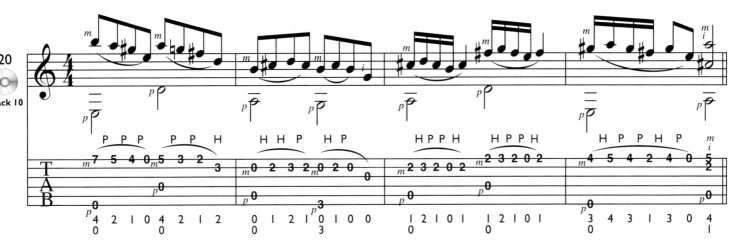

Example 21 introduces double-stop hammer-ons and pull-offs. There is nothing really new here, although it may feel new. In hammer-ons, make sure you are lifting and dropping both fingers together. In pull-offs, take care to pull both fingers off together. In both cases, strive to maintain a good balance between the parts—the upper and lower notes in each double-stop should sound at the same volume.

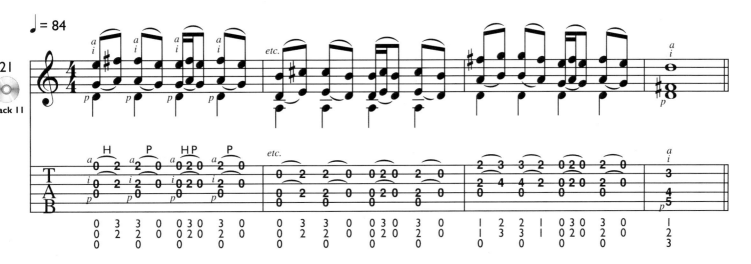

DESERT RIDE

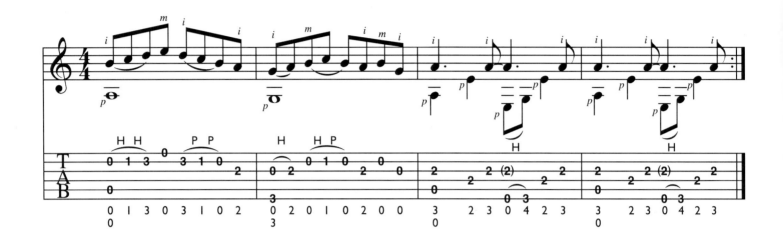

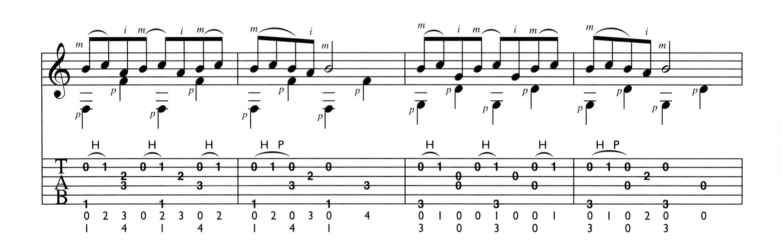

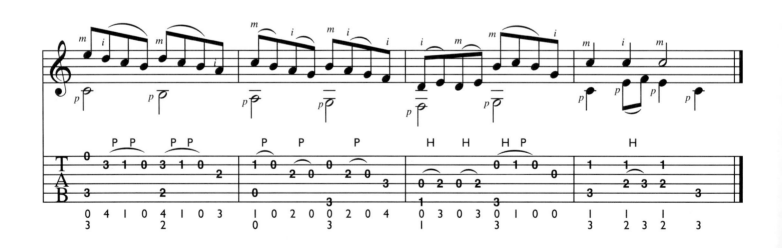

Tune your 6th string down to D for this one.

NIGHT OUT

Track 13

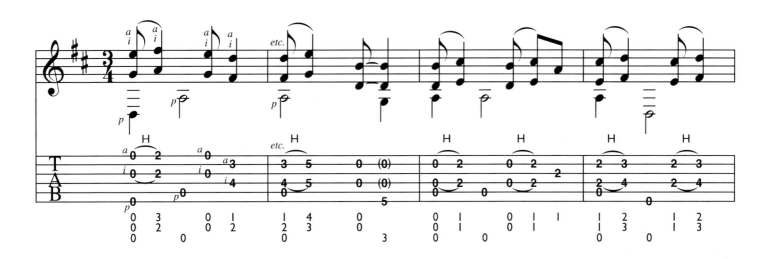

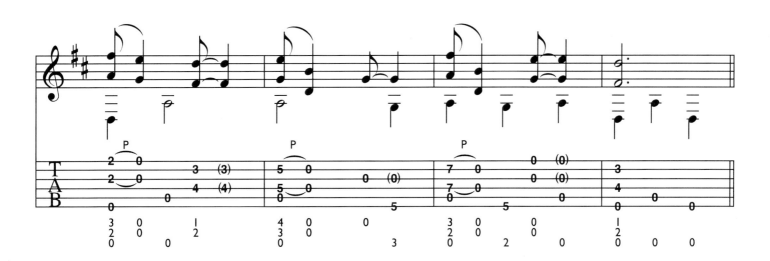

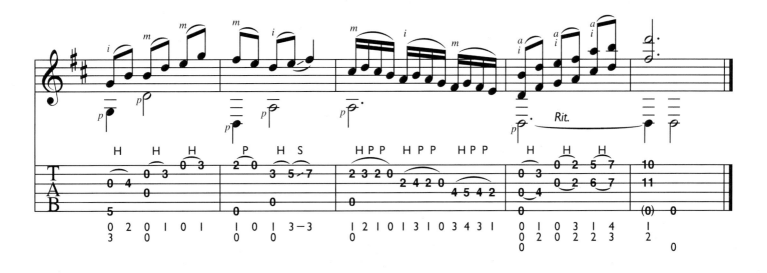

ARTIFICIAL HARMONICS

By now, you have certainly listened to lots of guitar music. You may have noticed occasional high chiming notes that have a bell-like tone. These were probably *harmonics*. Every musical note, or *fundamental tone*, is accompanied by an array of *overtones*. We aren't usually aware of them—they are just there, the way that many colors of the spectrum are there when we perceive a specific color. A harmonic is what happens when we touch the string in such a way as to isolate one of these overtones from the fundamental tone and most of the other overtones. These high, pure sounding tones are distinctive, and add a beautiful color to pieces. They can be very effective as highlights in the music. There are various ways to make harmonics on the guitar. On page 75, we covered natural harmonics. Now, it's time to discuss *artificial harmonics*.

While natural harmonics are made by touching the string lightly at certain points on the string with the left hand (the 12th, 7th and 5th frets are most common), artificial harmonics involve a different technique. Here is how to perform an artificial harmonic that sounds an octave higher than the fundamental tone:

- Finger the desired note normally with the left hand.

- With the *i* finger of the right hand, lightly touch the same string directly over a fret exactly twelve frets higher than the fingered note. For instance, if the fingered note is one the 1st fret, touch a spot directly over the 13th fret with the right hand.

- While touching the string with *i*, pluck the string with *p* or *a*.

- Immediately upon striking the note, quickly lift the right hand away from the string, allowing it to ring clearly.

Experiment with this for a little while. Remember that the as you change from note to note, the right hand will mirror the motion of the left hand fingers. As finger higher notes on a string, your right hand will move to the right. As you finger lower notes on a string, your right hand will move to the left. Work on the timing between plucking the string with *p* or *a* and lifting your right hand away of the strings so that the notes ring clearly. Notice the diamond shaped note heads in the example below, indicating harmonics. Unless marked otherwise, all of he artificial harmonics are as described above—twelve frets higher than the fingered note.

In Examples 22 and 23, pluck with *p*.

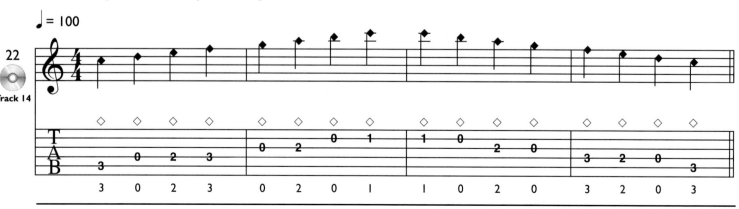

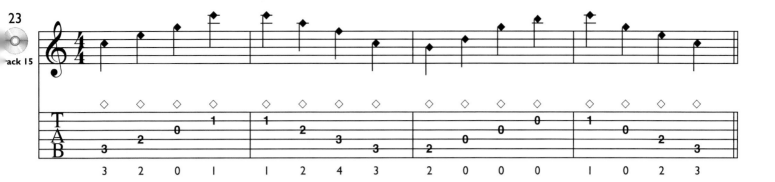

In Example 24, artificial harmonics are mixed in with normal notes. Since the artificial harmonics are fingered on the lower strings, continue to pluck them with *p*. But here's something you may never have tried before: pluck the normal notes with your pinky (*c*)! Yes, this will take some getting-used-to, but it works out well because your right hand will be tilted towards the pinky so that *p* can pluck the harmonics. Have fun.

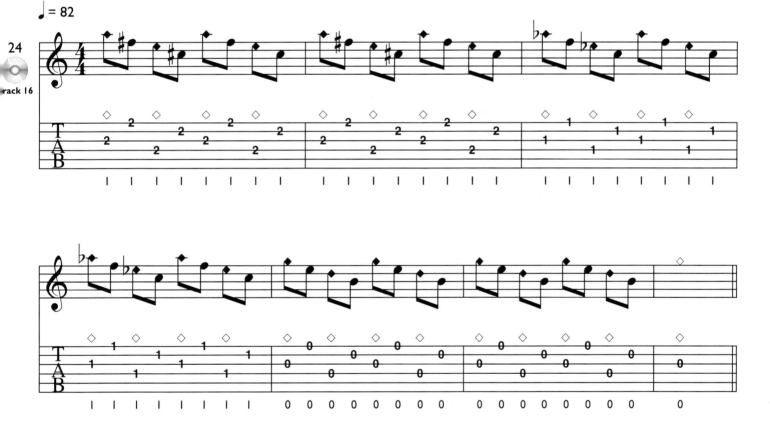

Now it's time to try plucking artificial harmonics with the *a* finger. Continue to use *i* to lightly touch the strings above the desired frets. This technique is usually used when the harmonics are played on the upper three strings. Learn the harmonics in Example 25 before putting them together with the bass notes, which are played with *p*.

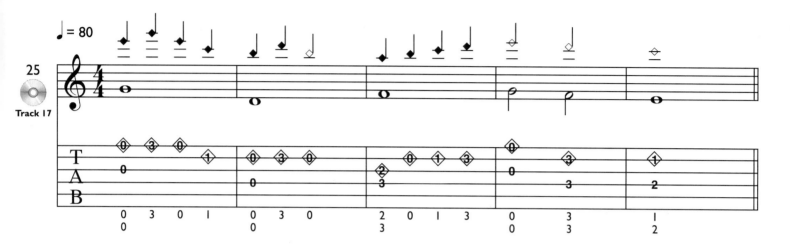

Here is yet another artificial harmonics technique. Pluck the normal notes (stems down) with your pinky, and pluck the harmonics (stems up) with *p*!

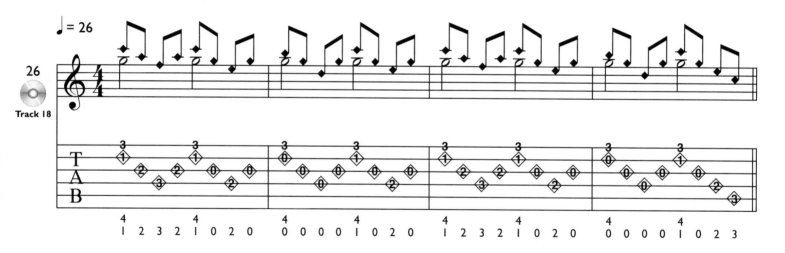

In the following piece, play all the harmonics with *i* and *p*. All other notes should be plucked with your picky.

STAR CATCHER

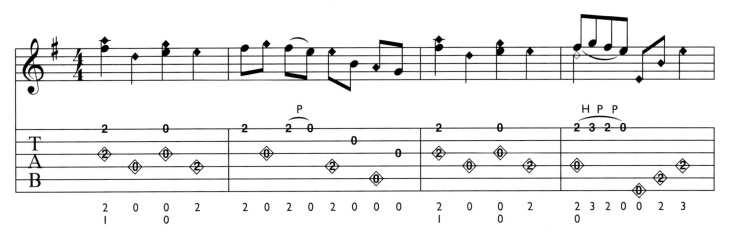

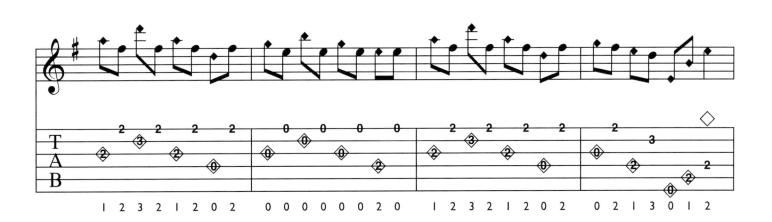

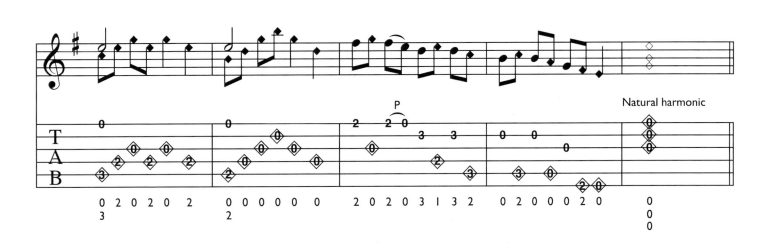

CHAPTER 4

Barre Chords

THE TECHNIQUE

Barre chords are an essential technique for all guitarists. The most important feature of barre chords is that they contain no open strings. This simple fact makes these chords indispensable because, since they contain no open strings, they can be played in any key anywhere on the neck.

To perform a barre, lay your 1st finger across all six strings just to the left of the fret. For now, try this on the 5th fret. Pull your left elbow in towards your side slightly. This will help you to use the thumb side of the 1st finger, thus avoiding the indentations at the joints of the finger, increasing your leverage and making it easier to use the other fingers. Try to use just enough strength to allow all six strings to ring clearly when plucked. Try to keep the 1st finger fairly straight—parallel to the fret. Slowly pluck all six strings. If one string doesn't ring clearly, try adjusting your left hand up (towards the ceiling) or down (towards the floor) to put slightly more or slightly less finger over the neck. Make sure you have your left elbow in closer to your side than normal. We all have different sized hands and need to experiment to find the right position for each barre.

Another important variable in playing barre chords is, believe it or not, your guitar. Some guitars have a "low action," where the strings are very close to the frets and easy to push down. Some guitars have a "high action," and are more difficult to play. While barre chords require a bit more strength than other notes and chords, if you are using your elbow, hand and finger positions to their best advantage, they shouldn't require *that* much strength. If you find barres unreasonably difficult to play even after considering all the technical variables, maybe you should have your action adjusted down or consider a lighter set of strings.

Another important variable for playing barre chords is the number of strings being barred. For instance, if you are playing a chord where the 6th, 2nd and 1st strings are barred and the other strings are taken with other fingers, your barre need only work on the three barred strings. You can work on controlling which part of the 1st finger works the hardest.

ROOT 6 AND ROOT 5 BARRES

The two most common types of barre chord are the root 6 and root 5 barres. As you know, every chord has a root. Root 6 barres have their roots on the 6th string, root 5 barres have their roots on the 5th string. The neat thing is, if you know all the names of the notes on these two strings, you can play any barre on any root. A♭ Minor? No problem, just find an A♭ on the 6th or 5th string and play the appropriate barre chord!

As you will notice when studying the chart on page 123, the root 6 chords are based on the open position E chords, and the root 5 chords are based on open position A chords. Check it out! Make sure you memorize and master all the chords on the chart. Have fun.

ROOT 6 BARRES

Major
1 3 4 2 1 1

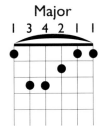

Minor
1 3 4 1 1 1

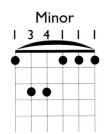

7th
1 3 1 2 1 1

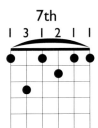

7th
1 3 1 2 4 1

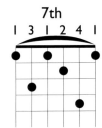

ROOT 5 BARRES

Major
x 1 2 3 4 1

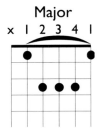

Major
x 1 3 3 3 1

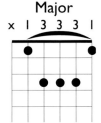

(Alternate Fingerings)

Major
x 1 3 3 3 x

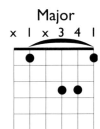

Major
x 1 x 3 4 1

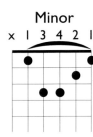

Minor
x 1 3 4 2 1

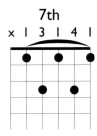

7th
x 1 3 1 4 1

ALTERNATIVE BARRE FINGERINGS

Here are some alternative fingerings that can be useful when you need your 4th finger free to play melodies in a barre chord context: Notice the muted string (x) and the use of the left hand thumb (T).

Major
T x 3 2 1 1

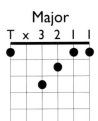

Major
1 x 3 2 1 1

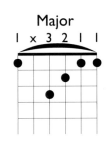

Minor
1 x 3 1 1 1

Minor
T x 3 1 1 1

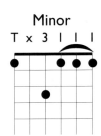

Example 27 will exercise your root 6 chops. These are all root 6 major chords. The pattern begins on the 1st fret (the root is F—the 1st fret of the 6th string) and moves up by a whole step to the 3rd fret (G) and by a whole step again to the 5th fret (A). You might want to study the right hand pattern before practicing the barres.

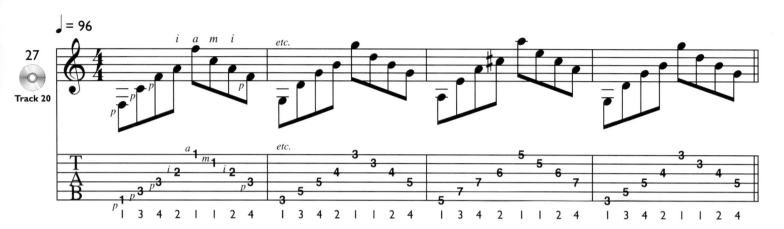

Try the same whole step pattern with other barres and fingerpicking patterns.

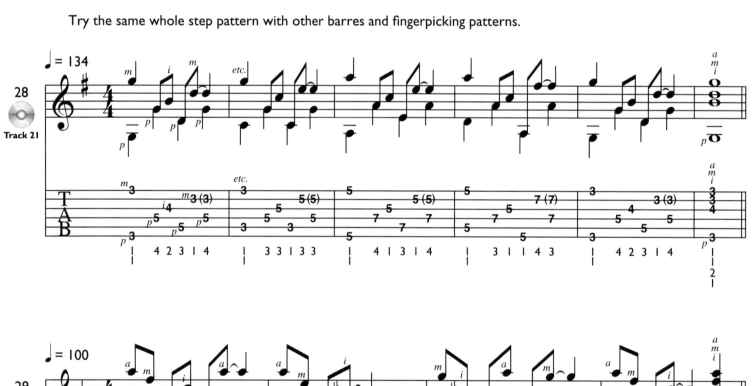

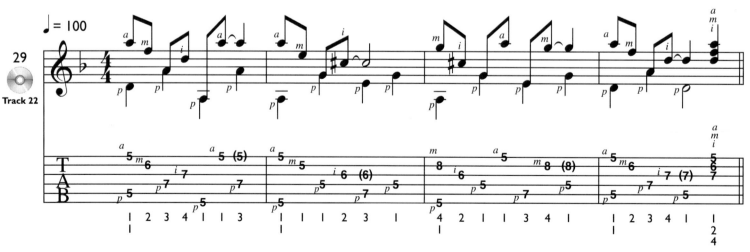

Handle the Barres will flex your root 6 muscles. Be sure to swing the eighths.

 HANDLE THE BARRES

Track 23

Spanish Nights uses root 5 barres.

SPANISH NIGHTS

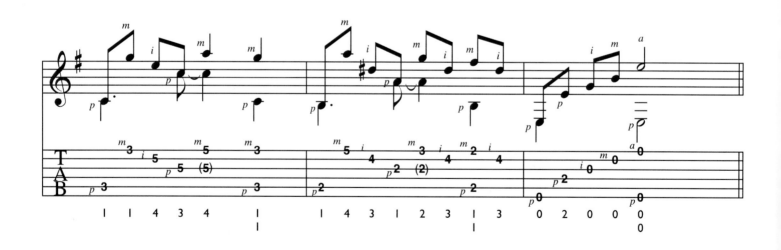

This piece, in the key of A Minor, relies heavily on minor barre chords.

A MINOR DETAIL

Track 25

CHAPTER 5

More Fingerstyle Patterns

So far, we've covered fifteen different fingerstyle patterns, plus, if you've been paying attention, you've noticed numerous other variations in the pieces throughout this book. Well, ladies and gentleman, here for your further fingerpickin' enjoyment are four more.

PATTERN #16

This one is really a $\frac{3}{4}$ version of Pattern #10 (see page 109) with quarter notes in the bass.

Example 31 will give you some practice with this pattern.

Pattern #17 is another alternating bass pattern, much like Pattern #14. There is a nice syncopation in the 3rd beat going into the 4th, spicing up an otherwise straightforward rhythm. Technically, it's easy. Repeating the *m* finger on the first two beats imparts a pleasant, bouncy feel. You may want to watch your right hand at first, to make sure you are crossing from the 1st to 2nd string accurately.

PATTERN #18

Perform the first two beats of Pattern #18 just as you would Pattern #9 (see page 109). As you play the *i* stroke on "&" of "2," extend *a*, *m* and *p* to play. After *a* and *p* play, *m* follows into the palm as you re-extend *p* to begin again.

Pattern #19 is another variation on the alternating bass, Travis picking pattern. While maintaining the pulsing alternating bass, perform an *i, m a* arpeggio as in Pattern #1 (see page 108), but start it off the beat by inserting an *m* stroke on the first half of the first beat and a tie over the third beat.

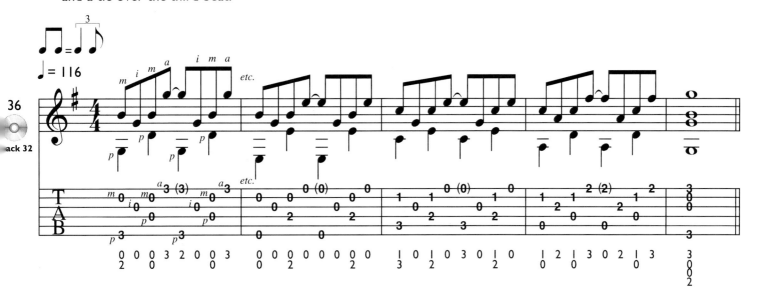

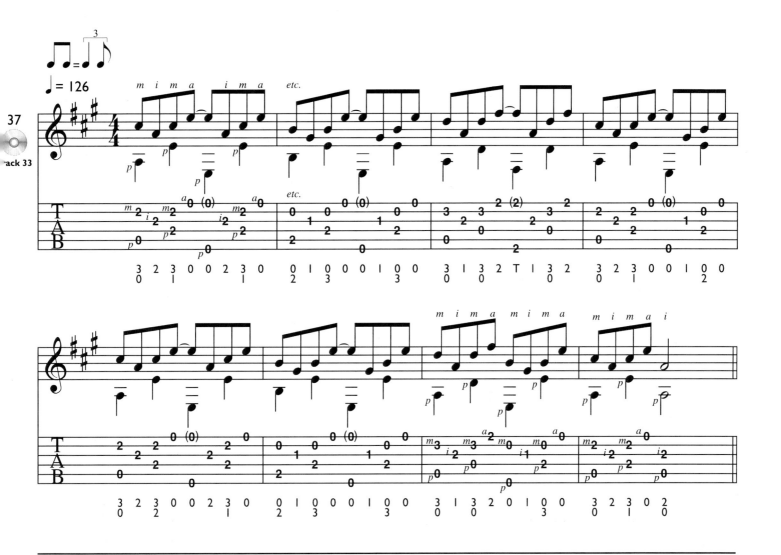

CHAPTER 6

Diatonic Harmony

This chapter will start with a review of what we have already covered regarding diatonic harmony and will then continue into unchartered territory. If you feel you have the major scale and diatonic triads nailed, there's no reason not to turn to the section on 7th chords on page 133.

THE MAJOR SCALE

In order to understand diatonic harmony, you must have a grasp of the major scale. This common scale can begin on any pitch and is made up of a series of whole and half steps. The *formula* of whole steps and half steps is:

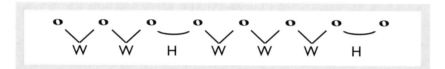

and W = Whole step

and H = Half step

The phrase, "Wendy Witch Has Wild, Wonderful, Wavy Hair" will help you memorize the major scale pattern.

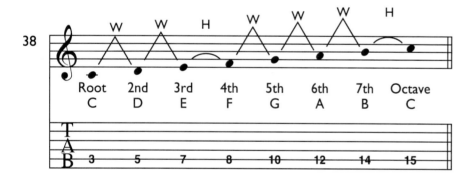

If we build a major scale starting on C, our formula gives us the notes C, D, E, F, G, A, B and C. Playing this scale horizontally up the fifth string, starting with the C on the 3rd fret, enables us to clearly see the pattern of whole and half steps on the neck.

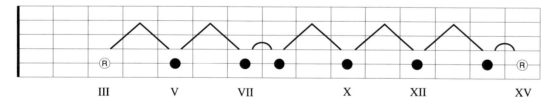

DIATONIC HARMONY—TRIADS

By now, you know the formulas for the most basic chords. Now, we need to see how they are related within one major key. The word *diatonic* means "within the key." For each of the seven different notes in the major scale, we can build a corresponding triad. These are the diatonic triads for that key. There will be a particular pattern of major and minor triads, with a diminished triad at the end, that is the same in any major key.

The following are the diatonic triads in the key of C Major:

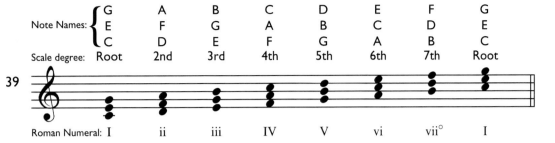

The preferred way to refer to triads is with a number that represents their diatonic position in the key. We use Roman numerals to write these numbers, upper case for major chords (I, IV and V), and lower case for minor (ii, iii and vi). For the diminished triad that occurs on the 7th degree, we add a small circle (○) to a lower-case Roman numeral (vii○). For a quick review of Roman numerals, see page 102.

Here is a summary of the diatonic triads for any major key:

> **I, IV and V** .....are always ..... **major**
> **ii, iii and vi** .....are always ..... **minor**
> **vii**○....................is always .... **diminished**

FOUR TYPES OF 7TH CHORDS

Now that you have brushed up on diatonic harmony with triads, it's time to put 7th chords into the mix. First, let's take a look at four important varieties.

THE DOMINANT 7TH CHORD
Frequently, the V chord has another tone added a *minor 3rd* (a distance of three half steps) above the 5th, which is a ♭7 above the root (1 - 3 - 5 - ♭7). This is a called a *dominant 7th* chord. The example on the right shows the V7 chord in the key of C, which is G7.

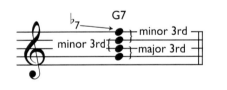

THE MINOR 7TH CHORD
Frequently, the ii, iii or vi chord has another tone added a *minor 3rd* (a distance of three half steps) above the 5th, which is a ♭7 above the root (1 - ♭3 - 5 - ♭7). This is a called a *minor 7th* chord. The example on the right shows the ii7 chord in the key of C, which is Dmin7.

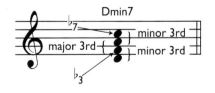

continued on next page...

THE MINOR 7♭5 CHORD

Frequently, the vii° chord has another tone added a *major 3rd* (a distance of four half steps) above the 5th, which is a ♭7 above the root (1 - ♭3 - ♭5 - ♭7). This is a called a *minor 7♭5* chord. The example on the right shows the min7♭5 chord in the key of C, which is Bmin7♭5. Notice that you can also think of this as a minor 7th chord with a lowered 5 (♭5).

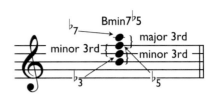

THE MAJOR 7 CHORD

Frequently, the I and the IV chords have another tone added a *major 3rd* (a distance of four half steps) above the 5th, which is a major 7 above the root (1 - 3 - 5 - 7). This is called a *major 7* chord. The example on the right shows the IV7 chord in the key of C, which is FMaj7.

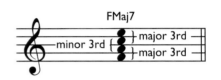

Here are some sample fingerings for the four types of 7th chords you have learned.

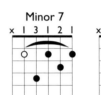

DIATONIC HARMONY—7TH CHORDS

Let's look at the diatonic 7th chords of C Major. Above the triads we generated on page 133, we add another diatonic 3rd. Here's what happens:

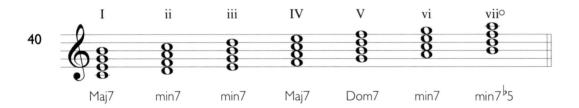

As with the diatonic triads, the diatonic 7th chords have a set pattern of qualities that holds true for every major key. Each triad quality is transformed into a specific quality of 7th chord:

The major triads on I and IV become Maj7 chords. The major triad on V becomes a dominant 7 chord. The minor triads on ii, iii and vi become min7 chords. The diminished triad on vii becomes a min7♭5 chord.

> **I and IV** ....are always ..... major 7
> **V** .... is always .... dominant 7
> **ii, iii and vi** ..... are always ..... minor 7
> **vii°** ....is always .... minor 7♭5

The following three pieces will get you acquainted with the sounds and applications of the 7th chords. Enjoy.

SEVENTH HEAVEN

Track 34

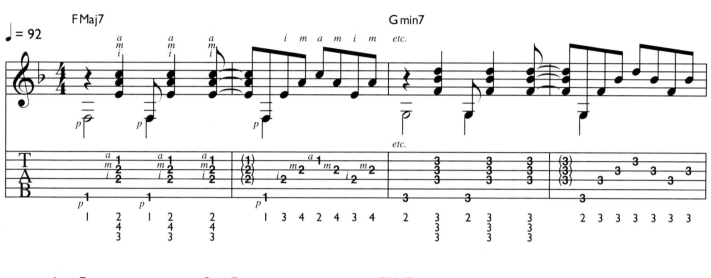

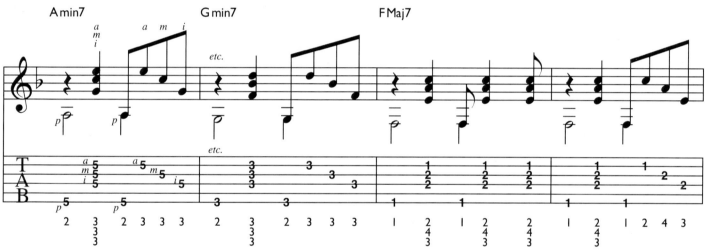

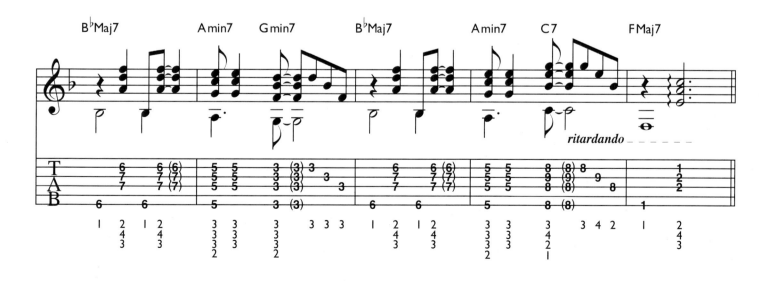

HORIZONTAL HOLD

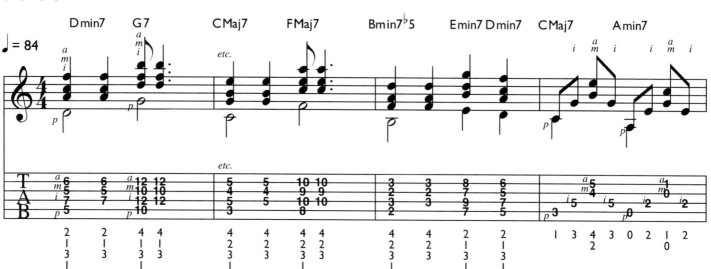

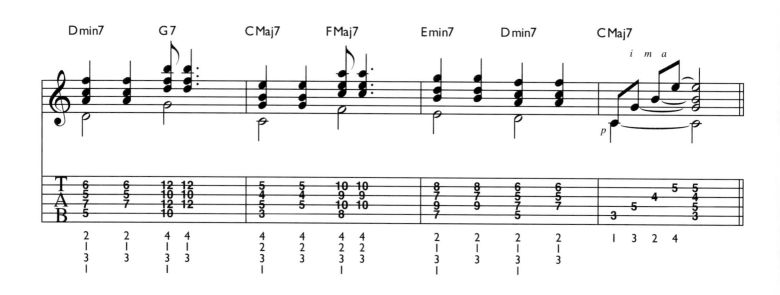

JAZZBERRY JAM

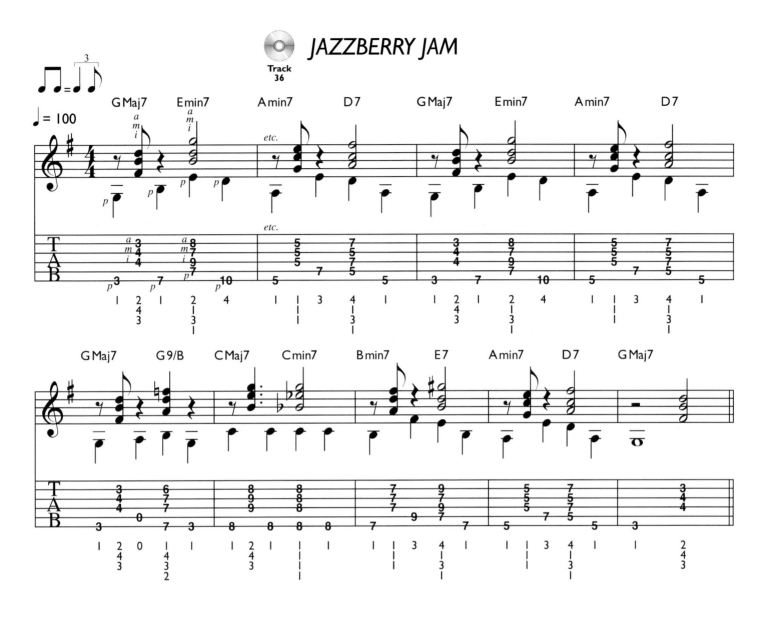

Leo Kottke (b. 1945) began his career on the leading edge of the fingerstyle guitar movement in the 1960s and '70s. His work—along with the work of a few others, such as John Fahey—inspired a whole new generation of fingerstyle players. Still active as a performer and recording artist, Leo Kottke's playing continues to inspire and instruct.

CHAPTER 7

Alternate Tunings

One of the most exciting and colorful things about fingerstyle guitar is the wealth of nonstandard or "open" tunings available to players. Many leading artists work with these alternative tunings exclusively, but even those who play mainly in standard tuning will have a few alternate tuning pieces in their repertory. You'll hear alternate tunings in the work of Adrian Legg, Leo Kottke, Michael Hedges, Joni Mitchell, Martin Simpson and almost any other major player.

You've already been introduced to two of the most common alternate tunings, Drop D and Open G. This chapter will review Drop D and Open G and introduce three more important tunings; Open D, DADGAD and Open C. To learn more about this fascinating area check out *Alternate Tunings* by Mark Dziuba, also published by Alfred and the National Guitar Workshop.

DROP D TUNING REVIEW

In drop D tuning we lower the 6th string (E) down a whole step to D. You can do this by using an electric tuner or by using either of the following two methods:

1) Play a harmonic at the 12th fret of the 6th string and tune the 6th string down to match the open 4th string.
2) Play the 7th fret of the 6th string and tune the 6th string down to match the open A 5th string.

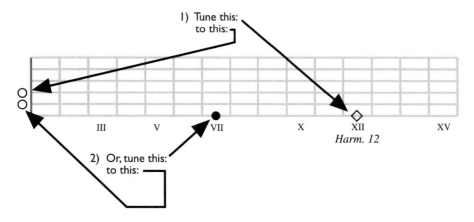

On the next page you will find a Drop D tune in the style of James Taylor. Notice how the hammer-ons, double-stops and syncopations combine to create this style.

NOTES TO JAMES

In open G, the strings are tuned D, G, D, G, B, D, from the 6th string to the 1st. The 2nd, 3rd and 4th strings do not change, but the others are lowered to their new pitches. Since a G Major chord is made up of the notes G, B and D, this tuning gives us the sound of a G chord by simply strumming the open strings.

Open G Tuning

Track 38

To tune to G from standard tuning, use an electric tuner or follow these steps:
1. Tune the 6th string down one whole step from low E to Low D. Match the harmonic at the 12th fret of the 6th string to the open 4th string.
2. Tune the 5th string down one whole step from A to G. Match the harmonic at the 12th fret of the of the 5th string to the open 3rd string.
3. Tune the 1st string down one whole step from E to D. Match the open 1st string to the 3rd fret of the 2nd string.

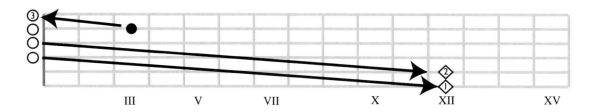

Here's a tune to play in Open G tuning. Be sure to notice the fingerstyle pattern, which is like a detail from the very beginning of Pattern #7 (see page 109). The pattern is *p-m-i-p-a-m* unless otherwise indicated.

ORPHEUS RETURNS

Track 39

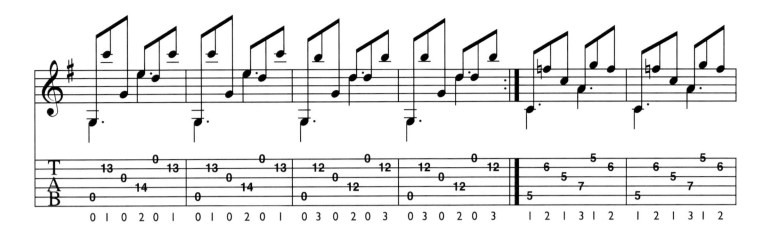

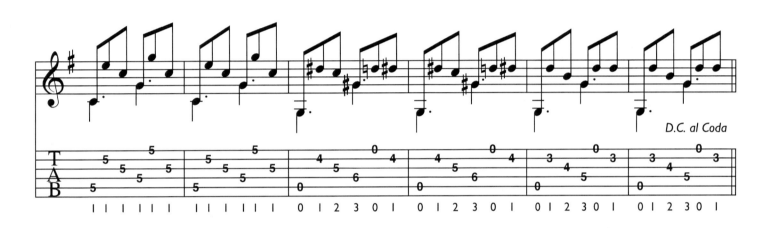

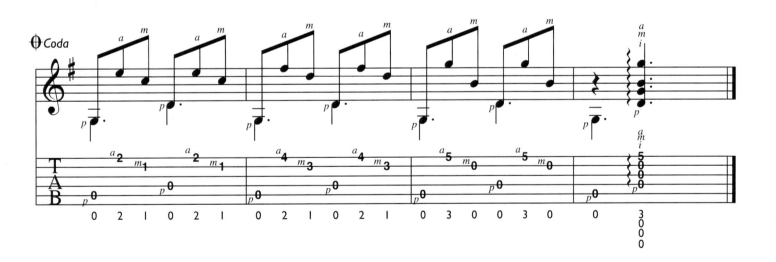

Open D tuning is very much like open G in that the open strings combine to create a major chord, in this case, D Major. The tuning of the strings, from 6th to 1st, is as follows: D-A-D-F♯-A-D.

Open D Tuning

Track 40

To tune to D from standard tuning, tune to track 40 on the CD, use an electric tuner or follow these steps:

1. Tune the 6th string down one whole step from low E to low D. Match the harmonic at the 12th fret of the 6th string to the open 4th string.
2. Tune the 3rd string down one half step from G to F♯. Match the open 3rd string to the 4th fret of the 4th string.
3. Tune the 2nd string down one whole step from B to A. Match the open 2nd string to the harmonic at the 12th fret of the 5th string.
4. Tune the 1st string down one whole step from E to D. Match the open 1st string to the harmonic at the 12th fret of the 4th string.

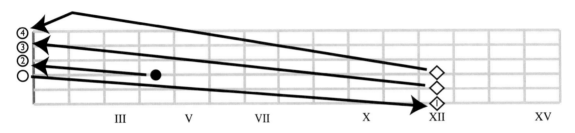

Here are a few chord shapes that will help you get started playing in this tuning:

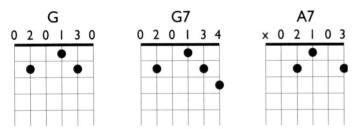

BENDING

Open D lends itself well to the blues style. Accordingly, the next piece, *Blues for Taj*, is in the blues style. It just wouldn't be the blues without a *bend* or two. A bend is accomplished by placing a finger firmly on the string, often with the support of one or two other fingers, and pushing the string up toward the ceiling (1st, 2nd and sometimes 3rd strings) or down toward the floor (6th, 5th, 4th and sometimes 3rd strings). This causes the string's pitch to smoothly move up to the desired pitch. It is an unmistakably bluesy sound that has also become an important tool for rock guitarists. And yes, even we fingerstyle folks have been known to bend a few strings. Check out the work of Adrian Legg. He is one of the world's premier string benders.

In *Blues for Taj* there are two bends. The first, on the very first note of the piece, is a bend on the F on the 8th fret of the 2nd string. This is a half step bend, meaning you only need to bend the string up enough to push the F up to an F♯. Play the F♯ (9th fret, 2nd string) first to learn the sound of the note, and then bend the F up to match that pitch. At the end of the 2nd measure there is a quick bend and release from the F up to F♯ and back to F♯. Simply bend up to F♯ as before, and then quickly release the string back to it's original position. Have fun!

SLIDES

When it comes to playing the blues, *slides* are right up there with bends as an expressive tool. And they're easy. Simply place your left hand finger on the string one or two frets below the destination pitch, such as the F♯ on the first beat of the seventh measure, and slide up to the destination. Keep an even pressure on the string as you slide, so that you hear the sliding sound. Slides are usually performed right on the beat.

BLUES FOR TAJ

Track 41

DADGAD tuning (said dad-gad) is one of the most important alternate tunings used by fingerstyle guitarists. Some of the guitar's greatest exponents, such as Jimmy Page and John Renbourne, have used this tuning. The brilliant French Algerian guitarist, Pierre Bensusan, uses DADGAD almost exclusively. This tuning has a very unique sound and, when paired with some of the expressive devices introduced in this section, will produce the highly distinctive sound we associate with Bensusan.

Track 42

To tune to DADGAD from standard tuning, use an electric tuner, tune to Track 42 on the CD, or follow these steps:

1. Tune the 6th string down one whole step from low E to low D. Match the harmonic on the 12 fret of the 6th string to the open 4th string.
2. Tune the 2nd string down one whole step from B to A. Match the open 2nd string to the harmonic on the 12th fret of the 5th string.
3. Tune the 1st string one whole step from E to D. Match the open 1st string to the harmonic at the 12th fret of the 4th string.

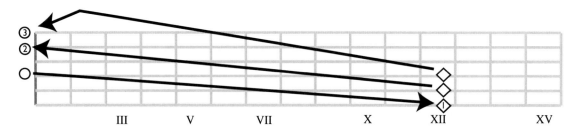

Here are some useful DADGAD chord shapes that you should learn:

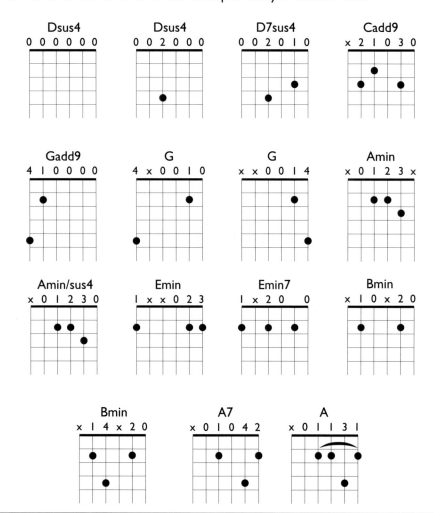

| Dsus4 | Dsus4 | D7sus4 | Cadd9 |
| 0 0 0 0 0 0 | 0 0 2 0 0 0 | 0 0 2 0 1 0 | x 2 1 0 3 0 |

| Gadd9 | G | G | Amin |
| 4 1 0 0 0 0 | 4 x 0 0 1 0 | x x 0 0 1 4 | x 0 1 2 3 x |

| Amin/sus4 | Emin | Emin7 | Bmin |
| x 0 1 2 3 0 | 1 x x 0 2 3 | 1 x 2 0   0 | x 1 0 x 2 0 |

| Bmin | A7 | A |
| x 1 4 x 2 0 | x 0 1 0 4 2 | x 0 1 1 3 1 |

EXPRESSIVE DEVICES THAT SOUND GREAT IN DADGAD

If you want to play in the style of the great Pierre Bensusan, or use his style as an inspiration to find your own voice, you should learn these techniques.

Here are four examples demonstrating how well the *harp technique* you learned on page 71 works in DADGAD. The notes of a scale are played across different strings, allowing them to ring through one another.

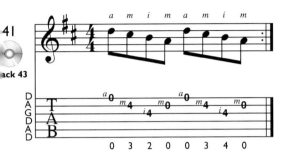

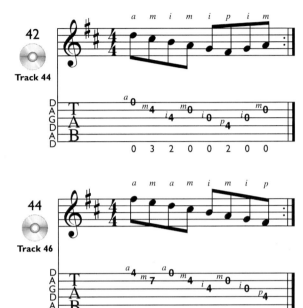

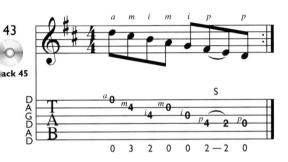

Example 45 involves *palm muting*. Place the pinky side of your right hand palm on the bass strings (6th, 5th and 4th) just next to the bridge. Strike the bass strings with *p*. This will produce a slightly muffled but still pitched sound.

This is a great technique. Sometimes called a "*Bartok Pizz.*," sometimes called a "*pop,*" this percussive effect is made by pulling the string out slightly from the guitar with the right hand and letting it go, causing it to slap against the frets.

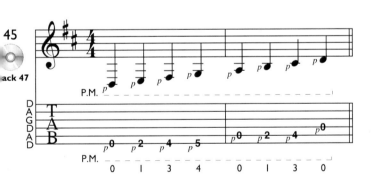

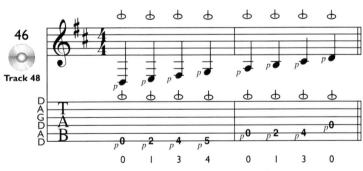

P.M. = palm mute

✧ = pop or Bartok Pizz.

Try mixing palm muting and popping. Use the *p* finger to do both.

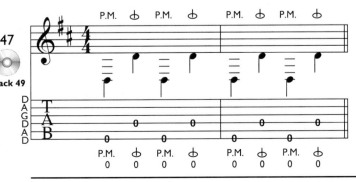

Now try adding a melody to the groove you created in Example 47. Use *m* and *i* on the melody and *p* on your palm mute and pop bass figure. Just be careful to mute only the bass strings so that the melody will sing clearly.

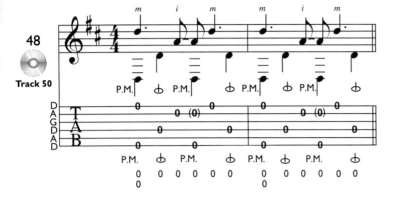

Example 49 includes palm muted notes that are also popped. For extra expressivity, a wide, intense *vibrato* 〰 is added to the syncopated C♯. The vibrato is performed by rapidly pushing the string up and down a small distance, causing a very small pitch waver, similar to a vocal vibrato.

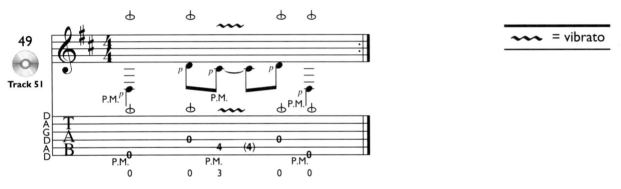

〰 = vibrato

This example puts all these new techniques together: harp technique, palm muting, popping and vibrato. Then, dig into *For Pierre* on the next page and have fun!

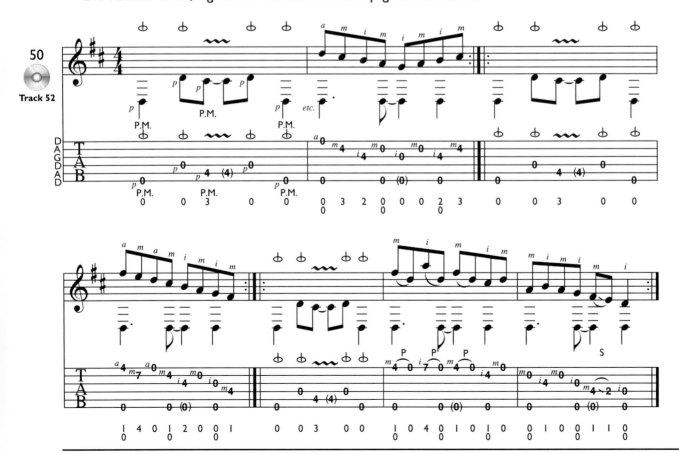

FOR PIERRE

This is another great example of an open tuning. When the open strings are strummed, they sound a C Major chord. In open C, the strings are tuned C-G-C-G-C-E from 6th to 1st.

Track 54

To tune to open C from standard tuning, use an electric tuner, tune to Track 54 on the CD, or follow these steps:

1. Tune the 6th string down two whole steps from E to C. Match the harmonic at the 12th fret of the 6th string to the 3rd fret of then 5th string.
2. Tune the 5th string down one whole step from A to G. Match the harmonic at the 12th fret of the 5th string to the open 3rd string.
3. Tune the 4th string down one whole step from D to C. Match the open 4th string to the harmonic at the 12th fret of the altered 6th string.
4. Tune the 2nd string up one half step from B to C. Match the 2nd string open to the harmonic at the 12th fret of the altered 4th string.

PHOTO COURTESY OF KAMAN MUSIC

Badi Assad (b. 1966) is one of the most unique and gifted artists to appear on the scene in the 1990s. She combines classical technique, Latin rhythms and unusual vocal techniques to create a completely original style of music.

SEEING YOU AGAIN

CHAPTER 8

Inversions

INVERTING THE TRIADS

Every triad can be inverted. An inverted triad is one whose bass (lowest note) is one other than the root. Because there are three notes in a triad there are only three basic ways to voice (arrange) a triad.

> **A root position triad has its root in the bass.**
> **A 1st inversion triad has its 3rd in the bass.**
> **A 2nd inversion triad has its 5th in the bass.**

For instance, a root position C Major triad has C as the bass. In 1st inversion, E is the bass, and in 2nd inversion G is the bass. The arrangement of the notes above the bass (voicing) is up to you. If all three chord tones appear at least once, the chord is correct.

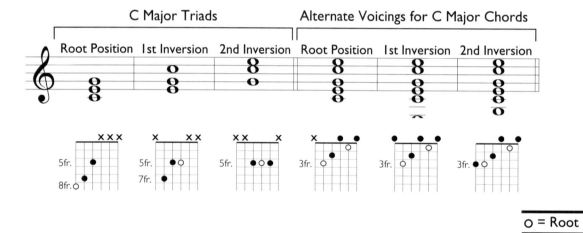

SLASH CHORD NOTATION

Slash chord notation is a common method for notating inversions. In slash chord notation, the root of the chord is written, followed by a slash and the name of the lowest note of the chord. In slash notation, a 1st inversion C Major triad would be written as **C/E**. C is the root, and E is the bass. A 2nd inversion C Major triad would be written as **C/G**. C is again the root, and G is the bass. The example below shows basic triads, and typical voicings of these chords, as slash chords.

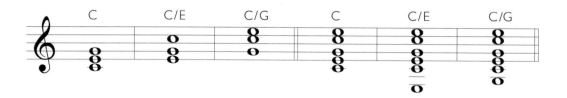

The next three exercises will help you get more familiar with inverting triads. Each of the examples harmonizes the diatonic triads in the key of C on the top three strings (1st, 2nd and 3rd) over the first twelve frets. Notice that minor and diminished chords are inverted in exactly the same manner as major chords. Play through each example slowly at first, and pay close attention to the fingerings for each inversion of each chord type. Each example will begin with whatever triad falls in open position.

ROOT POSITION TRIADS IN C MAJOR

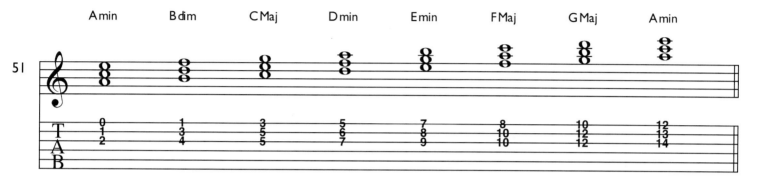

1ST INVERSION TRIADS IN C MAJOR

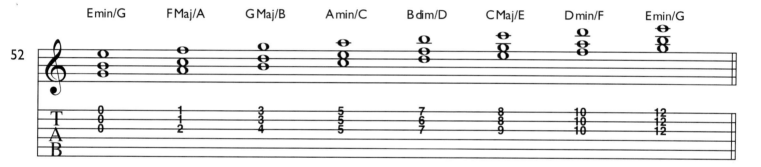

2ND INVERSION TRIADS IN C MAJOR

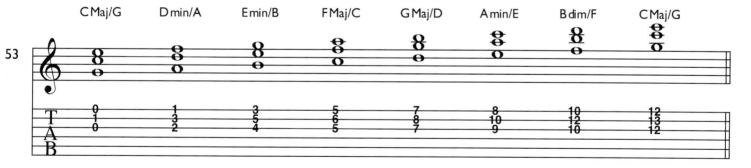

By now, you have played hundreds of inversions, whether you knew it or not! For instance, every time we play an alternating bass, we are playing root position chords alternating with 1st and 2nd inversion chords. Go back and look at some of the fingerstyle patterns and you'll see inversions all over the place. They are an integral part of fingerstyle playing. Now that you have studied them specifically, learn the following selections in which inversions were used to create the pieces. Try to be aware of which inversion you are playing at any given time. Have fun.

BUDDY'S BACK

Track 56

THREE'S IN THREE

Track 57

The following examples, in A Major this time, will familiarize you with the inversions on the 4th, 3rd and 2nd strings. Master them before moving on to the next piece. Each example will begin with whatever triad falls in the open position.

ROOT POSITION CHORDS ON THE 4TH, 3RD AND 2ND STRINGS

1ST INVERSION CHORDS ON THE 4TH, 3RD AND 2ND STRINGS

2ND INVERSION CHORDS ON THE 4TH, 3RD AND 2ND STRINGS

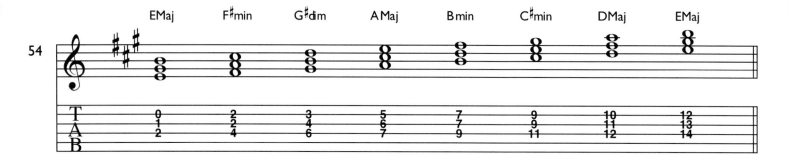

HAMMERING AWAY

Track 58

CHAPTER 9

Exploring Bass Lines

One of the coolest things about playing fingerstyle guitar is that we can play all the parts of a piece or arrangement simultaneously—we can play the melody, accompaniment and bass line all at once. Do you remember hearing that piece that got you interested in fingerstyle guitar? *"You mean to tell me that's ONE guitarist?!"*

In large part, that's what it's all about to play fingerstyle. And, to a very significant degree, a strong piece or arrangement is one with a really strong bass line. As fingerstylists, we spend a lot of time—maybe too much time—playing alternating bass lines (as in Travis picking). But to be stuck in that style of playing is very limiting. One of the most important things you can do to expand your horizons as an arranger, composer or player is to break away from the alternating bass and start working with lines. We began exploring this topic in Chapter 10 of the *Beginning* section and will expand on it in this chapter.

WALKING BASS LINES—REVIEW

Walking bass lines are scale passages played by *p* in the lower strings. In some pieces, these bass lines are so distinctive they make the chords, and even the melody, seem secondary. The chord pattern and melody can be created to fit the bass, rather than the other way around. Ideally, the bass fits the melody like a glove.

Study this walking bass line. Then learn *Walking Around* on page 157 and notice how it fits the melody and moves through the different harmonies.

WALKING AROUND

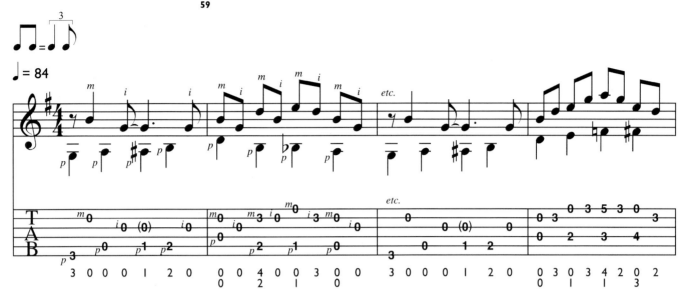

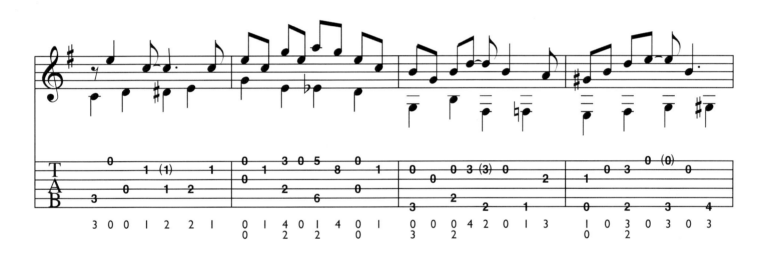

GOIN' DOWN

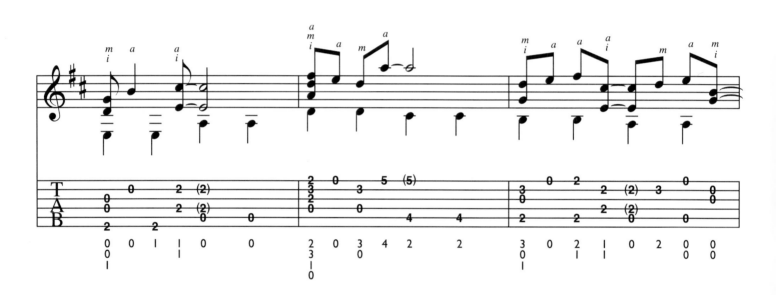

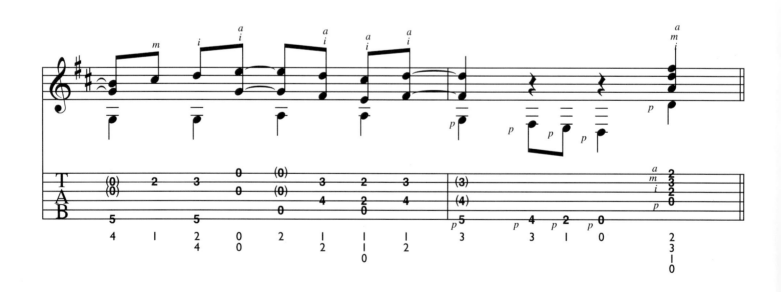

BOOGIE BEAT

As you learned on page 23, in an arpeggio the notes of a chord are played individually, rather than all together. Arpeggios are the fingerstyle guitarist's bread and butter. They are useful for accompaniments (virtually all of the fingerstyle patterns you have learned are arpeggios), they can include melody and accompaniment and they make great bass lines.

Here's are two arpeggio bass lines that you will probably recognize. The 1950s and '60s may have been cancelled without them. Use your theory knowledge to figure out what they are (turn the book upside down to read the answer at the bottom of this page).

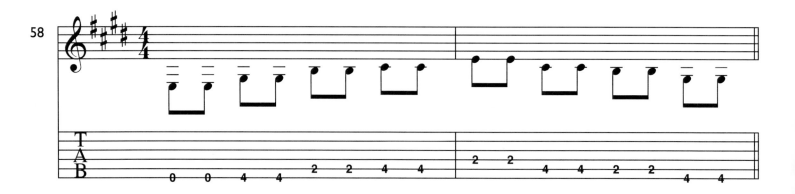

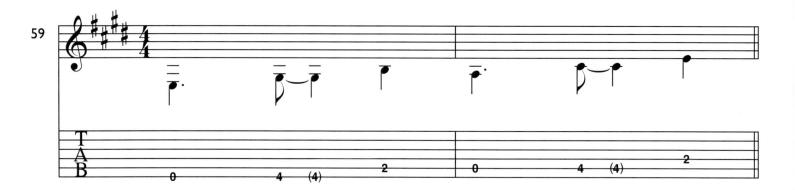

Ray's Rockin' on page 161 is a great example of a piece using an arpeggiated bass line. Learn it well and enjoy!

Answer: E Major and A Major.

RAY'S ROCKIN'

Track 62

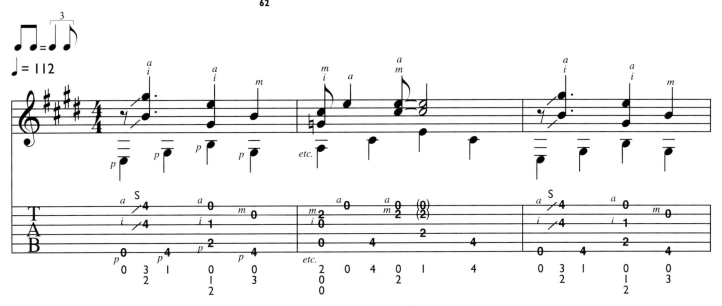

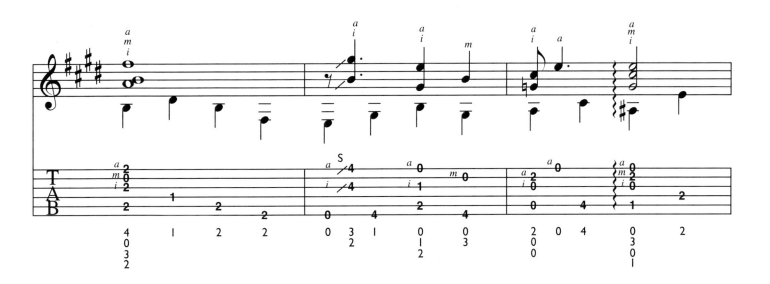

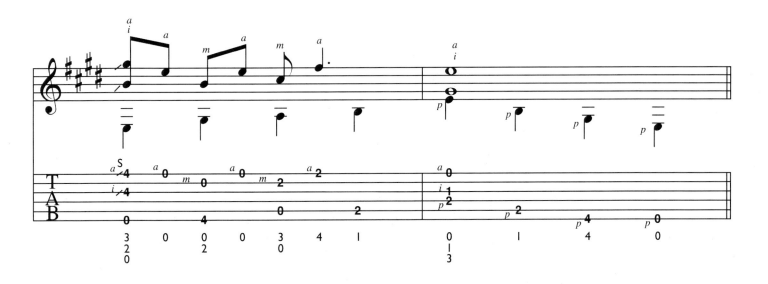

CHAPTER 10

The Modes

Every type of scale evokes a certain mood which is related to how the half steps fall in the scale pattern. The familiar major scale (also called the Ionian mode) has a "bright" or "up" feeling. The natural minor scale (Aeolian mode) that we examined on page 36 has a more somber or "dark" quality.

By starting a scale from each note of the major scale, and using the same set of notes belonging to that major scale, we can create all the *modes* of the major scale. In other words, a mode is a re-ordering of the notes of a scale. This approach to viewing the modes is often called the relative approach. You can also view each mode as being parallel to a major scale of the same root. These are exactly the same concepts as the relative and parallel minor that you learned about on pages 36 and 37.

Besides the Ionian and Aeolian modes the two modes of the major scale most common to rock music are the *Dorian* and *Mixolydian* modes. These names come from the names of Greek tribes whose music was originally associated with these sounds.

The following example shows the modes of the C Major scale and the chord type most related to each mode. For instance, we think of a minor 7th chord as being closely related to the Dorian mode because that is the chord that results from building a diatonic 7th chord up from the root of the Dorian mode. The numbers above the scales refer to the parallel major scales and the alterations needed to get to the mode. For instance, if you lower the 3rd and 7th degrees of a D Major scale (♭3 and ♭7) you will have a D Dorian mode.

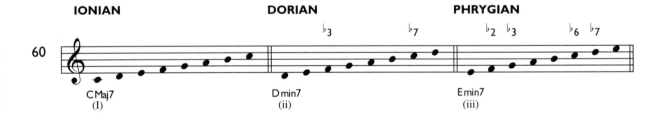

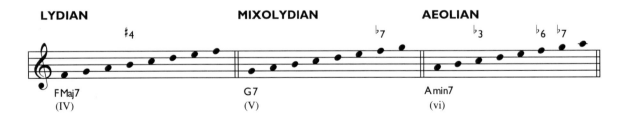

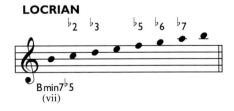

As you have just learned, every mode can be viewed in one of two ways:

The relative view—Every mode can be viewed as being a scale that occurs when you play a major scale starting and ending on a note other than the root. The Dorian mode occurs when playing a major scale starting and ending on the 2nd degree. The Mixolydian mode starts when playing a major scale starting and ending on the 5th degree.

The parallel view—Every mode has a formula of it's own. The Dorian mode is what happens when you take any major scale and lower the 3rd (♭3) and 7th (♭7) degrees. The Mixolydian mode is what happens when you take any major scale and lower the 7th (♭7) degree.

To prepare for the next two pieces—*A Dorian Mood* in the Dorian mode and *All Mixed Up* in the Mixolydian mode—let's take a look at the Dorian and Mixolydian modes from a parallel point of view.

A DORIAN MOOD

ALL MIXED UP

CHAPTER 11

Counterpoint

By now you have learned many fingerstyle pieces. Also, you have probably learned other pieces from other sources. Maybe you have learned some of the pieces that initially inspired you to play fingerstyle guitar. Fantastic!

This chapter, and the one following on arranging, are about getting your own creative juices flowing. If you are a naturally creative person, you have already tried composing or arranging fingerstyle pieces. That's great, because mostly we learn by doing. The materials discussed in this chapter are meant to help you along in that process.

THREE KINDS OF MOVEMENT

As you know by now, one of the coolest things about fingerstyle guitar is the ability to play more than one part. This means *counterpoint* is available to us as a tool. Counterpoint refers to playing two or more melodies (voices) at the same time. This often referred to as *contrapuntal* playing. There are three ways that moving lines relate in counterpoint:

1. Similar motion—The voices move in the same direction.
2. Oblique motion—One voice moves and the other doesn't.
3. Contrasting motion—The voices move in opposite directions.

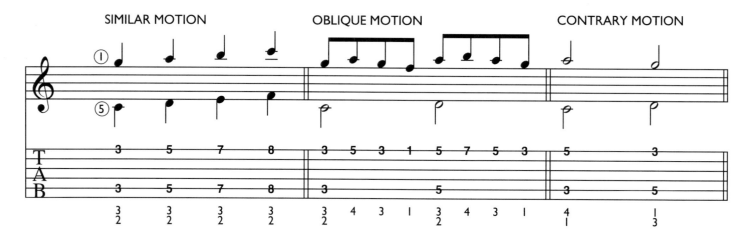

Over the next several pages we will take a look at these three types of contrapuntal movement applied to the guitar.   We are going to be using the C Major scale as grist for our mill, so let's check it out.

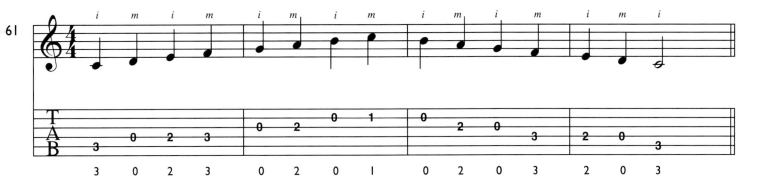

Here's the scale again, this time going over all six strings in the first position. Make sure you have thoroughly familiarized yourself with this material before going on.

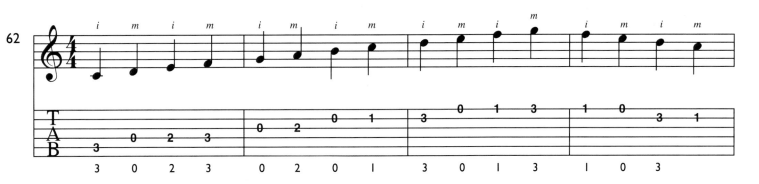

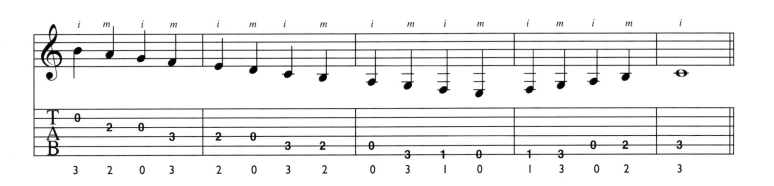

Example 63 is a good demonstration of basic counterpoint using oblique motion. The low voice, or bass, moves very slowly through the C Major scale, starting on C on the 3rd fret of the 5th string and moving down to the low E on the open 6th string. The high voice, or *treble*, moves more quickly up and down through the scale.

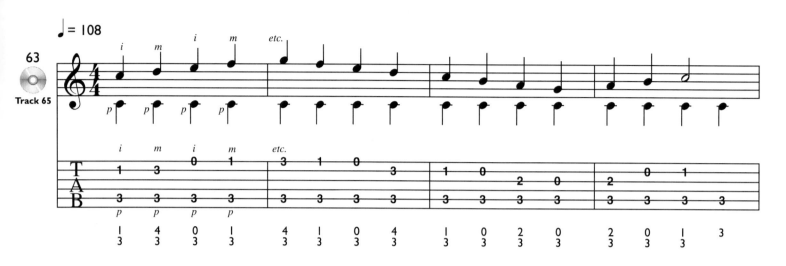

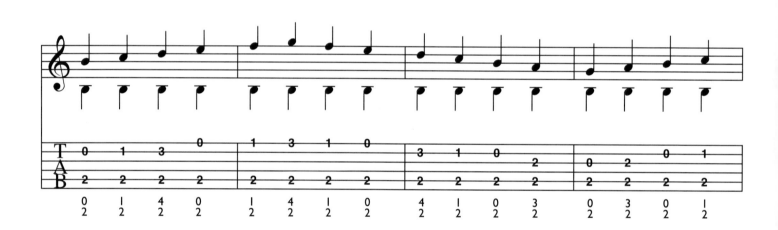

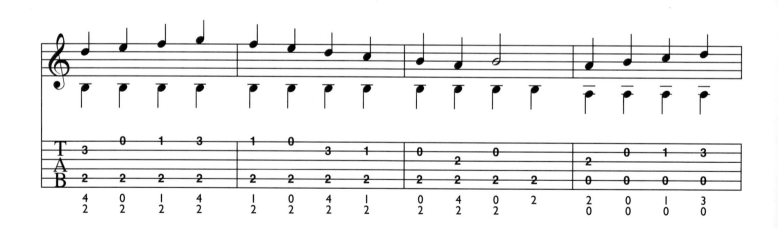

Example 64 uses a combination of oblique and similar motion. The first measure, for instance, uses oblique motion—the bass stays still while the treble moves up and down. But the movement from the first measure into the second is similar motion—the treble descends to C as the bass descends to B. Notice that the B and C are *dissonant* (they clash). This is OK because the treble resolves up to the D, which is *consonant* (harmonious) with the B on the very next eighth note.

The alternating bass in Example 65 results in an ongoing mixture of similar and contrasting motion.

This piece is in the key of A Minor, which is the relative minor key of C Major. The only different note in A Minor is the G♯. Notice how the bass and treble voices relate, and see if you can identify the different kinds of counterpoint, the kind of bass line being used, etc. Have fun and swing those eighths!

THE CAT'S MEOW

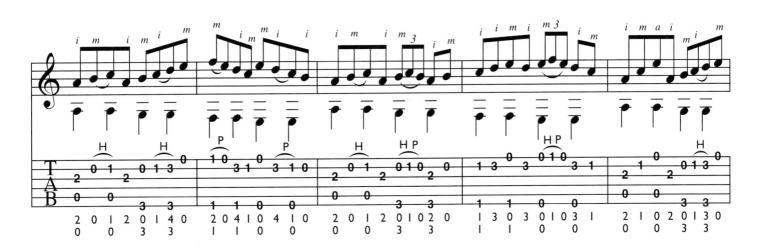

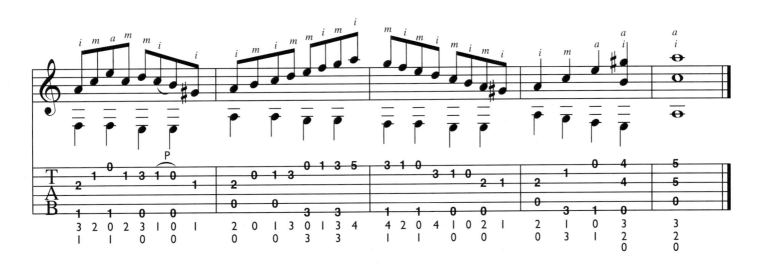

CHAPTER 12

Arranging

Arranging has always been a big part of fingerstyle guitar playing. In fact, it is fair to say that plucked string instruments did not enter the realm of solo instrumental playing until people starting doing plucked arrangements. Believe it or not, it all started back in the 15th century. It was then that the *lute* players (a lute is a sister instrument to the guitar with a bowl shaped body and an angled peg head) started arranging choral works by famous composers for their instrument. Not long after, guitar players and other pluckers got the idea—"Hey! We can play something other than dance tunes. Cool!"

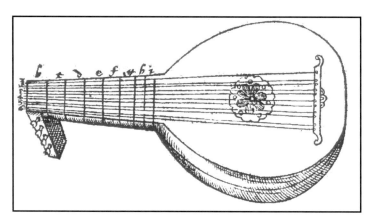

A lute.

Now, while the lute's day has past, arranging for plucked strings is a great guitar tradition. For some players, such as Chet Atkins, it's a specialty. Many other players, such as Ed Gerhard, Martin Simpson and Pierre Bensusan include arrangements of traditional tunes in their repertoire.

At it's heart, arranging is simply the placing of a melody in a new context. The melody can be left essentially untouched, but the harmony or feel may be changed. The melody itself can be altered or used as a basis for creating a new melody. Almost any musical element, from rhythm to time signature to the bass line—anything you can think of—is fair game to the arranger.

In this book, we will deal with basic arranging. We will use the timeless melody of Scarborough Fair to develop the ideas. First, we'll learn the traditional melody. Then we will begin to add various elements to the tune, finally arriving at a full-blown arrangement. Dig in!

Ed Gerhard *came on the national scene in the late 1980s. Not only is he a fine player and composer, he is a brilliant arranger.*

Since it is important to the arranger to be aware of the harmony, the chord symbols are included in the music.

SCARBOROUGH FAIR—MELODY

Now that you have the melody in your ears, let's add a simple bass part. The best way to begin building your bass part is to simply play the roots of the chords. Just one bass note per measure. It won't sound fancy, but it will sound right.

SCARBOROUGH FAIR—MELODY AND SLOW BASS

Track 70

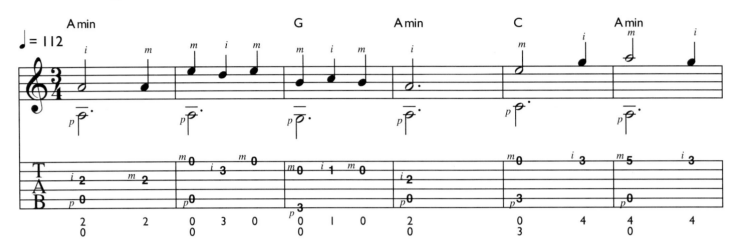

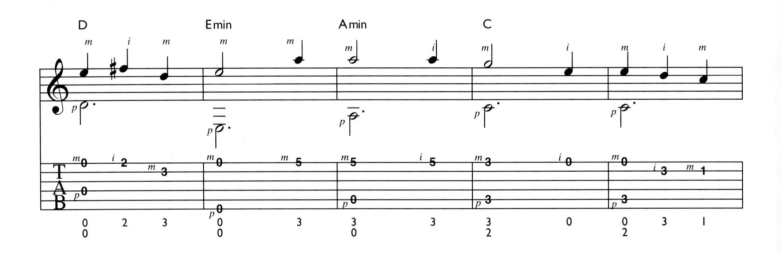

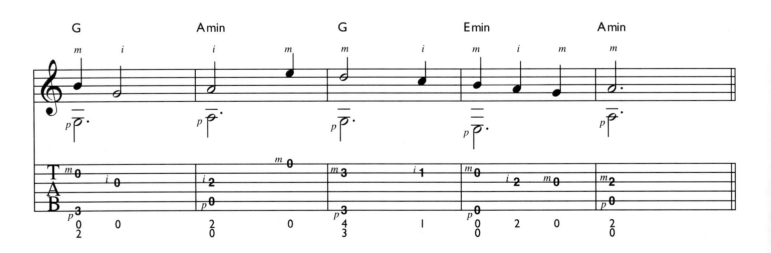

It's time to add a little window dressing to your arrangement. For now, stay with just the two voices, melody and bass. Develop your bass line using the devices you know, such as arpeggios and walking bass. Study the chords in your arrangement and find ways to arpeggiate them on the bass strings. When there is a long note in the melody, such as a half note, move your bass line through an arpeggio. While the melody is moving, do less in the bass. Learn the sample arrangement below bass line first. Now that both the bass and melody are moving, there will be new challenges for the left hand. Practice small sections, slowly, before putting it all together.

SCARBOROUGH FAIR—MELODY AND QUICKER BASS

If you like, you can call your arrangement done. Some of the most brilliant arrangements are the most simple. Listen to Martin Simpson's arrangement of *Lord Jamie Douglas* on his "Cool and Unusual" CD. Very few notes can make a powerful statement.

But, assuming you need more, try adding a third, middle voice to your arrangement. Just use other notes from the chords that work well with your melody and bass line. You may have to alter a fingering or two to make it work.

SCARBOROUGH FAIR—IN THREE VOICES

Track 72

One of the most interesting things you can do to compliment a melody is to create a second melody to play with it. These are often called *counter melodies*. Let's put the information from Chapter 11 to work in our arrangement of *Scarborough Fair*. In this case, we have added counter melodies below the main tune, in both the bass and the middle parts. In the first six measures, the counterpoint is mostly two-voiced—treble and bass. In measures seven through eleven, a third voice is added in the middle. Try playing each voice separately before putting them together.

SCARBOROUGH FAIR—CONTRAPUNTAL

Track 73

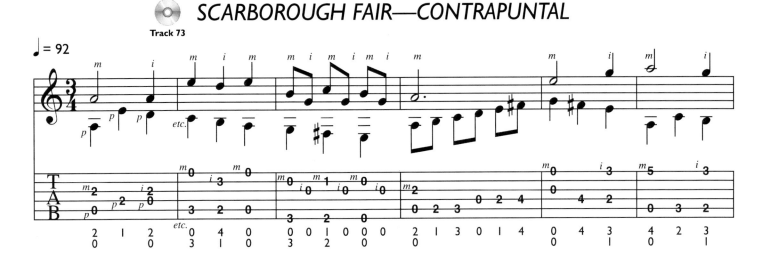

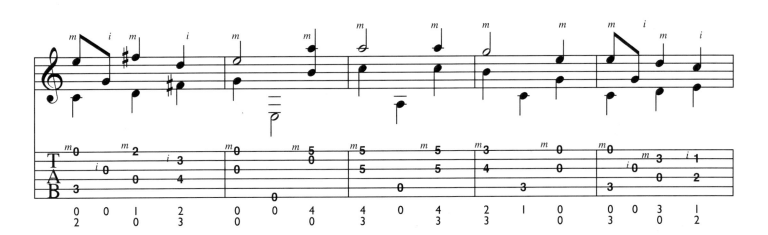

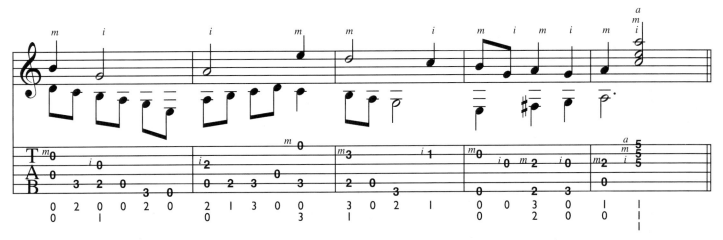

If you haven't done so already, start creating your own arrangements of tunes you love. This topic will be taken up again in the *Mastering* section, where we will continue to experiment with *Scarborough Fair*. Let's see how far you can develop this skill until then.

EXPLORING THE STYLES

DANCING DREAMS

Track 74

In the Style of John Fahey

Tune to: E B G E B E

(*RH Thumb plays all notes on this line.)

gradually increase tempo

RISE AND SHINE

In the Style of Leo Kottke

Notice that there are no plucked notes in this piece—all the notes in the left hand part are hammered-on or pulled-off. Also note the *slap harmonics* in the right hand part (R.H.). These are executed by slapping directly over the indicated fret with the thumb side of your *i* finger. If you hit just the right spot hard enough, harmonics will sound. A *right hand tap* (R.H. Tap) is done by hammering the indicated fret quite hard with *i* or *m*, sounding the note without plucking, as in a hammer-on. Modern techniques such as this are covered thoroughly in the *Mastering* section.

L.H. = Left Hand
R.H. = Right Hand

THE ROAD TO YOU

Track 76

In the Style of Michael Hedges

Tune to: DADGBE

♩ = 126

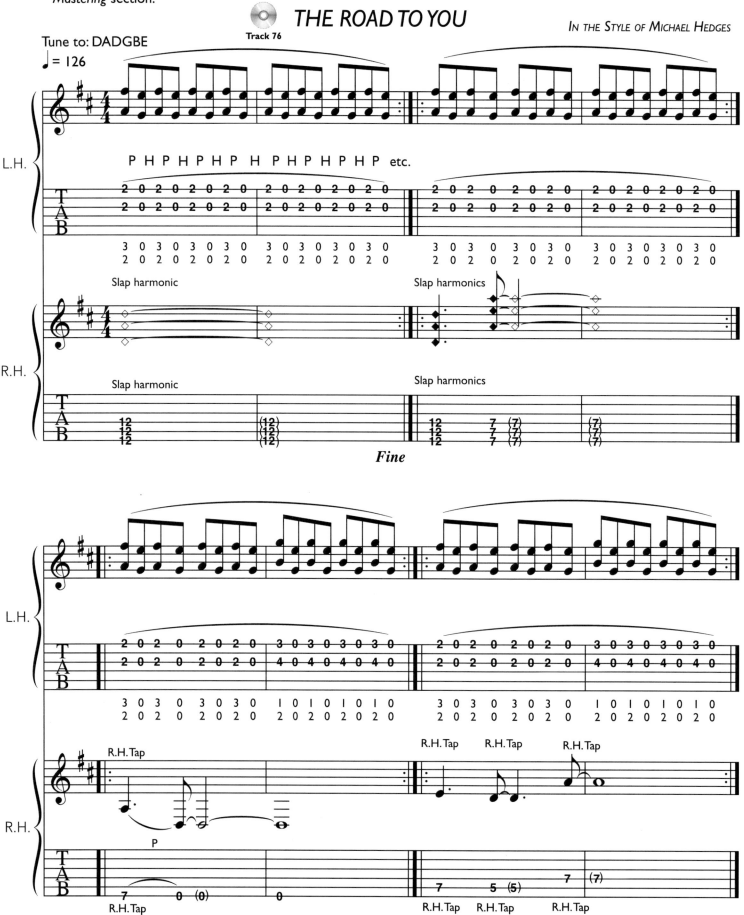

Fine

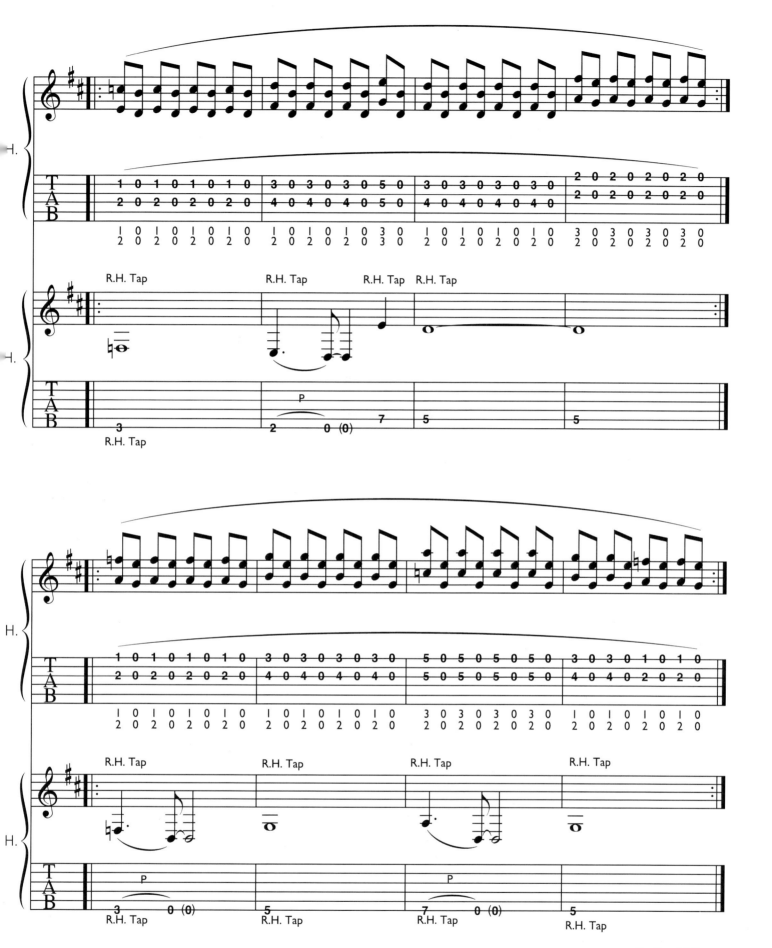

D.C. al Fine

THANKS TO JOSIE

In the Style of Adrian Legg

SMASH THE WINDOWS

Track 78

An Irish Tune

SI BEAG SI MOR

An Irish Classic by O'Carolan

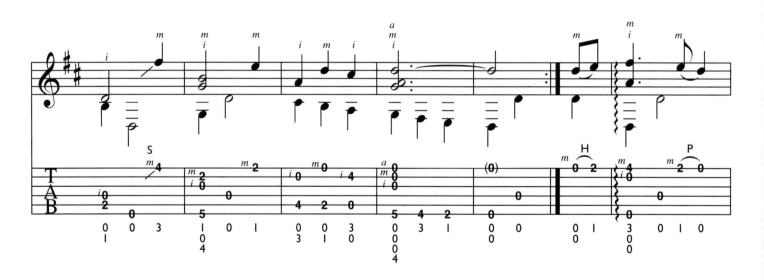

HOT PEPPER BLUES

FINGERSTYLE BLUES

FINGERSTYLE BLUES

Track 81

AFTER DARK

Track 82

Fingerstyle Blues

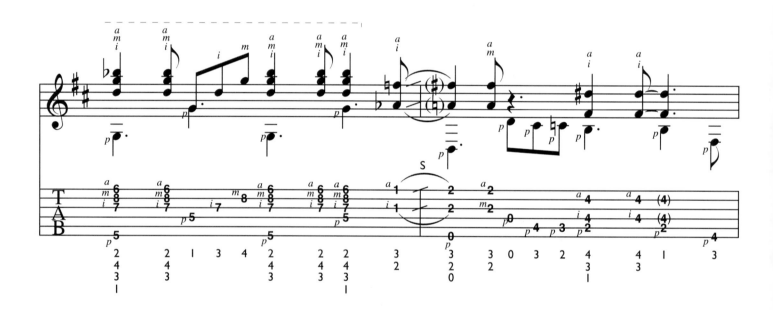

THE REVERAND'S RAG

FINGERSTYLE BLUES IN THE STYLE OF REV. GARY DAVIS

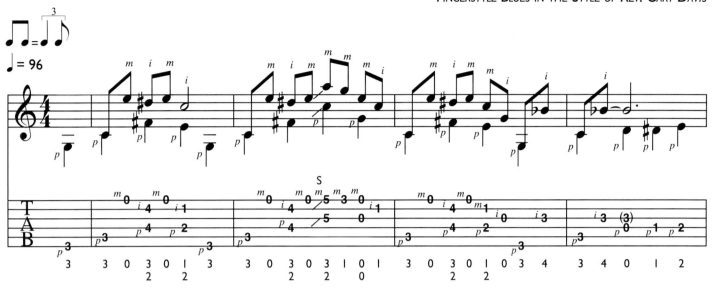

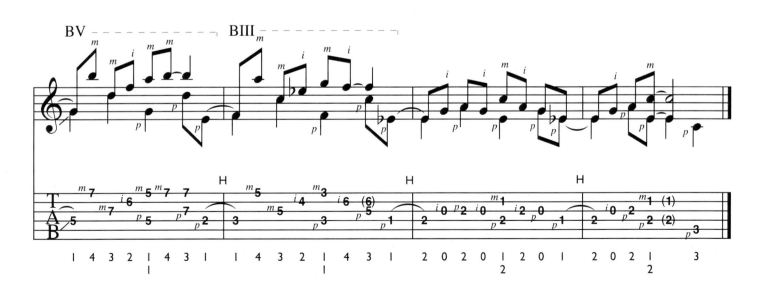

AFTERWORD

Congratulations. You have traveled quite a distance since the beginning of this book. We hope the process of learning has been fulfilling and joyful, and that you will continue to challenge yourself by moving on to the *Mastering* section.

By now, you have mastered many fingerstyle patterns and learned lots of tunes. You have picked-up some important standard techniques, such as hammer-ons, pull-offs, slides, vibrato, barres, harmonics and bends, and even a couple of less traditional techniques such as slap harmonics and right-hand tapping. You have studied the basics of counterpoint and arranging. It is fair to say that you have a good grasp of the basic possibilities available to fingerstyle guitarists. In terms of technical development, however, you have only just begun. Practically speaking, there is virtually no limit to what a player can accomplish technically. The only real limit is your imagination. The only thing that can limit your imagination is a lack of curiosity. Listen to what other artists, from all styles of music, have done on the guitar. For instance, listen to the incredible speed of jazz guitarist Tal Farlow, fusion player Al Di Meola or classical guitarists such as John Williams. Observe the sheer power of the blues master B. B. King's vibrato, or the absolute clarity and evenness of classical virtuoso, Manuel Barrueco. Look at what Eddie Van Halen accomplishes with tapping. If you only listen to fingerstyle players—even though this is an incredibly diverse group—you will be missing a lot. We have something to learn from every guitarist.

This is true of your expressive and creative powers, too. The more you have heard, the more you can imagine. Yes, you have looked into the expressive devices of artists such Pierre Bensusan and Michael Hedges, but that is just the beginning. Consider the emotional power of Yehudi Menuhen's violin playing, or the manipulations of time (*rubato*) used by great jazz or classical pianists. Investigate the contrapuntal mastery of J. S. Bach, the free improvisations of John Coltrane and the songwriting of the Beatles. Your ability to create interesting, moving and satisfying music will depend upon how many different types of music you have heard and how well you have listened.

Your "book learning" is important, too. While some successful musicians claim a limited knowledge of music, there is nothing to gain by purposefully choosing to remain uninformed. There are great books on theory (such as *Theory for the Contemporary Guitarist* by Guy Capuzzo), technique (take a look at *Pumping Nylon* by Scott Tennant) and ear-training (check out *Learn How to Transcribe for Guitar* by Tobias Hurwitz). Your local colleges may offer classes on music theory and history that you can take. While you should never let schooling get in the way of a good education, remember that Michael Hedges, one of our most creative fingerstylists, had a college degree in classical composition!

The world of music is so vast that a lifetime of listening and exploration is not enough to experience it all. This is why music is such a wonderful pursuit. The more you learn, the more you will realize there is left to learn. We wish you a long and satisfying musical journey, and much happiness along the way.

APPENDIX

Open Chords

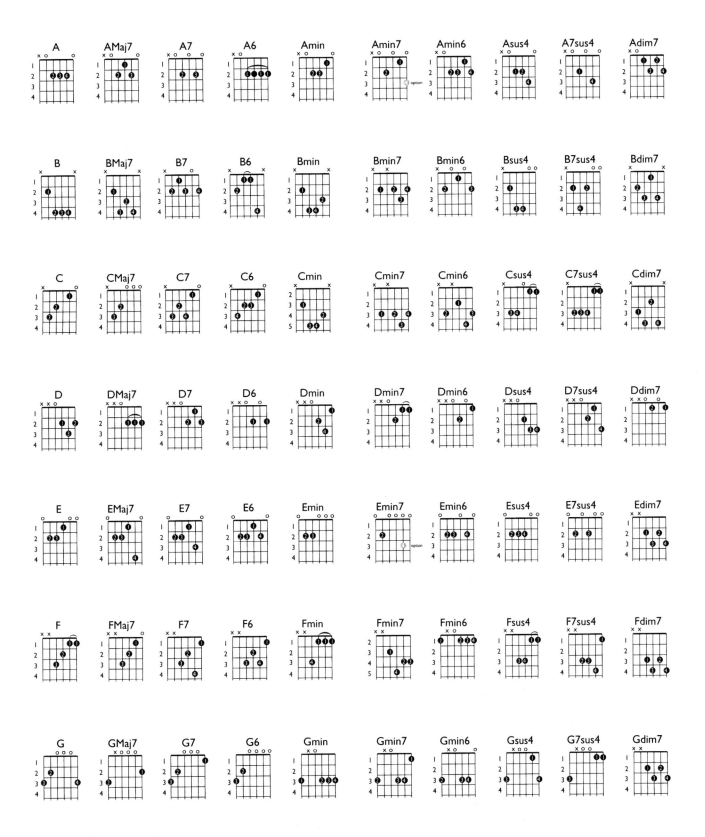

FINGERSTYLE

STEVE ECKELS

Audio tracks recorded and engineered at Bar None Studio, Northford, CT
Performed by Steve Eckels

Contents

ABOUT THE AUTHOR

Steve Eckels received his Bachelor's degree in guitar from Berklee College of Music and his Master's degree in guitar and jazz at New England Conservatory. His teachers have included Robert Paul Sullivan, Gene Burtoncini, William Leavitt, Chuck Wayne, Barry Galbraith, Gary Burton and Pat Metheny. In addition to concert and public engagements, he now teaches guitar at New Mexico State University at Las Cruces. He is the author of seven guitar folios, and has recorded 18 albums and CDs.

ACKNOWLEDGEMENTS

I would like to express a special thank you to those authors from whom I have learned so much: Joseph Schillinger, Yehudi Menuhin, Ivan Galamian, George Van Eps, Vincent Persichetti, Lee F. Ryan, Mark Hanson, Mick Goodrick and John Stropes. Special thanks to my violin teacher, Dr. Frank McDonald, to my friend Joe Mancilla for assistance with alternate tunings and to my editor, Nat Gunod, for his meticulous attention to detail and pedagogy.

00

Track 1

An MP3 CD is included with this book to make learning easier and more enjoyable. The symbol shown at bottom left appears next to every example in the book that features an MP3 track. Use the MP3s to ensure you're capturing the feel of the examples and interpreting the rhythms correctly. The track number below the symbol corresponds directly to the example you want to hear (example numbers are above the icon). All the track numbers are unique to each "book" within this volume, meaning every book has its own Track 1, Track 2, and so on. (For example, *Beginning Fingerstyle Guitar* starts with Track 1, as does *Intermediate Fingerstyle Guitar* and *Mastering Fingerstyle Guitar*.) Track 1 for each book will help you tune to the CD.

The disc is playable on any CD player equipped to play MP3 CDs. To access the MP3s on your computer, place the CD in your CD-ROM drive. In Windows, double-click on My Computer, then right-click on the CD icon labeled "MP3 Files" and select Explore to view the files and copy them to your hard drive. For Mac, double-click on the CD icon on your desktop labeled "MP3 Files" to view the files and copy them to your hard drive.

INTRODUCTION

Welcome to the *Mastering* section, in which you will be introduced to new musical ideas and subtle techniques that will help you reach your potential as a fingerstyle player, arranger and composer. To help guide you along your way, I have prepared examples that are musical, educational and enjoyable. Since my approach is based in art and nature, which are things common to us all, you may find yourself saying, "Of course, why didn't I think of that?" Don't worry, you don't have to reinvent the wheel. Contained in the following pieces of music are gems of wisdom that I have gathered from studying the masters of guitar, violin and composition for the past thirty years.

One of the most satisfying parts of this book was composing the examples for the sections on alternate tunings and modern tapping and drumming techniques. If your background is in the traditional approach to guitar, as mine was, you might find yourself a bit hesitant about venturing into these areas. The good news is that the learning approach presented here is based on what you already know. You can and should learn to perform in alternate tunings and incorporate drumming and tapping into your playing. Primordially speaking, I think we are all drummers at heart. These modern techniques are satisfying and can greatly expand your creative potential.

Another component of this section that I feel will be very helpful to you is the chapter on developing your sense of touch. In learning guitar, touch is one of the most neglected areas of discussion. It is assumed that you just press down on the fret, and that's it. There are some subtleties involved can make your playing more effortless and flowing.

One of the advantages of studying out of a book such as this is that you can make steady progress, page by page. Nevertheless, be open to the idea of making a giant step forward in your playing. It can happen.

CHAPTER 1

Tone and Balance

Wellness is important.

Take good care of yourself.

As goes your mind and body, so goes your guitar playing....

FINGERNAIL CARE

Playing with fingernails is optional. Using fingernails however, expands your tonal possibilities. You can vary your tone from mellow to crisp by simply adjusting your hand position so that either more skin, or more fingernail, contacts the string.

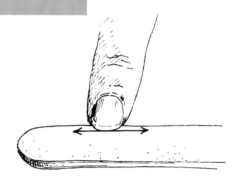

Shape the nail by moving a file back and forth over the edge.

The nails need to be shaped so that they glide smoothly across the strings without snagging on any rough edges. The actual shape is a matter of individual preference, so you will need to experiment to find out what works best for you. Use the following tools, in the following order, to shape and polish your fingernails:

- Fingernail file (the more expensive the better)
- 600 grain sandpaper (or finer)
- Cheesecloth

The sandpaper and cheesecloth are available at most hardware stores. You may keep all of your supplies organized by storing them in a box or pouch. Use the fingernail file to shape the nails by lightly rubbing the file under the edge of the nail. Use the sandpaper to remove the roughness left by the file. Hold the right hand still and move the paper back and forth with the left hand as shown in the illustration on the right. Finish by rubbing the bottom and top of the edge with the cheese cloth, making the nail glassy smooth.

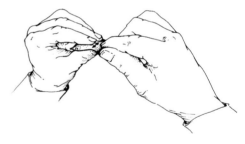

Remove the roughness with sandpaper and then buff with cheesecloth.

THE FREE STROKE

The free stroke is the most commonly used stroke for fingerpicking.

Action:
In order to produce a full tone, the string should be pressed downward and inward before being released. The plucking finger moves up and into the palm and does not touch the adjacent string before continuing its motion. This stroke requires a curled finger position.

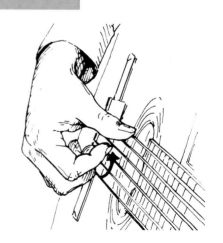

Variations for Example 1:
- Let all open strings sustain.
- Mute the open strings with your left hand, using the side of your left hand fingers opposite your fingernails.

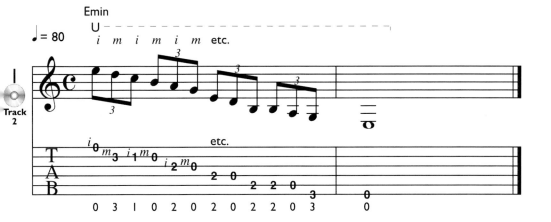

△ = Rest Stroke
U = Free Stroke

THE REST STROKE

The primary benefit of the rest stroke is fullness of tone. It is used where special emphasis is desired.

Action: The weight of the finger is directed downward and inward so that it lands (rests) on the adjacent string before it continuing its motion Think of the string more as a trampoline than a bow and arrow. Your fingers need to be less curved to execute this stroke.

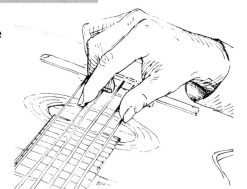

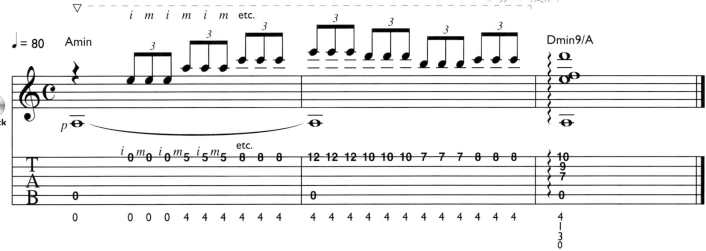

THE THUMB

In addition to plucking strings, the thumb is also used to provide stability and as a mute.

Practice the preceding free stroke exercise as follows:
- To provide stability, rest the thumb tip on the low E string.
- To provide a dry sound, lay the thumb across the strings, from 6th to 3rd, and drag it ahead of the plucking fingers.

Improve the tone of your free strokes by matching its tone with the full tone of your rest strokes. Do this with minimal shifting of hand position. With practice, your free strokes will sound as full as your rest strokes.

△ = Rest Stroke
U = Free Stroke

CLEARER VOICES
Track 4

Practice Tip: Rhythm Reading
Ignore the pitches and play the rhythm of the example using open strings only. Rhythm reading will be beneficial with many of the examples in this book.

PLANTING

Incorporating "preparation gestures" such as planting will improve your control. Where you see the unfilled notes ♩, or circled plucking fingers in the TAB (*i* = index, *m* = middle, *a* = ring), *plant* (place, but do not play) the indicated plucking finger on the string as preparation to pluck the following note. These notes are not played—they just indicate a plant.

GARDEN SONG
Track 5

Practice Tip: Left Hand Preparation
In addition to planting the fingers of your right hand, you may also prepare the fingers of left hand. Where you see the unfilled notes, or circled plucking fingers in the TAB, lightly plant the next left hand finger on the string above the fret which they are preparing to play.

The following three practice principles—Rearranging Finger Order, Shifting Accents and Contrasting Groups will help you achieve balanced control of each individual finger. These practice principles apply to many musical situations. You will find yourself using them to master many pieces.

REARRANGING FINGER ORDER

The goal of the following piece is to attain equal control of each finger. Use the rhythm reading practice technique (page 200, bottom) as preparation if necessary.

THE GOLDEN LADDER

Track 6

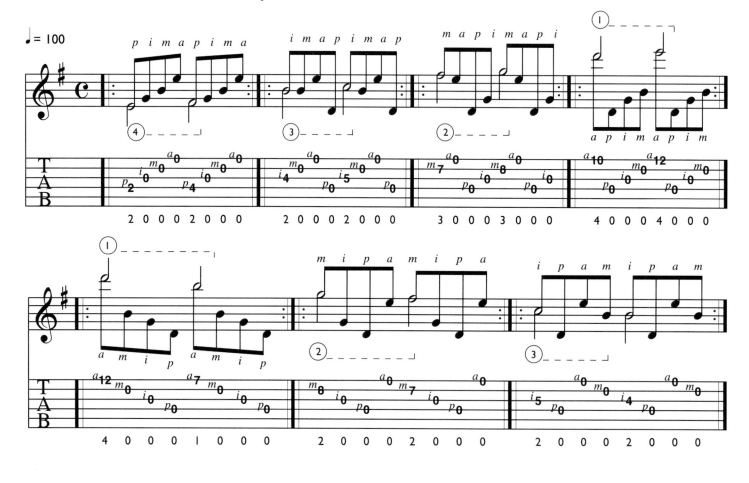

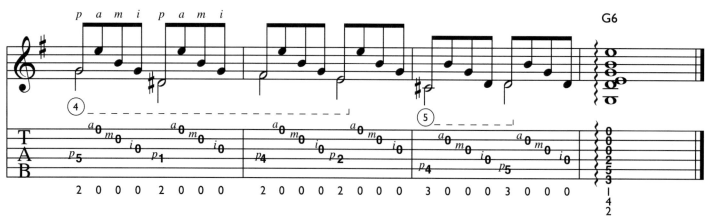

SHIFTING ACCENTS

As this piece progresses, the accent falls on different beats and different fingers. This is another way of improving your finger control.

SONG OF ASCENT

CONTRASTING GROUPS

Improve finger control by using finger groups of two or four notes (2's or 4's), to play rhythmic patterns of triplets (3's) and vice-versa. For instance, if the rhythmic pattern is triplets (groups of three notes in one beat), use a two-note pattern, such as *p-m-p-m*. Exaggerate the accents.

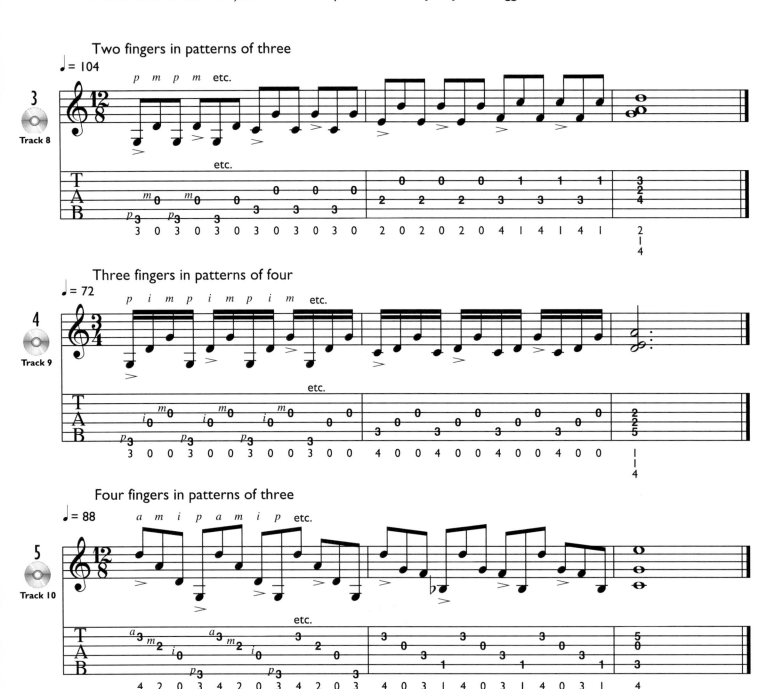

Practice Tip: Contrasting Groups

Use the preceding technique of contrasting finger groups of 2's and 3's with rhythmic patterns whenever you can. This is a very useful way of attaining balanced control of your fingers.

CHAPTER 2

Exploring the Harp

The guitar can be many things including a drum, a single-stringed instrument, a harp and a fretted instrument. The diverse nature of the guitar is a reflection of the historical evolution of instruments from ancient times until now—from the very simple to the complex—and is an important part of creating fingerstyle guitar music. In this chapter we will explore some fingerstyle patterns that address the harp aspect of the guitar's nature. It is essential to notice how the left hand accommodates the right hand.

Before you continue, it would be a good idea to experiment and see how many combinations you can discover for six strings plus the three fingers and thumb of your right hand. Always consider what left-hand patterns mirror these harp combinations. Try to write a piece of music that uses only open strings. Indicate the fingerings.

HARP FINGER PATTERN ON INDIVIDUAL STRINGS

Let's begin by exploring a right-hand pattern which will prepare you for multiple-string-patterns which have a more harp-like sound.

Playing the accent on the beginning of each beat in *River Song* prevents either finger from becoming predominant. During the *i, m* fingering, rest your thumb on the 6th string for stability.

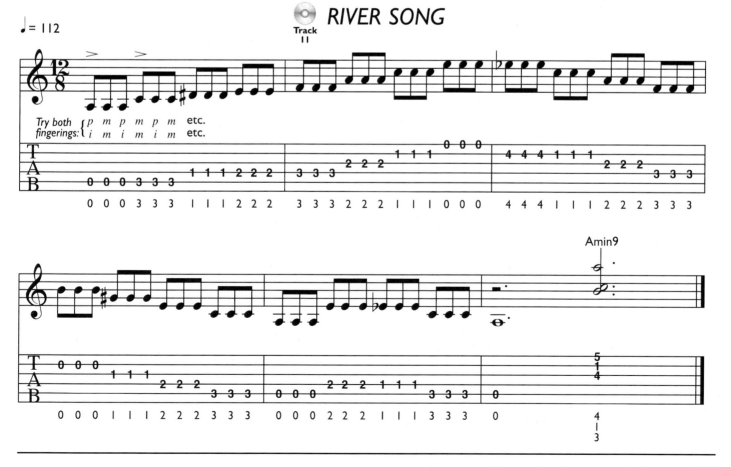

In *Drifting Breezes*, observe the constant *p-m* alternation in the right hand. The *m* finger remains on the 1st string, and *p* moves from to string to string to accommodate the left hand. Since *m* doesn't change strings, and the *p-m* alternation is constant, you need only think of how *p* and the left hand are working together. Simplifying your thinking will improve your playing many times over.

DRIFTING BREEZES

Track
12

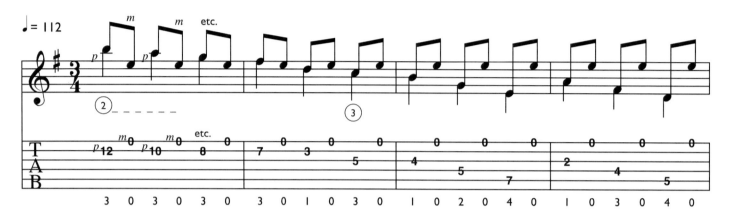

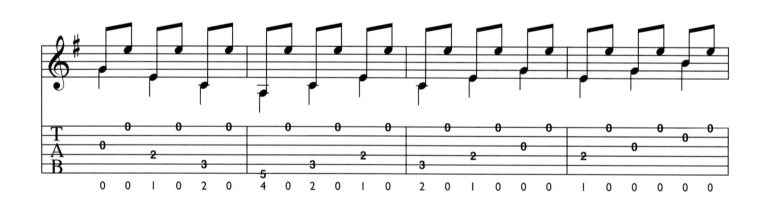

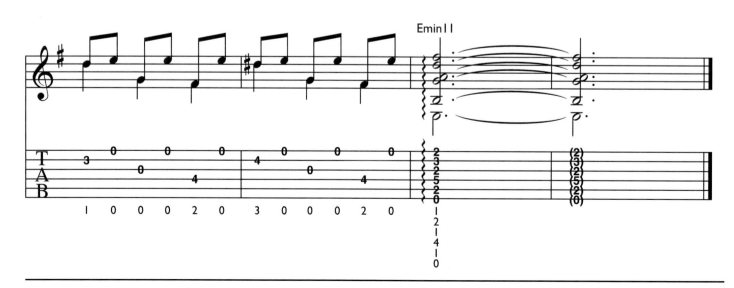

Notice how the left-hand positions in *Hand-Gliding* are designed to accommodate the right-hand harp activity. This type of "marriage" between the hands can be thought of as "right-hand harmony," the right hand being the male and the left hand being the female.   Instead of thinking, "Mr. Right Hand" and "Miss Left Hand," think "Mr. and Mrs. Right Hand Harmony."

HAND GLIDING

Track 13

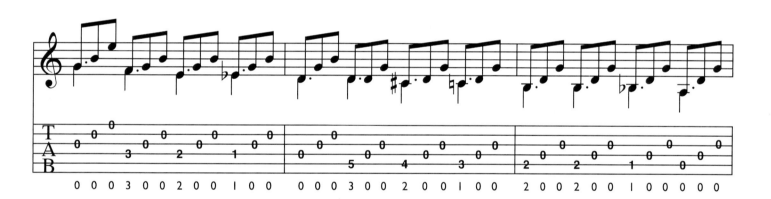

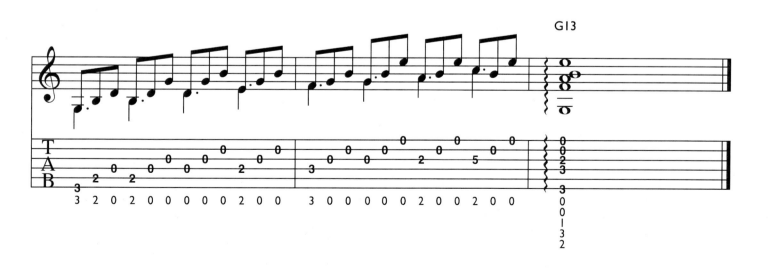

We need to consider how the left hand patterns presented in *Sun Dapples* might be expanded from one part of the neck to the entire neck. This expansive process can be referred to as "local into global," and is important for achieving unrestricted movement around the neck. Notice that the right-hand pattern, *p-i-m-a*, remains constant, but moves to different string sets to accommodate the left hand. Recognizing patterns will increase your fluency.

SUN DAPPLES

Track 14

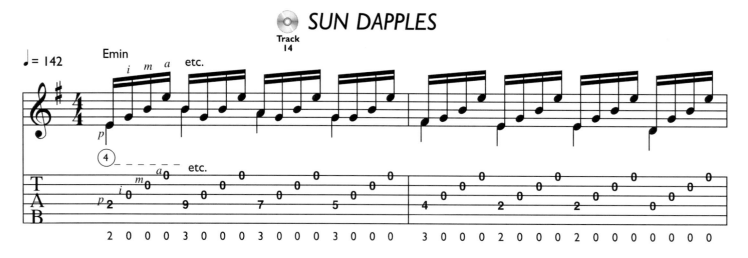

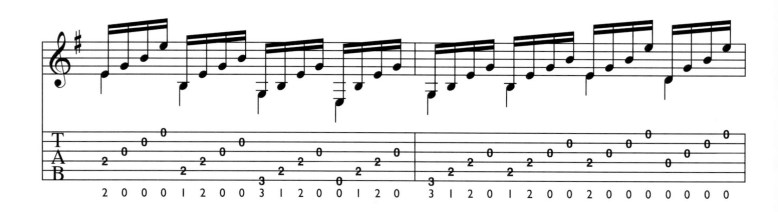

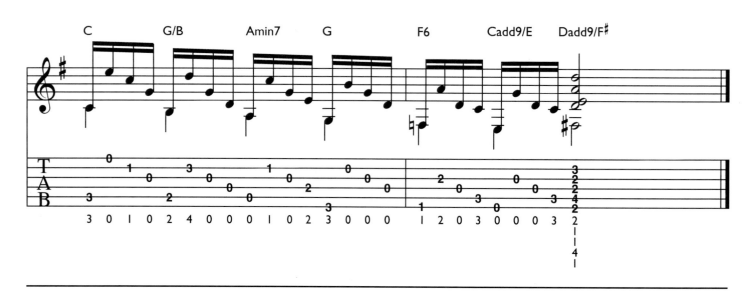

HARP FINGER PATTERN USING FIVE STRINGS

Memorize the chord forms in *The Crossing* and add them to your musical vocabulary.

Sometimes we play adjacent strings in an arpeggio by repeating *p* or *i*. This is called a *sweep*. They are marked in this example with arrows.

↗ = ascending sweep
↘ = descending sweep

THE CROSSING
Track 15

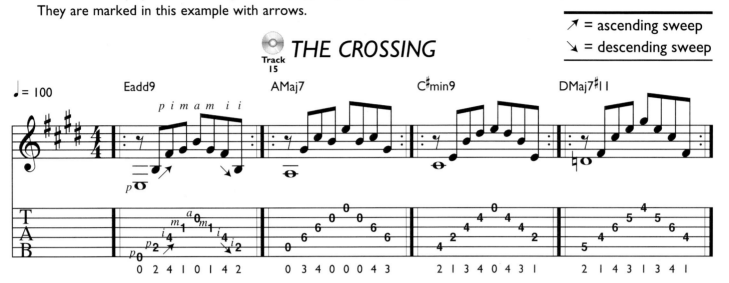

HARP FINGER PATTERN USING SIX STRINGS

The second chord in *Dancing Waves* is very interesting. It contains the notes for two different chords: GMaj7 (G, B, D, F#) and DMaj7 (D, F#, A, C#). Harmonies such as this, where two or more chords are juxtaposed, are called *polychordal*. This is a great way to create new sounds. Check out Chapter 3 on Chord Formulas beginning on page 210 to learn some more ideas for creating harmonies.

DANCING WAVES
Track 16

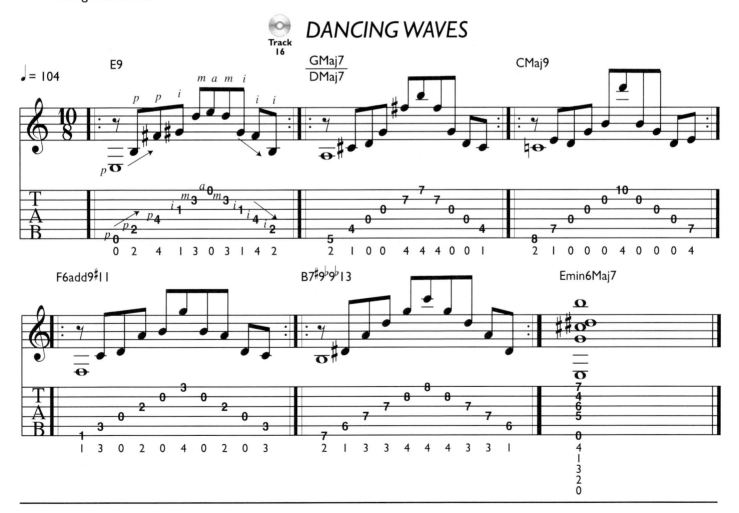

CHAPTER 3

Chord Formulas

Left-hand chord forms can be described as general or specific. For example, triads such as DMaj (D Major) or Dmin (D Minor), are specific whereas, "chords in 3rds" is a general formula. By thinking about a general formula rather than specific, you are freed from the need to use a specific label, and you are able to explore all combinations of the twelve notes in the chromatic scale and refer to them as "mixed intervals."

In the previous chapter, we explored the marriage between the right-hand movements and the left-hand patterns that interact with them. In this chapter our hands will change roles. Musical examples will be developed from left-hand movements and the right-hand patterns that interact with them.

Left-hand movements that are based on formulas simplify the right hand's responsibilities. In the musical examples that follow we will explore six formulas, each having it's own musical quality and fingerstyle implications.

FORMULA #1: CHORDS IN 2NDS

The idea of chords in 2nds is to use the interval of a 2nd, either a major or minor 2nd, as building material for harmonies. Playing a harmonic interval of a 2nd superimposed over a bass note creates a particular kind of sound that's fun to explore.

Marital Bliss is in A Minor. See how many diatonic 2nds in A Minor you can finger on the guitar. Try every position. Then, use your findings and your own creativity to extend *Marital Bliss* into a longer piece. Have fun!

MARITAL BLISS
Track 17

The following piece explores triads (in second inversion) superimposed over a bass note. Chord formulas such as chords in 3rds need not be limited to *triads* (three note chords). Explore the possibilities of two-, four- and five-note structures in 3rds. Just keep stacking those 3rds to create new sounds.

THE REVELATION BLUES

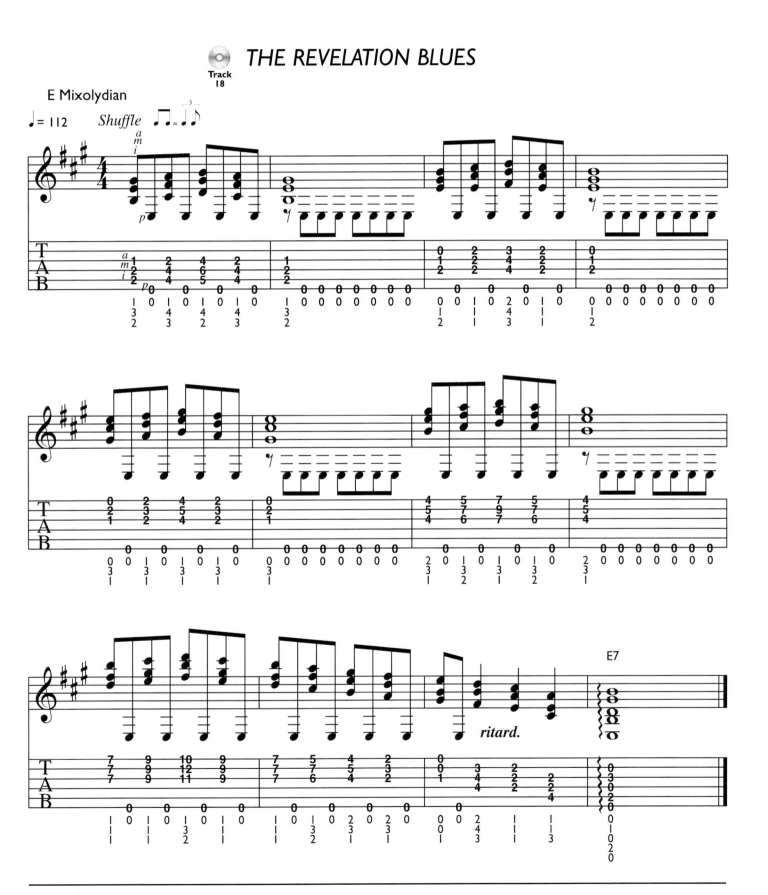

Performance Notes

Notice the open quality of 4ths in *Even-ing Sounds*. This is especially true when each note is plucked individually as in the next-to-last measure. This technique is called *arpeggiation* and can be used with any chord form.

EVEN-ING SOUNDS

Track 19

In *Driftwood Song*, intervals of 5ths and 7ths superimposed over a bass note are used. Use the palm of your right hand to mute the bass strings and create a driving rhythmic effect.

DRIFTWOOD SONG
Track 20

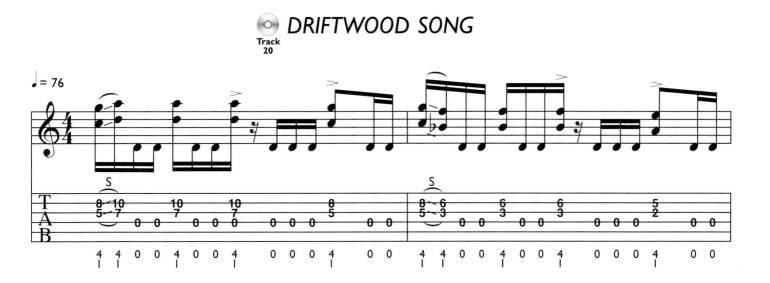

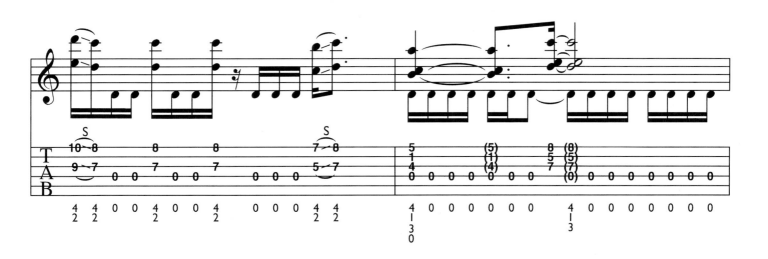

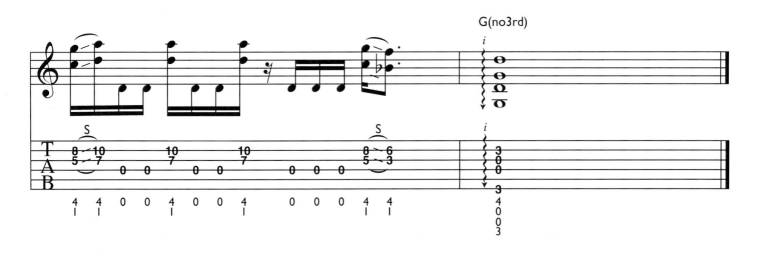

The *drop-two* formula is so named because the second voice (each note in a chord is called a *voice*) from the top of the chord is dropped one octave. For instance, in Example 6 the top voice is E and the 2nd voice from the top is C. Lower the C one octave and you have a drop-two voicing. Drop-two voicings work well for the "stride style" of fingerpicking used in *Sailing Song*.

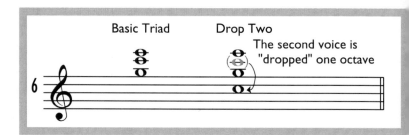

Chord formulas such as the drop-two can be modified with the addition of *auxiliary tones* or *non-chord tones*. This is sometimes referred to as *melodization* and is used in measures 5 through 7 of *Sailing Song*. In the last four measures, an open string that may or may not be a chord tone is added for color. This is a guitaristic way of using a *pedal tone* (a sustained or continually repeated note).

SAILING SONG

Track 21

The *drop three* formula is so named because the third voice from the top of the chord is dropped one octave.

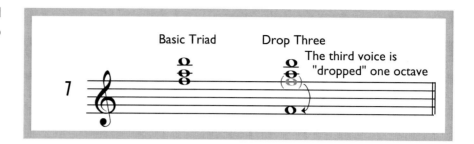

Play *Plain Song* first as written, in "block chords." Once you are familiar with the fingerings, fingerpick them with the variations found at the bottom of the page. Notice that variations D) and E) change the time signature and feel of the piece.

PLAIN SONG
Track 22

Variations

CHAPTER 4

Sense of Touch

In this chapter we will pinpoint specific body sensations through the use of exaggeration exercises. It is your job to remember these sensations and introduce them into your playing. Doing so will result in a relaxed, accurate and healthy playing style.

GRAY TONES

In their perfect state of relaxation, the fingers of the left hand are completely at rest on the strings. Their active motion is one of lifting. In the following example, be aware of the lifting motion of each finger. Then allow each finger to passively fall onto the desired pitch. You are now just resting lightly on the string, and not pressing down. When plucked, these tones will sound muted or "gray." Touched lightly enough, they will sound completely unpitched. Experiment. The three components of gray tones are rest, lift and fall.

The result of the marriage of the right- and left-hand fingerings in *Ghost Dance* is some tricky string crossings for *i* and *m*. Practice the right hand alone before adding the left hand.

×= Gray tone

GHOST DANCE

Track 23

GRAY TONES INTO CLEAR TONES

To produce a clear, ringing tone, use a lever action with your left-hand knuckles. Use only the amount of pressure necessary to make the note sing clearly. Do not push or squeeze. When the knuckles are allowed to rise, the natural weight of the fingers automatically stops the string.

Tone is note a matter of black and white, gray or clear. There are many gradations in between that you should become aware of. In the following example we will explore three such gradations:

1) Gray - A muted tone with no pitch (indicated with light gray ✕)
2) Semi Gray - A muted tone with pitch (indicated with dark gray ✕)
3) Clear - A normal tone (written normally)

As you progress from the gray tone to the clear tone, bring your awareness to the lever action created when the knuckles rise. The higher you rise, the more gray the tone. The four components of clear tones are rest, lift, fall and rise. In actual performance, these occur almost instantly as one motion.

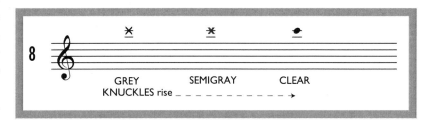

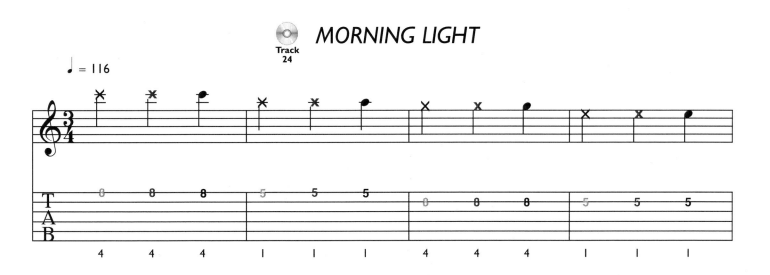

MORNING LIGHT

Track 24

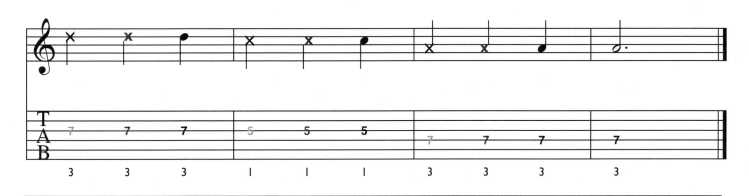

The ability to relax the left arm at will is extremely important to guitarists. Sometimes we have to correct a movement in the flash of an instant, and we are often called upon to shift from position to position very rapidly. Also, it's important in general to be loose and nimble. For these reasons, the left arm must be free and relaxed.

To perform the *Fast Pitch*, the left wrist needs to be flexible to move both up and down the neck, creating an oscillating motion with the forearm. In addition, the forearm should be allowed to rotate on an axis that runs through the arm, from elbow to fingers. Violinists use this type of motion to instantly adjust their intonation. Guitarists can use it to make immediate corrections and to develop a relaxed left arm.

In *Fast Pitch,* you will be either sliding up into, falling off (sliding down from), sliding up from or falling in (sliding down into) the notated pitches. Do all four of these motions with a loose wrist and arm, striving to be as free as possible.

Practice Variations:
    Do short slides and falls.
    Do long slides and falls.
    Repeat using the 2nd finger, then the 3rd and 4th.

FAST PITCH

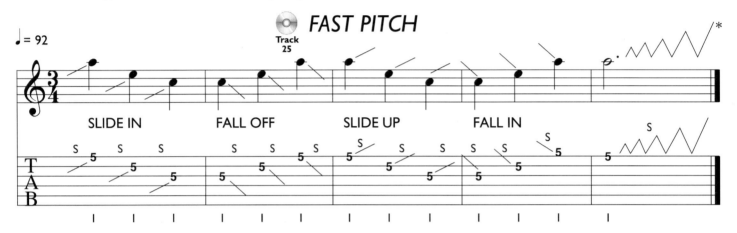

* This sign indicates a long slide that goes up and down in increasing amounts.

The idea in *Fingers Dance* is to move the arm freely to allow for rapid finger substitutions. Your arm should swing freely back and forth. To perform *Fingers Dance* your touch must be light, and your wrist and forearm must be supple and movable.

FINGERS DANCE

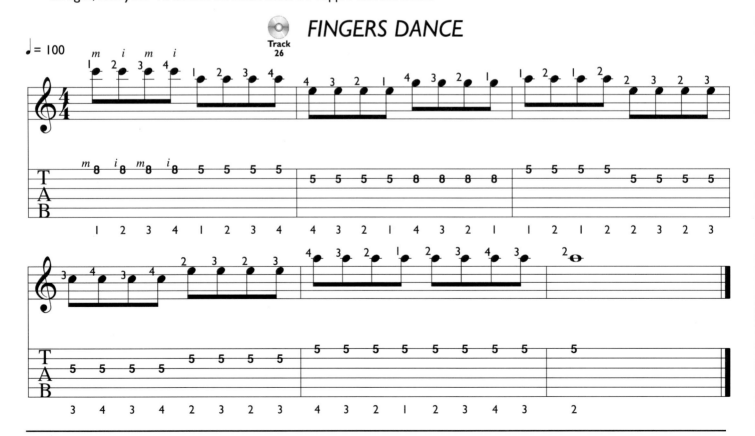

Now that you are sensitive to the left arm, it is time to investigate *shifting*—the act of moving from one position to another. To shift, we must give the correct amount of energy to the arm to cause motion of a specific distance. For instance, we need to know the amount of energy needed to shift from the first position to the fifth. The key to making this or any other shift is the efficient use of *impulse* and *momentum*.

Impulse is a mere spark of energy that starts the motion. Momentum is the follow through, or gliding part of the motion. Impulse and momentum are parts of one continuous motion.

Demonstration:

Using the thumb and the index finger of the right hand, gently clasp the wrist of your left hand. Keep the left hand completely limp, and the left forearm upright. With the left hand at rest, use the right hand to pull the left wrist toward yourself and then away. Notice the effortless movement of the limp left hand as it glides forward and backward with the movement of the arm and wrist. Also notice the whip-like relationship between the hand and forearm.

While playing *The Lucid Acrobat,* try to recreate the feel of the preceding demonstration by allowing your hand to glide to it's destination after the initial impulse starts each motion.

THE LUCID ACROBAT

Track 27

Pussy footing is a term coined by violinist Yehudi Menuhin. It refers to the action of two fingers in alternation on the neck, and is inspired by the frontal view of a cat walking. As one finger goes down, the other goes up, but not very much.

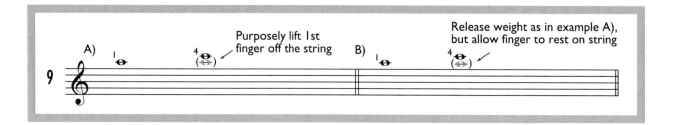

Play *The Kitten Walk* twice. The first time, exaggerate the motion by lifting one finger way off the string whenever another finger depressed a note. The second time through, allow the first finger to passively rest on the string, without pushing while the other finger plays. Pussy footing allows your muscles to remain soft and increases endurance.

THE KITTEN WALK

Track 28

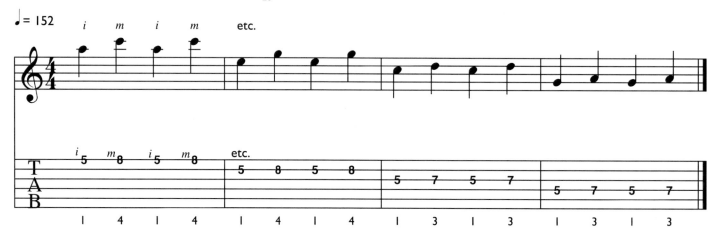

SQUARE AND DIAGONAL FRAMES

Certain positions that require the use of the 4th finger on the bass strings are facilitated by holding the palm parallel to the neck. This is known as the "square frame."

Shifting and vibrato however, are facilitated by holding the left hand so that the palm is at a moderate, oblique diagonal to the neck. This is referred to as the "diagonal frame." The diagonal frame is physically more natural and is used more often.

The diagonal frame provides another important benefit known as "double contact points." These contact points on the neck are 1) the base of the first finger and 2) the soft pad of the thumb. Awareness of double contact points greatly enhances stability and control.

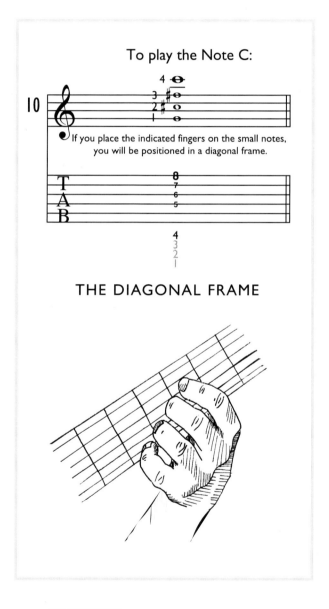

THE DIAGONAL FRAME

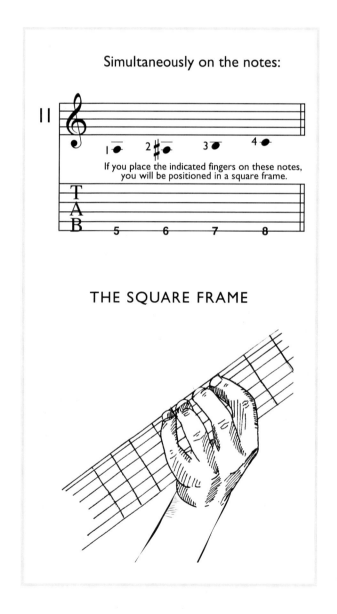

THE SQUARE FRAME

EXERCISE:

With the fingers simultaneously planted on the first string in a square frame, practice alternation between the square and diagonal frame. Also experiment with bringing your palm closer or further from the neck. These exercises increase finger flexibility.

Using vibrato enhances tone and facilitates movement. Although there are many artistic variations of vibrato, there are basically two types, classical vibrato and bending vibrato.

CLASSICAL VIBRATO

Supported by forearm rotation, the hand rocks repeatedly towards the bridge and back towards the nut. The fingertip loosens the string as it pushes toward the bridge, subtly lowering the pitch, and tightens the strings as it rocks towards the nut, subtly raising the pitch. This wavering of pitch causes the vocal-like vibrato used by violinists, violists, cellists and classical guitarists. Classical vibrato may vary in intensity depending on the amount of pressure the finger exerts against the fingerboard.

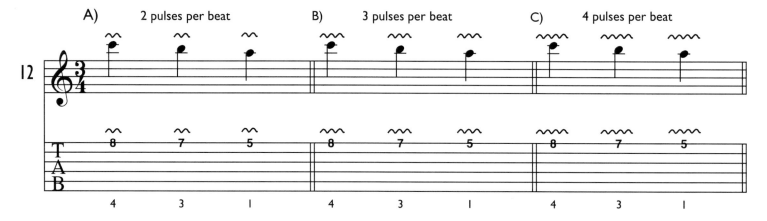

Vibrato speed should be played in a controlled manner. Play *Candela* three times. First with two pulses per beat, then three, then four.

CANDELA

Track 29

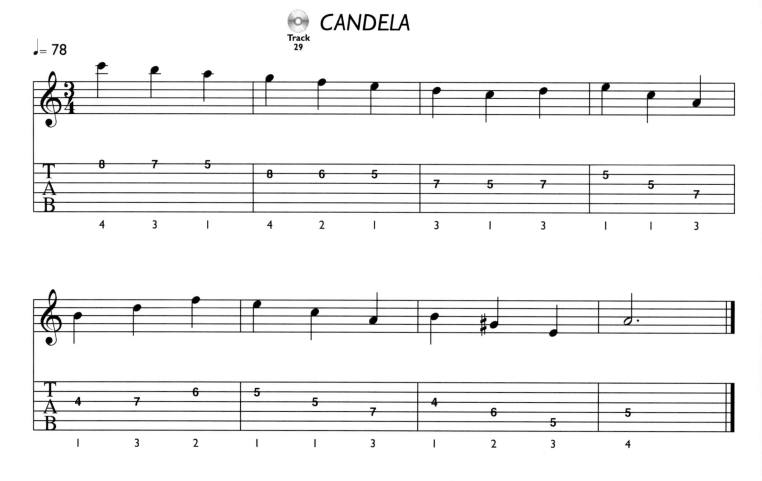

Bending vibrato is done by bending the string very slightly and quickly. Generally speaking, for strings 3, 4, 5 and 6, the fingertip bends the string by pulling it toward the palm of the hand. To do this more easily, reach over the string with the fingertip and allow all the fingers to move sympathetically in support of the vibrato finger. For strings 1 and 2 the string is pushed away from the palm of the hand. In both cases the result is the same: the note is pulled sharp and then released to it's natural pitch. When playing bending vibrato with the third finger, the first and second finger can assist by also pulling on that string.

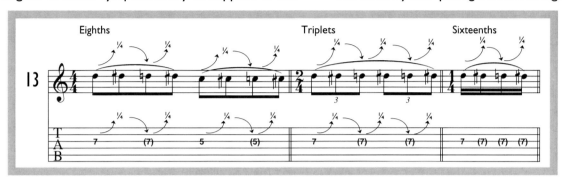

Since bending vibrato involves small bends—less than a half step—we will show them as quarter-tone bends. Even this is just an approximation. The width of the bend can vary. Play *Curve Ball* three times. Once with subtle pitch fluctuation, one with medium fluctuation and one with exaggerated fluctuation.

¼ ↗ = Bend up half way to to a half step. This is *quarter tone* bend.

♯ = indicates a quarter tone

CURVE BALL

Track 30

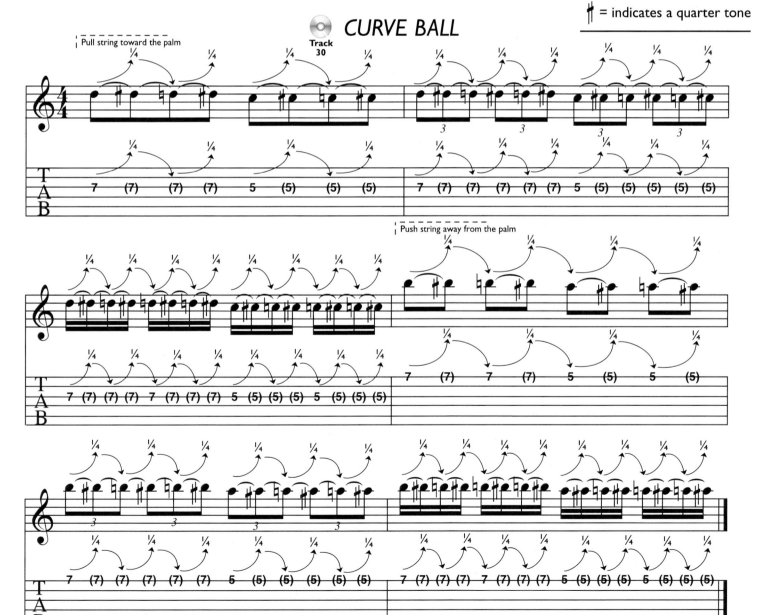

CHAPTER 5
Fingerstyle Speed

RIGHT-HAND PREPARATION FOR TREMOLO

A *tremolo* is a rapidly repeated note. This is an important flamenco and classical guitar technique that is great for all fingerstyle players to know. Developing a strong, controlled tremolo is good for your overall technique and creates various possibilities for left-hand finger patterns helpful for very fast playing.

Practice the examples below. Be sure to use the indicated fingerings and focus on the accents. Spend lots of time with these. They will help you develop a good tremolo technique.

Considerations:
    Move each finger firmly and with intent
    Maintain a strong sense of the upbeat
    Beware of fingernails that are too long and may catch on the string and inhibit the tremolo
    During practice, rest strokes may be played where accents appear

BALANCING

SHIFTING ACCENTS

CONTRASTING 2s AND 3s

PLANTING

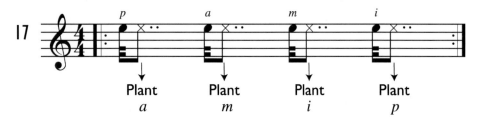

Play very short notes by planting the next finger immediately after each finger plays. For instance, immediately after *p* plays the 1st string, plant *a*, stopping the vibration of the 1st string.

COORDINATING LEFT-HAND PATTERNS WITH RIGHT-HAND TREMOLO

Any melody note can be surrounded with a series of secondary notes called *embellishments*. When these embellishments occur on one string they can be synchronized with right-hand tremolo. Melodic embellishments of this type are useful in fingerstyle improvisation because they simplify the thought process. For every one note that the mind conceives (target note), three or four notes are actually played (embellishments). In order to perform this technique, your right-hand tremolo must be perfectly coordinated with your left-hand movements.

SPEED BURSTS: Continue to extend this pattern

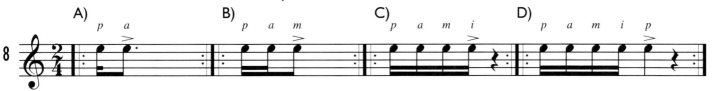

TEMPO CONTROL

3 FINGER TREMOLO: Practiced as contrasting 2's and 3's

In contrasting 2's and 3's, rhythmic groups of 2 or 4 are played with a three-note fingering, in this case *p-m-i*. A review of page 204 may be helpful.

2 FINGER TREMOLO:
Preparation

2 FINGER TREMOLO:
Practiced as contrasting 2's and 3's

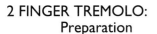

Change the right-hand pattern from *p-a-m-i* to *p-m-i* to *m-i* without pausing.

SEAMLESS TRANSITION: 4 fingers → 3 fingers → 2 fingers
Also practice seemless transition with sixteenth notes

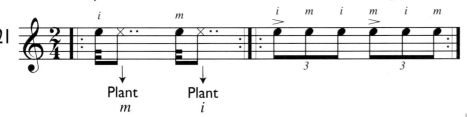

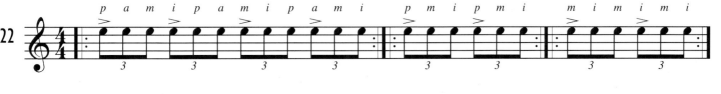

In the following three variations (A, B and C), the circled note is a primary note, and the other notes are the embellishments.

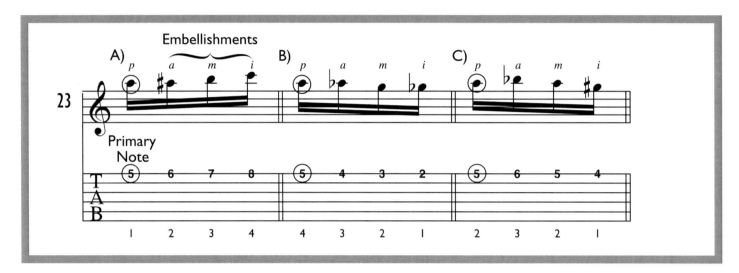

Treat each note in *Orbit Song* as a primary note. Play it three times, each time using a different one of the three embellishment variations in Example 23. For additional practice, play *Orbit Song* with all gray tones.

ORBIT SONG

Track 31

THREE-NOTE LEFT-HAND PATTERNS WITH RIGHT-HAND TREMOLO

In the following two variations (A and B), the circled note is the primary note and the other notes are the embellishments.

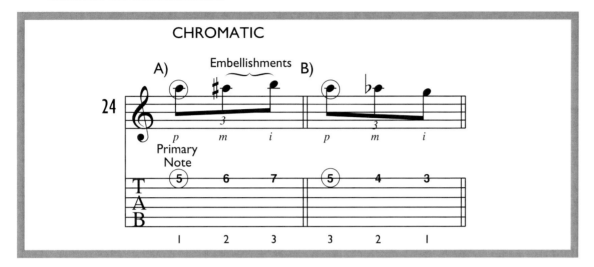

Treat each note in *Blast Off* as a primary note. Play it twice, each time using a different one of the two embellishment variations.

BLAST OFF

Track 32

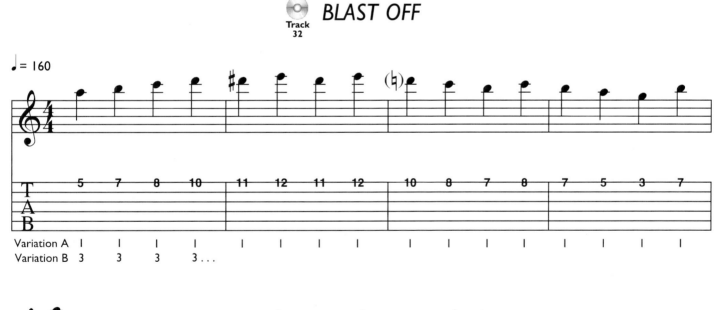

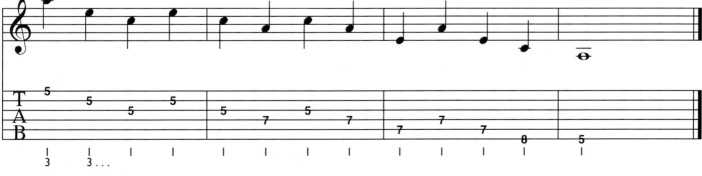

TWO-NOTE LEFT-HAND PATTERNS
WITH RIGHT-HAND TREMOLO

In the following three variations (A, B and C), the circled note is the primary note and the other notes are the embellishments.

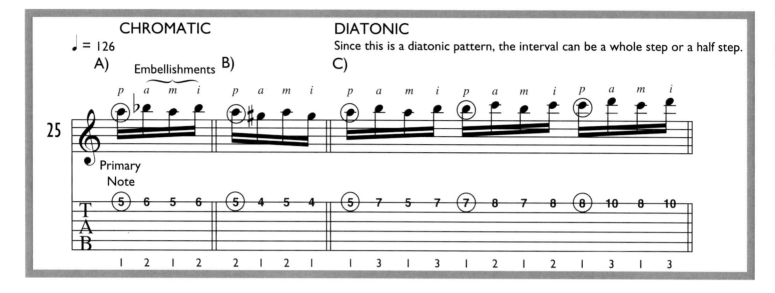

Treat each note in *Asteroid Bodies* as a primary note. Play the piece three times, each time using a different one of the three embellishment variations in Example 25. Incorporate the "pussy footing" concept discussed on page 220.

ASTEROID BODIES

Track 33

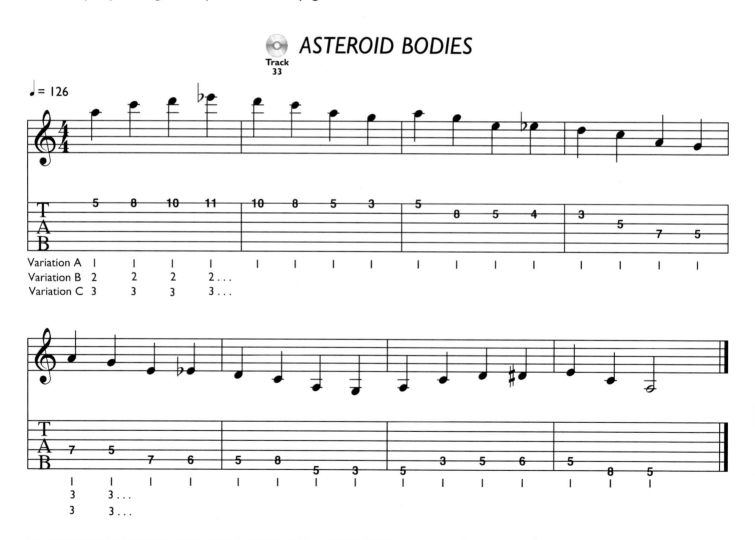

ONE-FINGER LEFT-HAND PATTERNS WITH RIGHT-HAND TREMOLO

The following pattern is an easy way to achieve lots of movement with minimum effort.

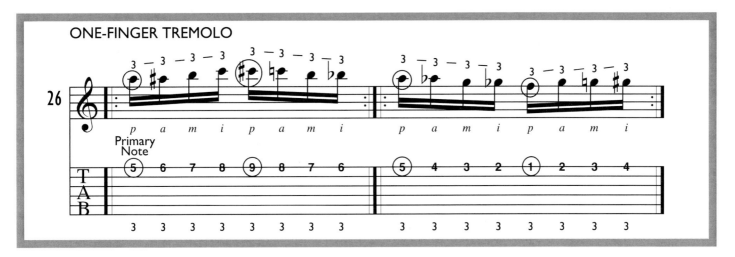

ONE-FINGER TREMOLO

Treat each note in *Overflowing Creation* as a primary note. While sliding from primary note to primary note, maintain a continuous tremolo. Playing this exercise, which is inspired by violin technique, helps develop your sense of touch and of distance. If you press too hard, you can't slide. If you don't press hard enough the notes sound unintentionally gray. Note that you can slide a small or large distance, and the larger the distance, the faster the left hand must move.

OVERFLOWING CREATION

Track 34

CHROMATIC SLIDING THROUGHOUT

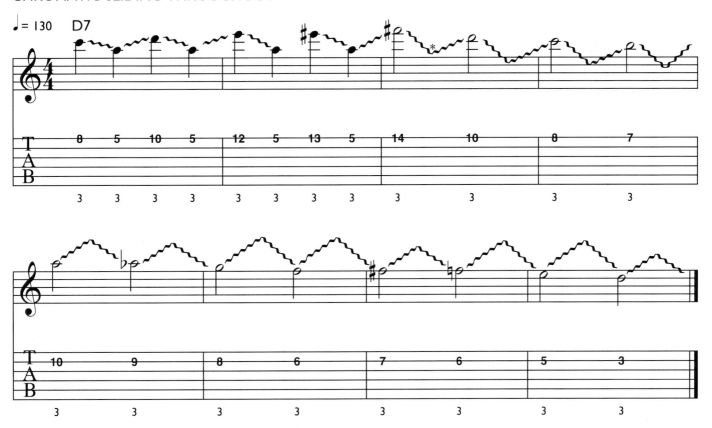

* The distance of the slides can vary as long as you arrive on the next primary note in time. Experiment! Keep the speed of your tremolo constant (even sixteenths), and try it using the other left-hand fingers.

Blues Tremolo Etude would be great as part of an ending for an exciting, virtuosic piece. Be sure the notes are of equal volume and length. In the last measure, continue the right-hand tremolo in even sixteenths during the up and down left hand slides.

BLUES TREMOLO ETUDE

Track 35

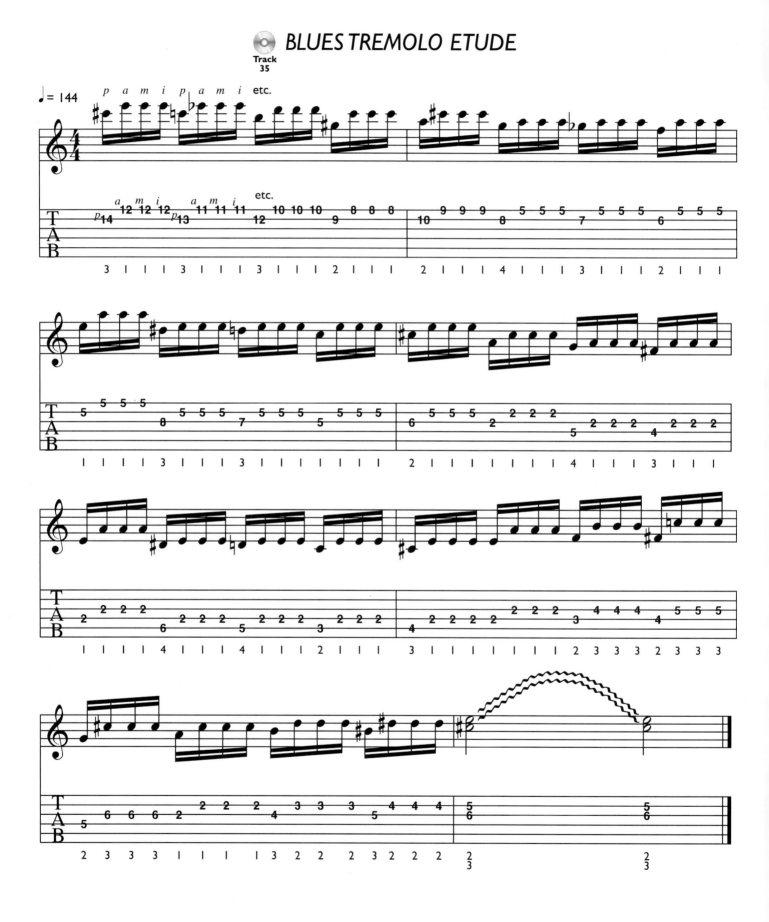

One way of developing speed is to start slowly and gradually speed up. Another way is to play two notes very rapidly, then play three, then four, and so on. This latter method, known as *speed bursts*, has the advantage of conveying the feel of speed. Also, one of the most difficult aspects of speed is endurance. It is easier to play two notes quickly than it is to play eight notes quickly. So, each of the following exercises should be mastered before going on to the next. Measure your progress with a metronome. Speed bursts may be practiced as gray tones, clear tones or somewhere in between.

Notice that the preparation exercise (Example 27) demonstrates how each burst should be followed by a plant. The next finger that would play is placed on the string as if ready to continue playing at the same speed.

SPEED BURSTS
Preparation: Extend this pattern

Add a plant after each of these bursts.

Sequences are repetitions of musical phrases at different pitch levels. These patterns continue from one part of an instrument's range to another part. Like embellishment patterns, sequences simplify the thought process. Sequences can occur up and down the neck or across the strings.

TWO-STRING SEQUENCE
The right- and left-hand fingerings for sequences that move up and down the neck are similar or identical for each part of the sequence. The repetitive fingering of both hands simplifies the thought process.

LUDWIG'S VAN
Track 36

Sequence on the A Harmonic Minor Scale

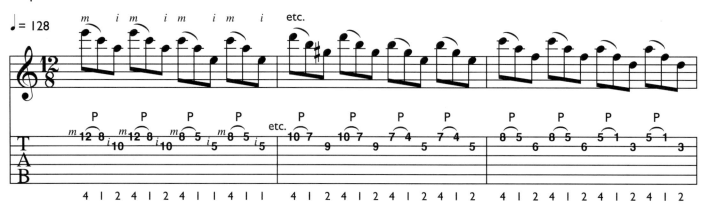

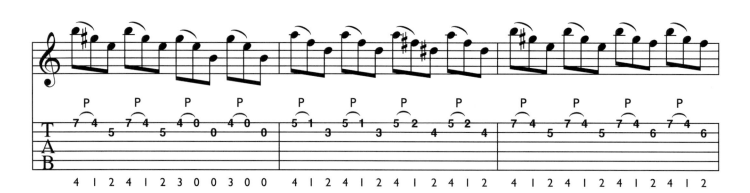

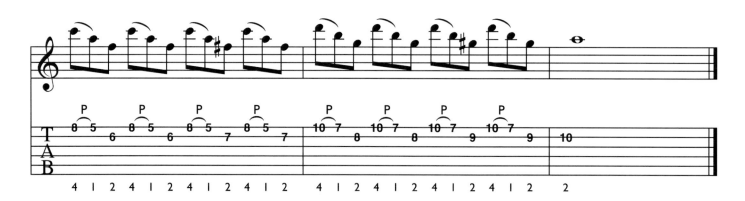

> **Practice Tip: Local into Global**
> Invent a two string sequence in a mode of your choice. Transpose it to each scale degree of the mode and perform it seemlessly from as low as possible to as high as possible. This technique is referred to as "local into global."

THREE-STRING SEQUENCE

Notice the use of gray tones in the second to the last measure. Gray tones may serve as filler material when you are not sure which actual pitches to use. Gray tones also create a percussive, funky type of effect.

WOLFGANG'S GATEWAY

Track 37

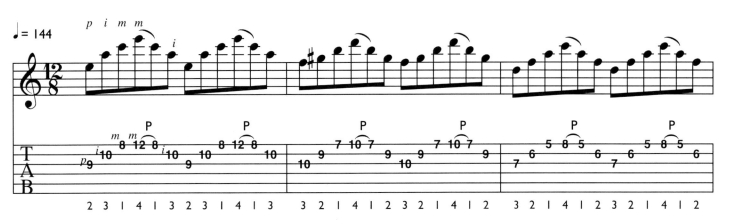

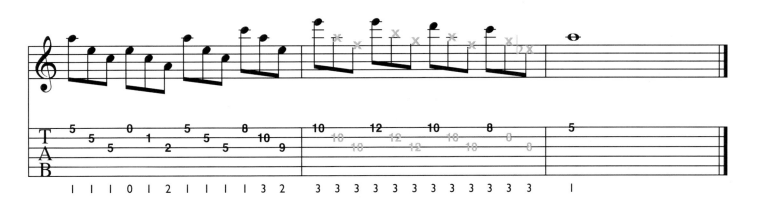

Practice Tip–Gray Tones

Add one, two or three gray tones above or beneath any series of primary notes. In *Wolfgang's Gateway*, the notes on the first, fourth, seventh and tenth eighth notes in each measure are primary notes. Use the second to last measure as an example and experiment on your own elsewhere in the piece.

CHAPTER 6

Modern Techniques

EXPRESSION & INVENTION

Rock rhythms and tapping techniques, access to ethnic music from around the world and the improved use of amplified acoustic instruments have resulted in more expressive possibilities for the fingerstyle guitarist than ever before.

In the following pages you will methodically develop the ability to play many of these popular techniques. The creative guitarist, however, should always be open to inventing new ones.

PHOTO COURTESY OF NAKED EAR MUSIC

Michael Hedges died tragically in a car accident on November 30, 1997. He will be remembered as one of the greatest innovators and composers for fingerstyle guitar.

The next four examples are based on a blues in D Minor. They explore left-hand tapping (indicated TL in the music and TAB) alone at first, and then in combination with a variety of other techniques. Left-hand tapping is done by hammering the desired fret with a finger of the left hand. It's like the second half of a hammer-on—you hammer-on to a note without ever having plucked the string with the right hand.

As a preparation gesture for each tap, lift the tapping finger out further than usual. Accelerate the tapping fingers fall into the fret with a trigger-type action, but do not use excessive force. Deliberately sustain notes to avoid unintentional staccato (short) sounds.

FERTILE GROUND

Track 38

♩ = 132

Shuffle

In *Planting Seeds*, left-hand tapping is combined with pull-offs. Tap the notes as usual with fingers the left hand where marked "TL." The pull-off action should be almost parallel to the frets, in effect plucking the string with the left hand. The tapped notes and the pull-off notes should be equal in volume. Care should be taken to make sure that tapped notes and pull-off notes receive accurate durations—the rhythm should swing (note the "shuffle" indication).

PLANTING SEEDS

Left hand tapping with pull-offs

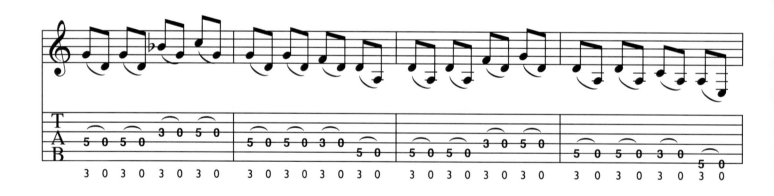

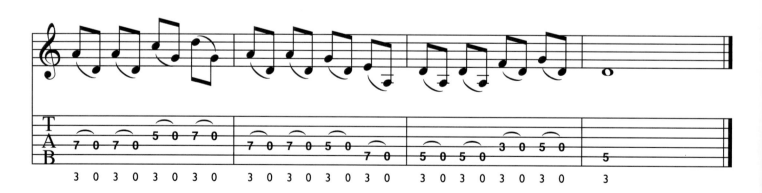

LEFT-HAND TAPPING WITH RIGHT-HAND DRUMMING

Right hand drumming ("R.H. Drumming") is done by lightly hitting the treble strings, just above the sound hole, with the right hand. This is indicated in the music and the TAB with an "×."

In *Tribal Connection,* tap the notes as usual with fingers the left hand where marked "TL." Lightly drum on the treble strings above the sound hole with the fingers of the right hand on the up beat (indicated with the ×). Be sure the drumming fingers remain on the strings long enough to prevent the open strings from unintentionally ringing.

TRIBAL CONNECTION

Track 40

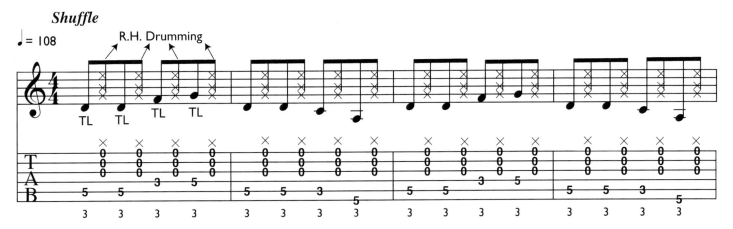

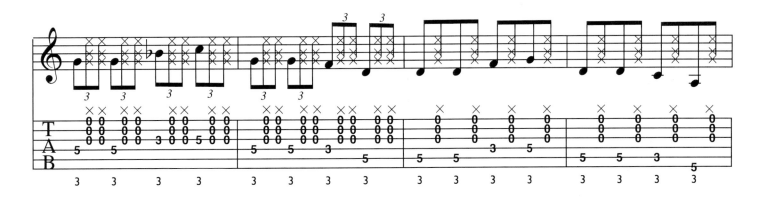

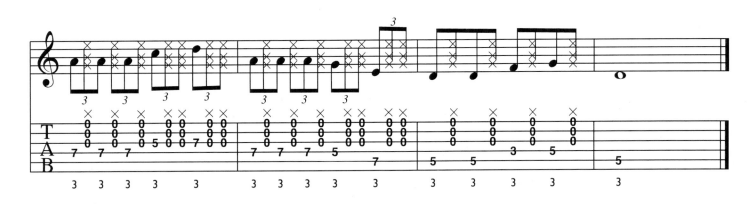

LEFT-HAND TAPPING WITH LEFT-HAND DRUMMING

Left hand drumming ("L.H. Drumming") is done by lightly drumming on the strings with the fingers of the left hand at the indicated pitch. This is indicated with a gray "×" at the indicated pitch in the music, and with a gray "×" above gray numbers in the TAB.

Note the alternation between tapped and drummed notes in *Knuckle Ball*. The right hand is not needed at all in this piece! Lightly drum on the strings with the fingers of the left hand at the indicated pitch.

KNUCKLE BALL

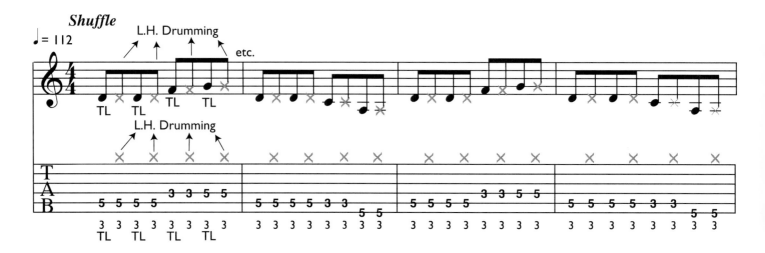

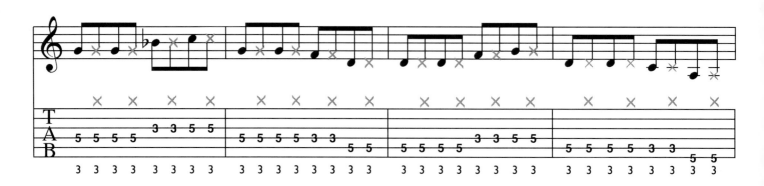

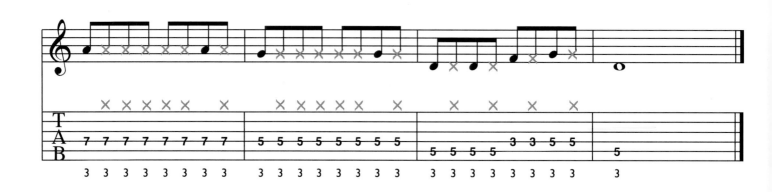

The next four examples use a typical blues riff in the key of A to explore left-hand tapping with double stops alone, then in combination with a variety of other techniques.

LEFT-HAND TAPPING IN DOUBLE STOPS

The technique for tapping double stops with the left hand is the same as for tapping single notes—lift the tapping fingers out further than usual and use an accelerated fall to the string. Be sure both notes of each double stop sound simultaneously.

SONIC BOOMER

Track 42

LEFT-HAND TAPPING IN DOUBLE STOPS WITH PULL-OFFS

The considerations for *Warp Factor* are basically the same as for *Planting Seeds* on page 236. Tap double stops as usual with fingers the left hand where marked "TL." The pull-off action should be almost parallel to the frets, in effect plucking the strings with the left hand. The tapped notes and pull-off notes should be very close in volume. Care should be taken to keep the rhythm swinging. This is another left-hand-only piece.

WARP FACTOR

Track 43

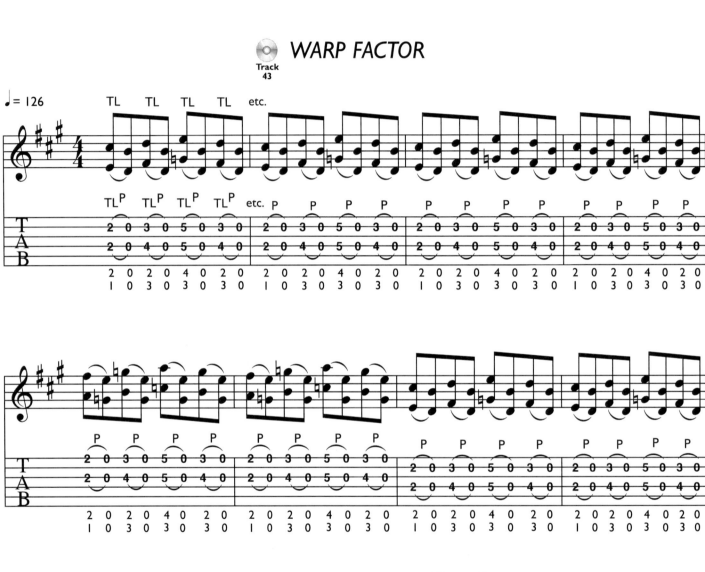

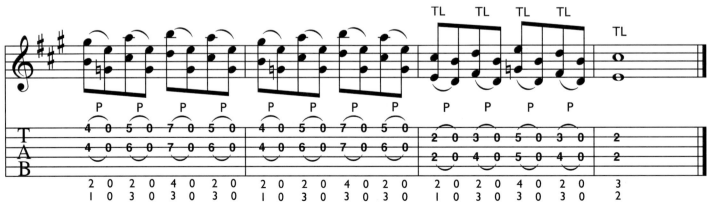

LEFT-HAND TAPPING IN DOUBLE STOPS WITH RIGHT-HAND DRUMMING

You may want to review *Tribal Connection on* page 237 before studying *Apollo's Theme*, since the techniques used are so similar. the difference here is the left hand is tapping double stops instead of single notes.

It is a good idea to practice the triplet section separately at first, since it requires a more rapid alternation between the left-hand tapping and the right-hand drumming.

APOLLO'S THEME
Track 44

LEFT-HAND TAPPING IN DOUBLE STOPS WITH LEFT-HAND DRUMMING

This combination gets your left hand working over-time! Tap double stops as usual with the fingers of the left hand where marked "TL." All of the drummed notes are marked with an "×". Avoid sounding the open strings accidentally.

POCO DIABLO

Track 45

Right-hand tapping technique (TR) opens the door to many expanded possibilities. It is done by hammering-on to the desired fret with a finger of the right hand. It is most common to use either *i* or *m*. You will find fingering suggestions above the TR marking in the music and below the 6th string in the TAB.

Right-hand tapping is as legitimate and important as traditional hammering-on and pulling-off, and is no longer an optional technique. Fortunately, tapping is easily learned. Technique alone however is not enough. Musicality must be applied.

Considerations:

- Rest the tip of middle finger on the fingernail of the index finger, then tap the desire note with the weight of both fingers.

- Important: For stability, the right-hand thumb should rest on the upper side of the neck.

- Review the instructions for successful left-hand tapping on page 235. The same principles of motion apply.

The next four pieces use a blues riff in the key of G to explore right-hand tapping alone and then in combination with a variety of other techniques.

FIRST TIME

Track 46

This one gets both hands tapping at once. Be sure all three notes sound simultaneously and with equal volume. Have fun!

HAPPY LANDING

Track 47

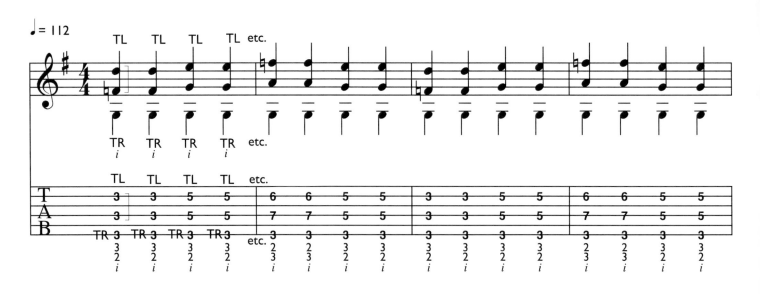

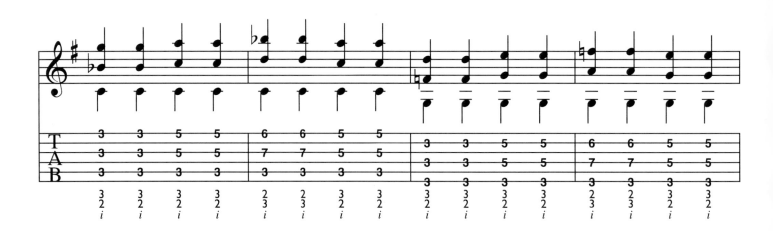

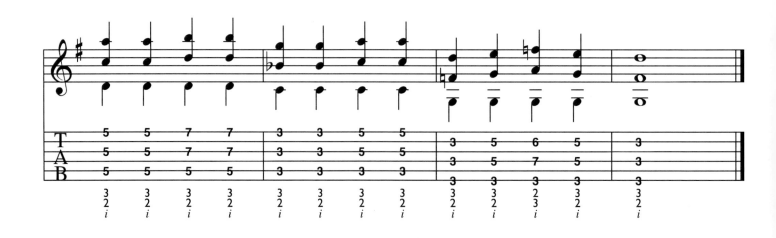

"The scrape" is basically a left-hand strum. "Scrape" the left-hand fingers from the previous chord, in this case the 2nd and 3rd fingers, across the strings in downward motion (towards the floor). The scrape is indicate, with this sign: Scr.

Notice the slide into the last, scraped chord in *Guru's Song*. The *i* finger slides up from the A♯ on the 6th fret to the B on the 7th fret as the left hand scrapes the open top four strings.

GURU'S SONG

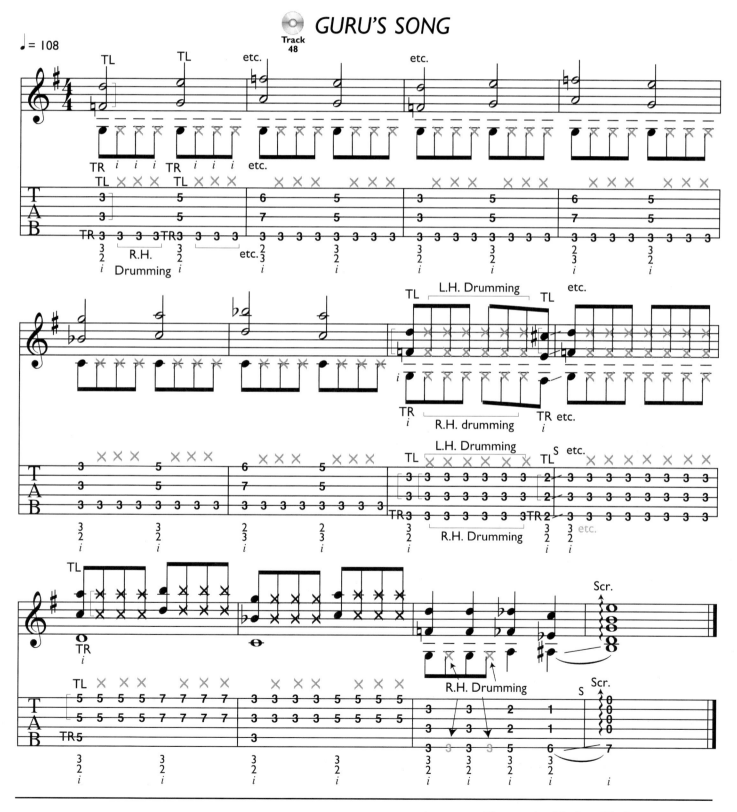

In *Guru's Dance*, be sure all of the notes are of accurate duration and even volume. Practice every group of triplets with the practice techniques of rearranging finger (note) order (see page 202), shifting accents (see page 203) and contrasting groups (see page 204).

GURU'S DANCE

Track 49

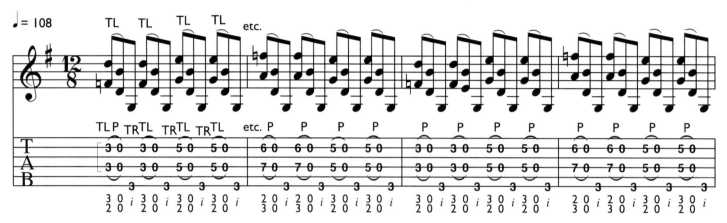

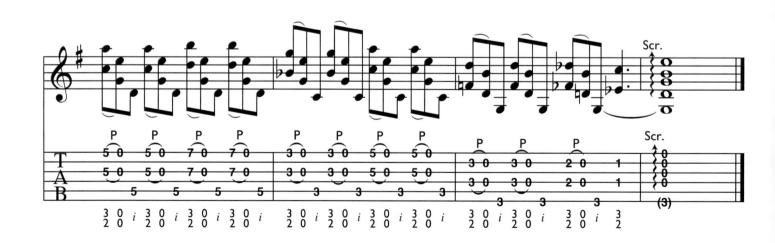

Slapping (SL) is what the name suggests. Snapping your wrist, slap the strings with the *m* finger of your right hand. Striking the strings this way will make your notes begin with a percussive attack. Also, in the second half of this piece there are some drummed notes ⅄. These drums are performed on the strings just above the sound hole with the palm of the right hand. The strings are muted during the drum, since the drum stops their vibration.

FLY BALL

Track 50

♩ = 108

There are as many ways to drum on the guitar as your imagination will allow. This time, try right hand drumming with the *m* finger over the fret board, so that the strings click against the frets. This will be written with a bold "X." Where you see a light "X," drum much lighter so that the strings do not click against the strings.

Notice that the left-hand fingering pattern in *Native Heart* is the same on the 6th, 5th and 4th strings as it is on the 5th, 4th and 3rd. As always, there is a subtle change when the 2nd string is involved because of the tuning of the guitar.

NATIVE HEART

Track 51

Pay special attention to the pattern in measures seven and eight of *Ping Pong Blues*. There is a pull-off from a note that has been tapped with the right hand, so the right hand performs the pull-off.

PING PONG BLUES

Track 52

♩ = 120

Shuffle

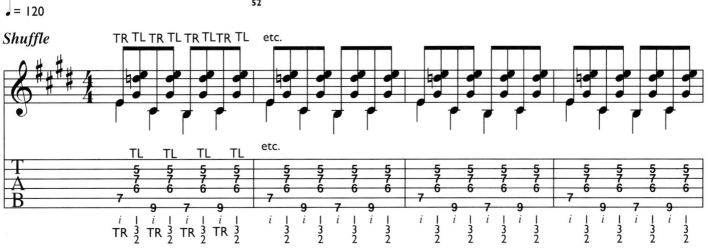

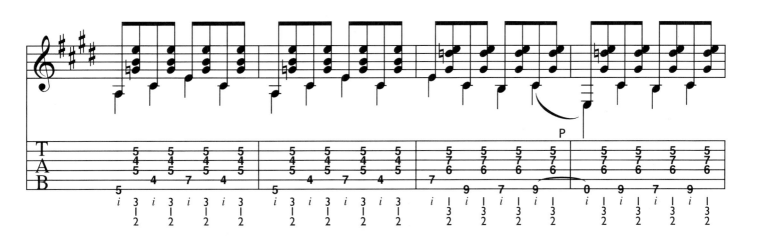

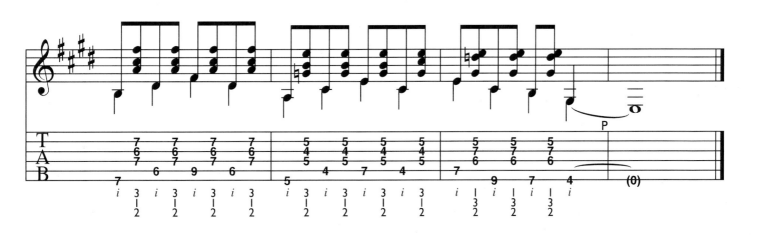

THE OSTINATO PATTERN, RIGHT-HAND STRING STOPPING AND SLAP HARMONICS

An *ostinato* is an accompaniment pattern that repeats. *String stopping* is the technical term used for pressing on the string at a desired fret. Traditionally it is done with the left hand, but it can also be done with a right-hand finger (usually *i*). When stopping a string with *i*, you will need to pluck with your *a* finger. This is indicated with a right-hand fingering where you would ordinarily find a left hand fingering, under the 6th string in the TAB and with (RS) in the notation. Another very cool technique is to create natural harmonics by forcefully slapping with the right hand the spot you would usually lightly touch with the left hand. This

technique is called *slap harmonics* and, as with right-hand stopping, it is indicated with a right-hand fingering for a natural harmonic (*m*) where you would ordinarily find a left hand fingering.

The repeating tapping rhythm *Judah's Harp* that begins after the fourth ending is an ostinato pattern. Where you see an "✕," gently drum on the body of the guitar with the middle finger of the right hand. The RS notes are tricky, and should be practiced alone before playing them in the context of the piece.

JUDAH'S HARP

Track 53

This is the technique made famous by guitarist Eddie Van Halen. Serious guitarists should give this tapping technique attention comparable to that of traditional slurs (hammering-on and pulling-off). The principles of movement are the same for both.

Review the instructions for right- and left-hand tapping pages 235, 236 and 243; the same principles apply. Plant the notes of the left hand at the same time the right-hand note is tapped. The index finger of the right hand should pull-off directly towards the palm of the right hand and touch the adjacent string in the process. During the right-hand pull-off, use the fingernail of the index finger to increase clarity. Resting the thumb of the right hand on the upper side of the neck greatly increases accuracy and stability. To achieve equality of duration and volume, practice any single group of triplets with the practice techniques of shifting accents, contrasting groups and rearranging finger (note) order. Important: make sure the tapped note is held for its full duration before pulling-off. Also, open strings tend to be louder than stopped notes. When pulling-off to an open string, be smooth and gentle.

BLAZING RIPPLES

Track 54

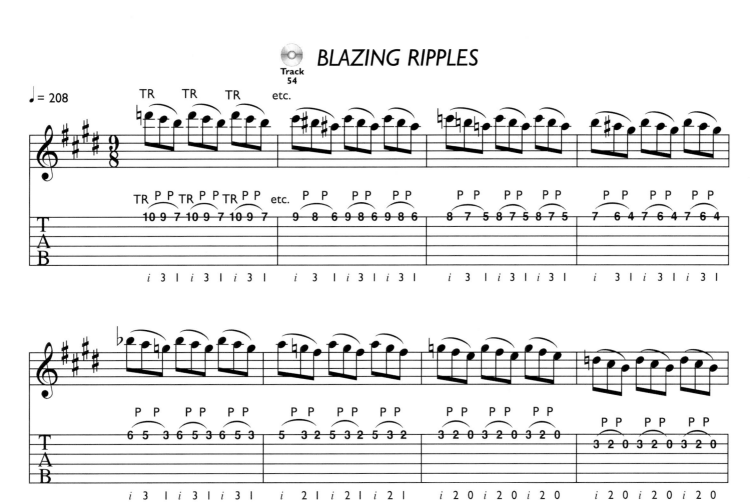

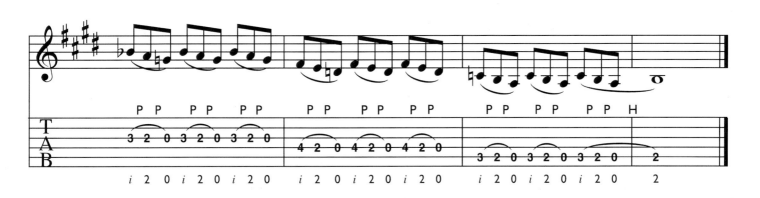

To achieve equality of duration and volume, practice any single group of sixteenth notes with the practice techniques of shifting accents, contrasting groups and rearranging finger (note) order.

DIGITAL SHOWERS

Track 55

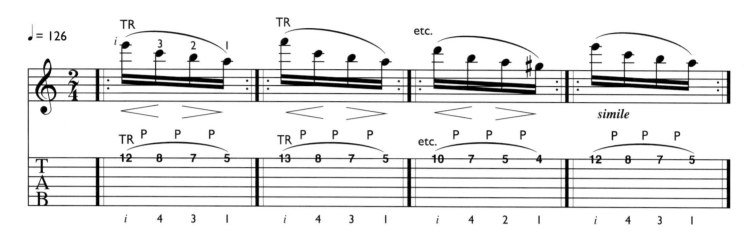

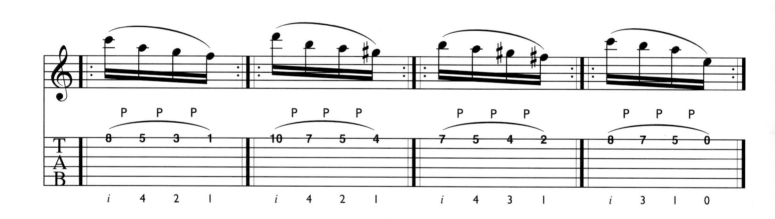

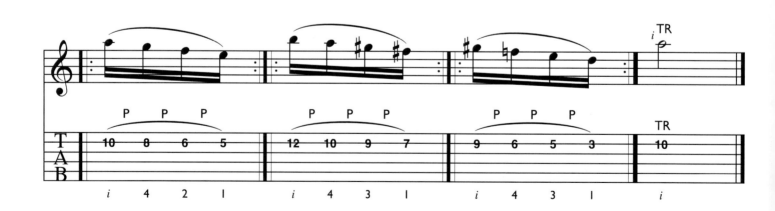

Planting prior to playing harmonics can greatly increase your accuracy. Practice the planting preparation gestures in Example 29 A) through E) before moving on. Timing is the key to successful planting.

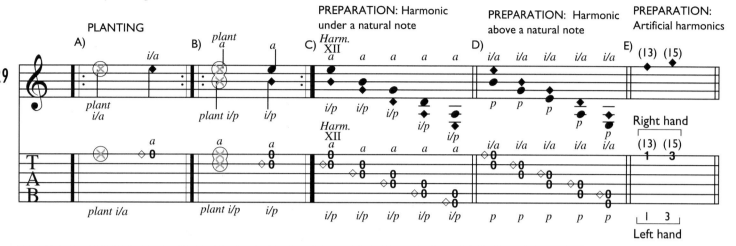

ARTIFICIAL HARMONICS

Artificial harmonics are harmonics that occur above fretted notes. As you know, the most common natural harmonic is found at the 12th fret—one octave above the fundamental tone. If you fret a note and then touch the fret that is twelve frets above it (one octave higher) with your *i* finger, plucking with your *a* finger, the result will be an artificial harmonic. See page 118 for a complete review of this technique.

Master the harmonics in *Celestial Bodies* first, before adding the non-harmonics. Play the harmonics firmly and loudly.

Celestial Bodies

Track 56

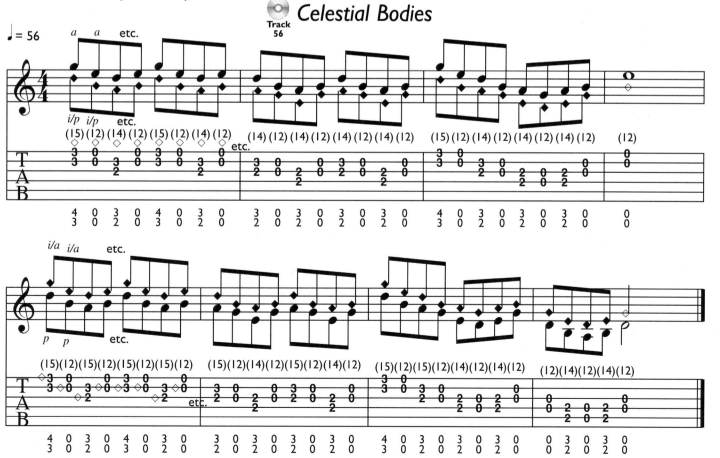

Use these exercises to prepare for the next piece.

A)

R.H. PREPARATION: Harmonic under

B)

R.H. PREPARATION: Harmonic Over

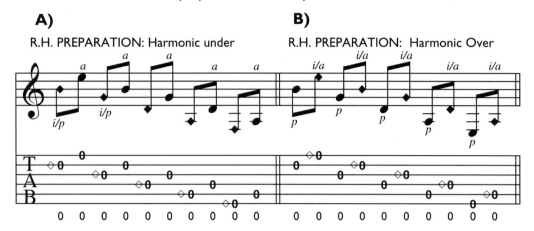

After you have mastered *Twinkling Gems* try this technique with wider intervals (skipping a string). The numbers in parentheses over the TAB indicate which fret to touch with the right hand.

TWINKLING GEMS

Track 57

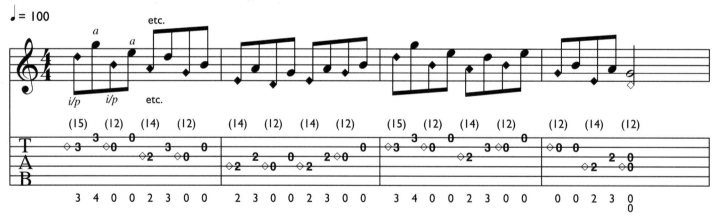

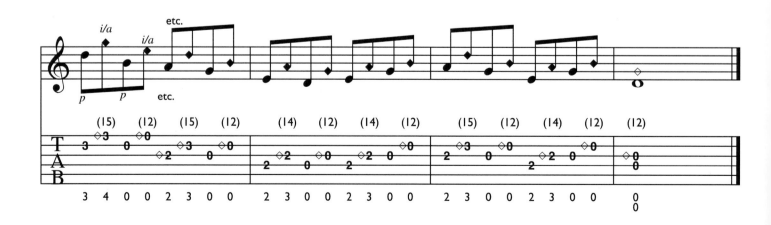

CHAPTER 7

Alternate Tunings

Understanding and using alternate tunings greatly expands the creative possibilities for the fingerstyle guitarist. Many guitarists are so conditioned to standard tuning fingerings that they hesitate to venture into the realm of alternate tunings. This fear of alternate tunings is unnecessary, because while the string to string relationships are different in alternate tunings, the characteristics of movement up and down an individual string are the same; twelve frets still represent one octave of the chromatic scale.

TUNING EXPLORATION #1: ONE STOPPED STRING

A stopped string is any string that is fingered (stopped) by the left hand. This exercise demonstrates the value of movement up and down the neck on a single string.

1. Re-tune your guitar to any set of notes that sounds good (usually lower and with the root on one of the bass strings.) The choice of notes is your creative decision.
2. On the 1st string, find a scale that sounds good in relationship to the open strings.
3. Create an improvisation using this scale in various combinations with other open strings.
4. Repeat this process by improvising up and down the neck on the 2nd string.
5. Continue with short improvisations on the 3rd, then 4th, 5th and 6th strings.

TUNING EXPLORATION #2: TWO OR MORE STOPPED STRINGS

1. Using a creative tuning of your choice, create an improvisation using similar motion between two stopped strings. Incorporate various combinations of open strings. For example, try various picking explorations with the stopped string set of the 5th and 1st strings (5/1) in combination with other open strings.
2. Repeat this process using other sets of two stopped strings.
3. Incorporate oblique motion and contrary motion into explorations of two stopped strings.

When working with two or more stopped strings, the relationship of the notes on one stopped string to another is important. These relationships hold to the following principles of movement:

    1. similar motion—two voices moving in the same direction
    2. oblique motion—one voice remains still as the other moves
    3. contrary motion—two voices move in opposite directions

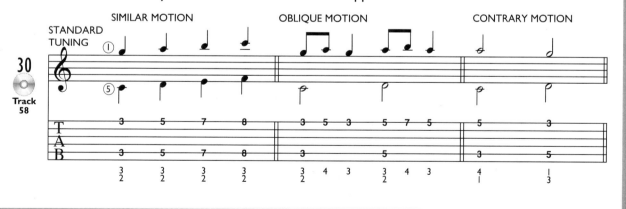

String Sets

In this chapter, string sets will be indicated in parentheses as follows: (5/1) means: the 5th and 1st string are stopped while the other strings remain open. (6/2/1) means that the 6th, 2nd and 1st strings are stopped while the other strings remain open. This system can apply to any combination of stopped strings.

TUNING INSTRUCTIONS FROM STANDARD TUNING:

Lower the 6th string E two whole steps to C.

Match the open 5th string to the 7th fret of the 6th string.

Match the open 4th string to the 5th fret of the 5th string.

Match the open 3rd string to the 3rd fret of the 4th string.

Match the open 2nd string to the 6th fret of the 3rd string.

Match the open 1st string the 5th fret of the 2nd string.

String intervals: 5th, 4th, ♭3rd, ♯4th, 4th.

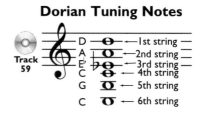

Dorian Tuning Notes

For tunings such as this one that are considerably below standard pitch, it is helpful to pick the strings somewhat closer to the bridge.

The right-hand drumming technique in measure three of *The Forest Sings* is accomplished by drumming the middle finger of the right hand on the bass strings. At [C], during the first chord, the 5th string is muted with the fleshy side of the 2nd finger. In fingerstyle playing, the left hand is frequently called on for muting purposes.

Observations by section:

[A] Arpeggiation of open strings

[B] One stopped string (1st string) in combination with open strings

[C] Two stopped strings (6/1) in oblique and similar motion

[D] Two stopped stings (6/1) in similar motion

[E] Left hand tapped ostinato with right hand tapped double stops

THE FOREST SINGS

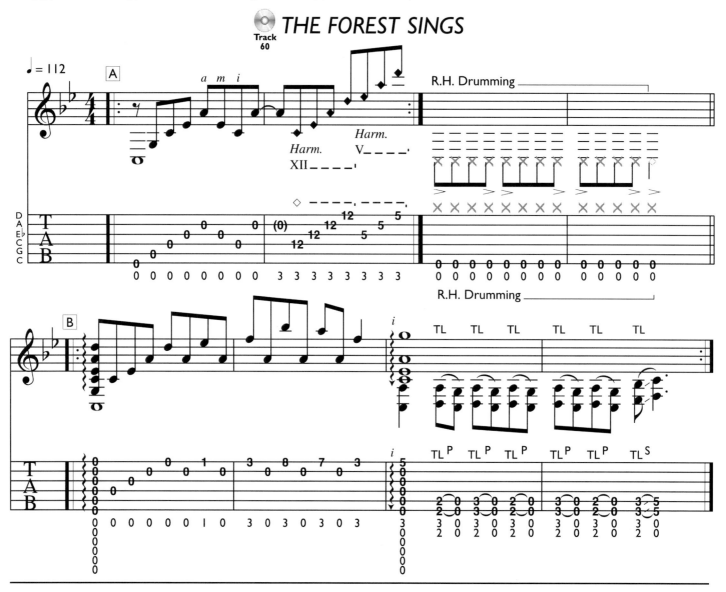

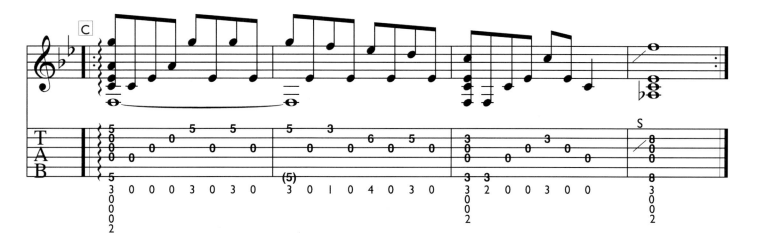

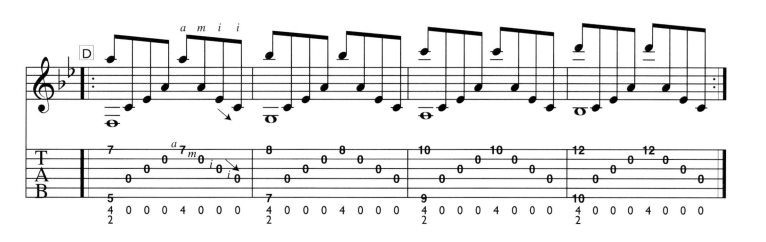

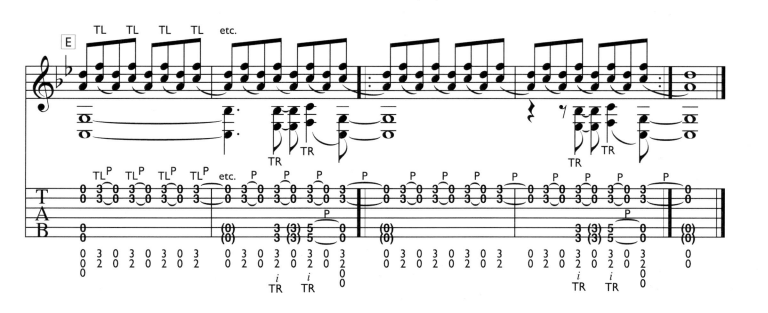

TUNING INSTRUCTIONS FROM STANDARD TUNING:

Lower the 6th string E two whole steps to C.
Match the open 5th string to the 7th fret of the 6th string.
Match the open 4th string to the 6th fret of the 5th string.
Match the open 3rd string to the 4th fret of the 4th string.
Match the open 2nd string to the 2nd fret of the 3rd string.
Match the open 1st string to the 5th fret of the 2nd string.
String intervals: 5th, ♭5th, 3rd, 2nd, 4th.

Phrygian Tuning Notes

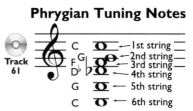

Track 61

Observations by section:

A Two stopped strings (1/2); similar motion; Travis picking pattern

B Partial bar with added melody note; measure three - banjo pattern

C Two stopped strings (6/5); similar motion with added melody note; Travis pattern.

D Two stopped strings (1/2) with pull-offs to open strings

E The right hand should drum on the open bass strings while the left hand drums on the
guitar where indicated by the ✕'s

F With the middle finger of the right hand, slap bass string where marked "SL." Where
indicated with the ✕'s, drum on the muted bass string with same finger. Muting
is accomplished by touching the string with the fingers of the left hand.

VIOLET STRATOSPHERE

Track 62

♩ = 152

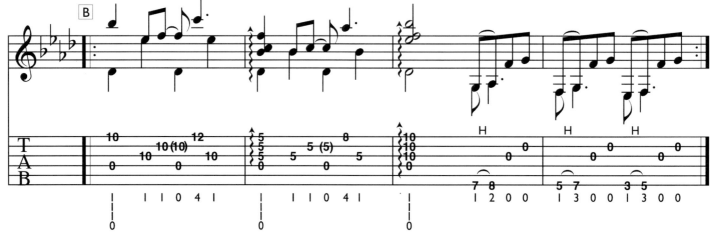

LYDIAN TUNING: C, G, D, E, F♯, B

TUNING INSTRUCTIONS FROM STANDARD TUNING:
Lower the 6th string E two whole steps to C.
Match the open 5th string to the 7th fret of the 6th string.
Match the open 4th string to the 7th fret of the 5th string.
Match the open 3rd string to the 2nd fret of the 4th string.
Match the open 2nd string to the 2nd fret of the 3rd string.
Match the open 1st string to the 5th fret of the 2nd string.
String intervals: 5th, 5th, 2nd, 2nd, 4th.

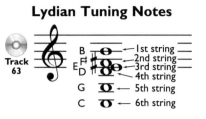

Lydian Tuning Notes

Track 63

Tonal Sculpture uses the following techniques:
SL = slap the strings percussively with the fingers of the right hand
TL = tap the note with the appropriate finger of the left hand

Observations by section:
A	One stopped string (6th)
B	Three stopped strings (6/3/2)
C	Two stopped strings (5/1); oblique motion
D	One stopped string (4)

CODA Metric modulation (third measure): the value of an eighth note remains constant but the rhythmic groupings change. The result is $\frac{9}{8}$ time.

TONAL SCULPTURE

Track 64

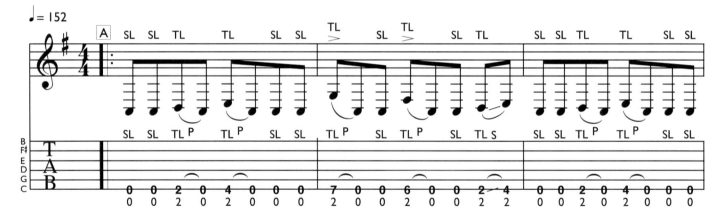

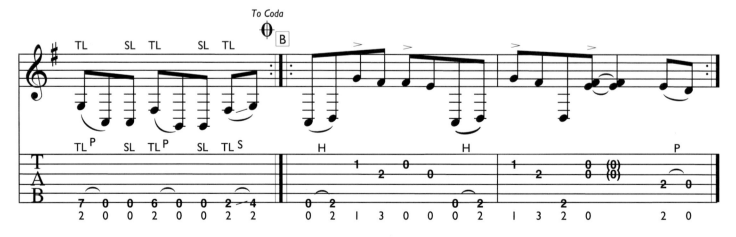

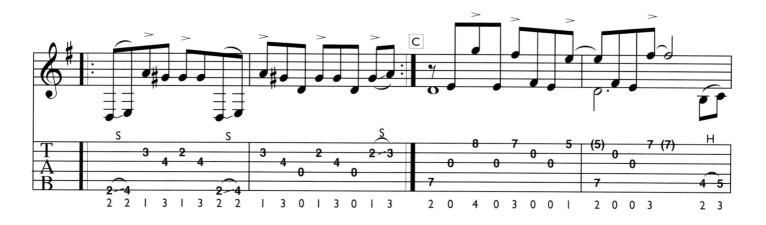

D. C. al Coda

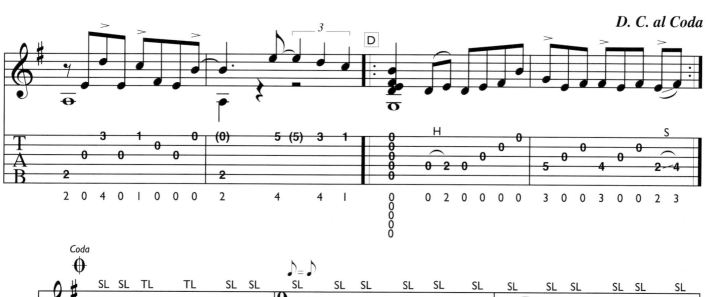

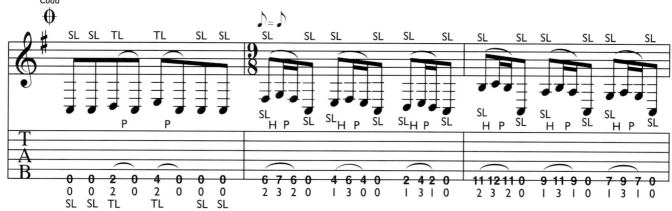

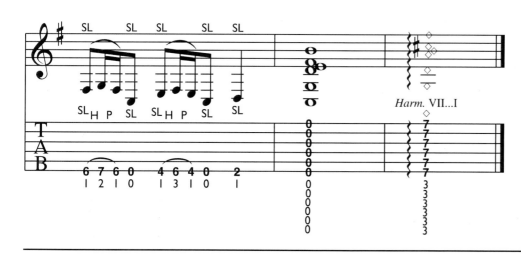

TUNING INSTRUCTIONS FROM STANDARD TUNING:

Lower the 6th string E two whole steps to C.

Match the open 5th string to the 7th fret of the 6th string.

Match the open 4th string to the 3rd fret of the 5th string.

Match the open 3rd string to the 6th fret of the 4th string.

Match the open 2nd string to the 3rd fret of the 3rd string.

Match the open 1st string the 5th fret of the 2nd string.

String intervals: 5th, ♭3rd, ♭5, ♭3rd, 4th.

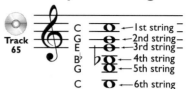

Mixolydian Tuning Notes

Track 65

In *Already Dressed*, watch the following:

    SL = slap the bass strings with the fingers of the right hand.

    In Section C, slide up to the first note, and down off of the following notes.

Observations by section:

A One stopped string (5th)

B Two stopped strings moving across the strings

C Two stopped strings (1/2) moving up and down the neck

D Use of a movable barre

ALREADY DRESSED

AEOLIAN TUNING: D, G, D, G, B♭, F

TUNING INSTRUCTIONS FROM STANDARD TUNING:

Lower the 6th string E one whole step to D.

Match the open 5th string to the 5th fret of the 6th string.

Match the 4th string to the 7th fret of the 5th string.

Match the open 3rd string to the 5th fret of the 4th string.

Match the 2nd string to the 3rd fret of the 3rd string.

Match the open 1st string to the 4th fret of the 2nd string.

String intervals: 4th, 5th, 4th, ♭3rd, 3rd.

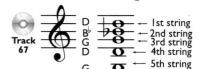

Aeolian Tuning Notes

Billowing Atmospheres uses the following techniques:

TL = Tap with the left hand

RS = Right hand string stopping. Stop the desired note with the *i*
finger of the right hand. Pluck the string with the *a* finger of the right hand. Right
hand string stopping *is* facilitated by allowing the weight of your arm to help push
the string to the fret. The plucking is facilitated by planting the *a* finger in advance
of doing the actual plucking.

Observations by section:

A One stopped string (6th) with pull-offs to open string

B Harmonics performed with the right hand above an ostinato tapped with the left hand

C Right hand string stopping above a left hand ostinato

D Two stopped strings (6/5) in combination with open strings

E Two stopped strings (5/1) with pull-offs to open strings

Notice the unusual groupings of beats throughout.

BILLOWING ATMOSPHERES

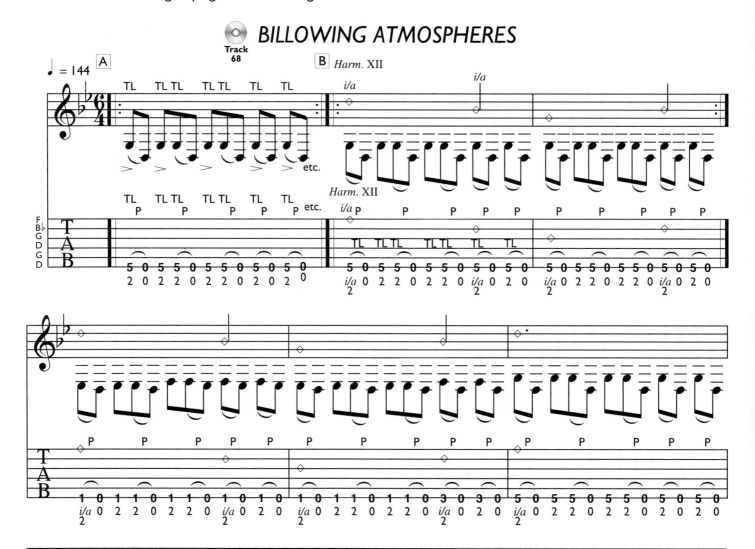

TUNING INSTRUCTIONS FROM STANDARD TUNING:

Lower the 6th string E one whole step to D.

Match the open 5th string to the 5th fret of the 6th string.

Match the open 4th string the 7th fret of the 5th string.

Match the open 3rd string to the 5th fret of the 4th string.

Match the open 2nd string the 4th fret of the 3rd string.

Match the open 1st string the 4th fret of the 2nd string.

String intervals: 4th, 5th, 4th, 3rd, 3rd.

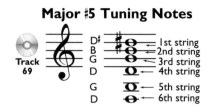

Major ♯5 Tuning Notes

Track 69

D♯	1st string
B	2nd string
G	3rd string
D	4th string
G	5th string
D	6th string

The Conqueror uses the following techniques:

    TL = Left hand tapping

    ✕ = Use the 3rd and 2nd fingers of the left hand to lightly drum on the strings, not producing a pitch.

In sections B through D, the bass line is highlighted in gray for the sake of clarity. In the D section: plant the *a* finger of the right hand resting on the first string for stability. The continuation of the ostinato through the two measures of this section is partially an illusion. It is impossible to maintain it in its exact form since the bass line uses the same strings. In the F section. since open strings tend to be louder than stopped strings, be gentle on the open first string.

Observations by section:

A	Two stopped strings (2/3) produce an ostinato that includes left hand drumming
B C D	An arpeggio builds with the right hand eventually spanning five strings while the ostinato continues
F	One stopped string (2) in combination with open strings in a Travis pattern

THE CONQUEROR

Track 70

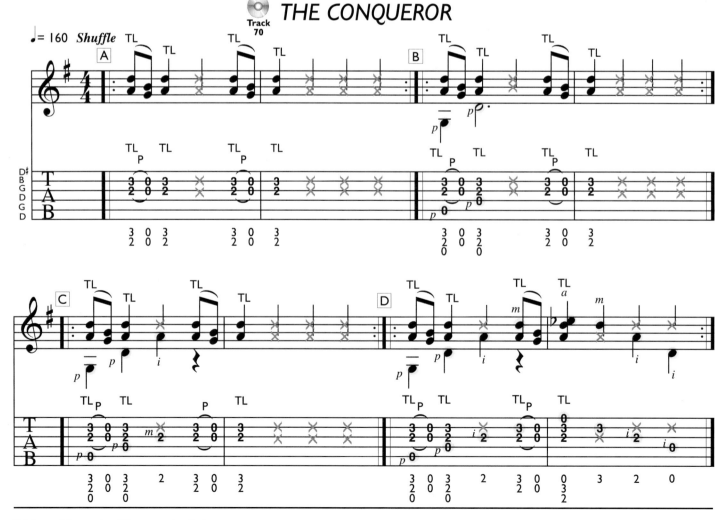

TUNING INSTRUCTIONS FROM STANDARD TUNING:

Lower the 6th string E two whole steps to C.
Match the open 5th string to the 5th fret of the 6th string.
Match the open 4th string to the 7th fret of the 5th string.
Match the open 3rd string to the 7th fret of the 4th string.
Match the open 2nd string the 2nd fret of the 3rd string.
Match the open 1st string to the 5th fret of the 2nd string.
String intervals: 4th, 5th, 5th, 2nd, 4th.

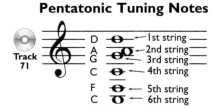

Pentatonic Tuning Notes

In the A section of *Global Unity*, drum on the strings with the fingers of the right hand where indicated with the ✗'s. In the B section, pluck the strings close to the bridge (*ponticello*). In the E section, lightly drum on the strings with the 4th and 3rd fingers of the left hand where indicated with the ✗'s. In the F section, use the wrist of the right hand to drum against the neck just above the soundhole where indicated with the ✗'s.

Observations by section:

A Two stopped strings (4/2) and (1/2)
B Two stopped strings (6/4)
C Three stopped strings (5/3/2)
D Two stopped strings (5/1); oblique motion
E Two stopped strings (1/2) create a left hand ostinato while the right hand plays
       harmonics and tapped triple stops
F Two stopped strings (4/2) as part of a strum pattern.

GLOBAL UNITY

Track 72

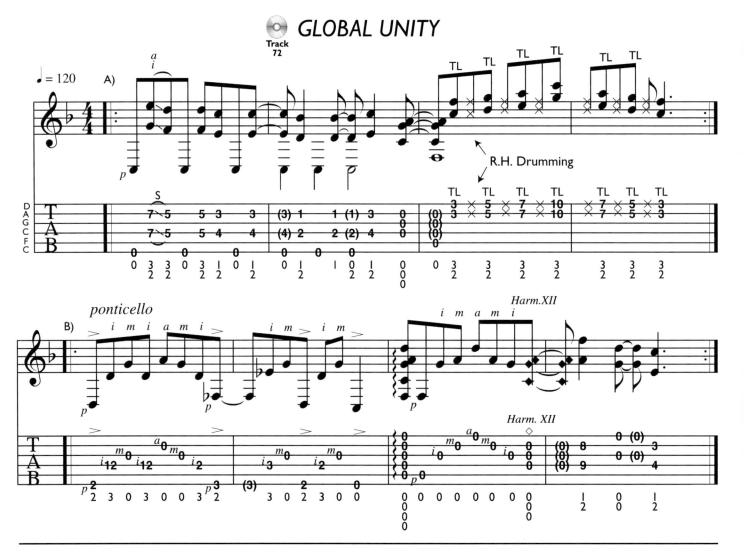

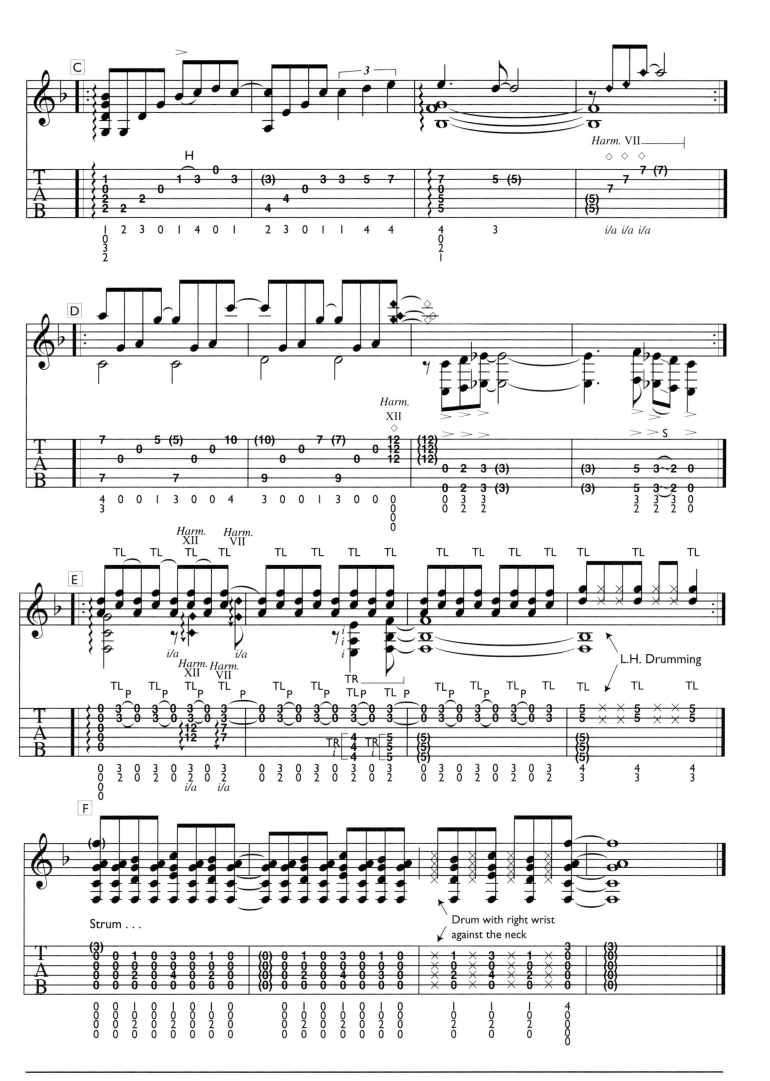

CREATING YOUR OWN ARRANGEMENTS IN ALTERED TUNINGS

Although bushwhacking through the wilderness on your explorations can be rewarding, at times it helps to have a compass to get your bearings. The blank template on the next page is provided for that purpose. You can use it, as demonstrated at right, to discover the names of the notes you're using. Studying it closely will also reveal guitaristic patterns and shapes for you to explore and develop.

At right is an example of how to use the blank template. The notes of the C Dorian scale have been written on the template. This is a great guide for composing and improvising in the C Dorian tuning. As you create your own tunings, create a chart such as this using your blank template.

Alternate Tuning Note Guide

ALTERNATE TUNING SUMMARY

- Playing in alternate tunings opens up new creative possibilities.
- Playing in alternate tunings is a required skill for the well-rounded fingerstyle player.
- The traditionally-schooled player can learn to play in altered tunings with the understanding of stopped string sets, and scale movement up and down the neck.
- Alternate tunings usually include the root tone of the mode or key suggested by the tuning on one of the bass strings.
- Alternate tunings contribute a unifying element to fingerstyle guitar compositions. Pieces using open tunings tend to involve lots of open strings. The frequency of the repetitions of these open strings creates a specific character that binds the piece together.

PROJECT:
Compose your next series of fingerstyle guitar compositions using a different tuning for each. Try tunings with root tones on various strings and in a variety of modes and keys.

ALTERNATE TUNING NOTE GUIDE
(A TEMPLATE FOR REPRODUCTION)

Tuning - ◯ ◯ ◯ ◯ ◯ ◯

Mode:

Root String: ◯

5fr.

7fr.

10fr.

12fr.

5fr.

7fr.

10fr.

12fr.

This page is provided to be photocopied as necessary. No other pages in this book may be reproduced by any means without written consent from the publisher.

CHAPTER 8

Arranging and Composition

Creativity is natural.

Seeds are gathered, planted and nurtured. Over time the seeds sprout. With continued sunshine and rain, a garden will grow and there will be a harvest. The cycle of birth and growth is governed by the laws of nature, and so is human creativity and musical composition.

Creativity is a science.

The professional guitarist does not always have the luxury of waiting for profound moments of enlightenment. Instead the professional sits down, gathers together the appropriate techniques and tools of the trade and follows a method that works. This is similar to the farmer who follows an agricultural method, or the scientist who follows the scientific method.

METHODOLOGY

The following is a description of a creative method using the seed metaphor.

- **Gather the seeds**— Find a musical model. The model should be similar in form and style to the one you intend to write.
- **Plant the seeds**— Make a diagram of the structure and characteristics of your model. This will serve as your outline or template (or the plot of ground for your garden). See page 286.
- **Nurture the seedlings**—If you are creating written music, keep the hand moving and don't think too much (like the farmer you will weed, prune and sort later). Have lots of paper on hand (and also a large waste basket). Playfully discover lots of variations and possibilities. If you are creating non-written music, have a small tape recorder on your desk to preserve ideas. Use your model as a guide, but feel free to follow your own impulses as they arise.
- **The Harvest**— Here is where you sort, organize and improve your ideas. Keep the best and disregard the rest. Arrange the best ideas into a beautiful bouquet.

Once you have successfully experienced a method that works for you, remember it. It is just as likely to recur again as the seasons of the year do. Don't rigidly stick to the method however, it is as likely to change just as the weather changes from year to year.

MUSICAL ARCHITECTURE, OR GUITARISTICS?
These are two distinct approaches to composing for the guitar. Knowledge and utilization of both increases the potential for an aesthetically pleasing works of art.
- Musical Architecture—Creating purely musical ideas and then transferring them to the guitar.
- Guitaristics—Using patterns and qualities unique to the guitar as the basis for the composition.

A "TO DO..." LIST FOR COMPOSERS AND ARRANGERS

- Start a file of your own guitar techniques and ideas. As you mature artistically, you will develop certain signature techniques. Write these down and save them. Referring to them in the future can help spark ideas.
- Sketch. Notate a composition without the use of a guitar. It doesn't matter if you have perfect pitch or the ear of Mozart. Using blank sheets of manuscript paper, jot down a musical fantasy indicating melodic contours, emotions and dynamics. Do this in real time (as if you were Mozart). Later, pick up a guitar and use your sketch as a guide. Refine the ideas into a finished composition.
- Develop your own code or shorthand. Sometimes creative ideas come faster than the can be notated. Shorthand techniques include using notes with no stems, no bar lines, light and dark notes, large and small notes, writing several options on top of each other, leaving lots of space in between notes, using footnotes to indicate several options for one section and others.
- Study the art of music notation. Music notation is an art in itself and enables you to share your compositions with others.
- Study sculpture, drawing and design. The same aesthetic principals, including unity, variety and balance, apply.
- Study creative writing. The same principles of discovery, drafting and revision apply.
- Find a Mentor. Choose a musical guru. Learning the music of one musical master in depth can take you to a higher level than dabbling in the work of many. While it is desirable to make personal contact with a living master, studying books, videos and recordings will also work.
- Research Sources of Inspiration. Inspiration can come from spirituality, nature, mythology, art history, nationalism, humor and other sources. Delving into these and other areas of inquiry is one of the great joys of creativity.
- Purchase an electric eraser. This valuable tool can be ordered from most office supply stores.
- Purchase a professional pencil. It is essential to use a pencil with lead dark enough to photocopy, and with a grip that is comfortable.

ARRANGING *SCARBOROUGH FAIR*

On the following pages are several variations on the traditional tune, *Scarborough Fair* (the original melody is shown below). Some of these are architectural in nature and others are purely guitaristic. Look for examples of both approaches. On page 286 you will find a sample structural outline and rhythm outline, and on page 287 there is list of melodic variation techniques, both of which will help your arranging.

SCARBOROUGH FAIR

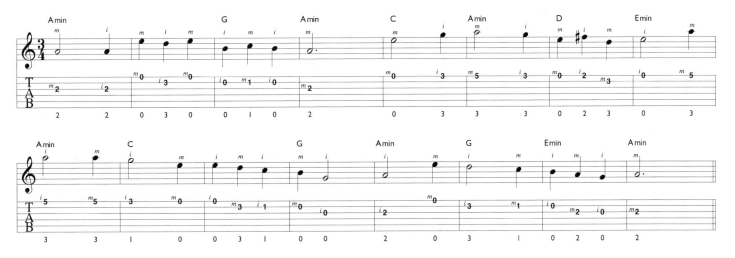

When approaching a new song, ask yourself, "What can I do that is a little different from other versions of this song?" In the following guitaristic variation, modern tapping techniques have been used to give the melody a fresh sound.

Scarborough Fair: Rhythmic Variations uses the following techniques:

- TL = Left hand tapping.
- TR = Right hand tapping.
- SL = String Slapping—With the fingers of the right hand, slap the strings percussively so that they click against the frets.

To play the last chord, pound the wrist percussively on the finger board. Be sure that the strings are muted.

SCARBOROUGH FAIR: RHYTHMIC VARIATIONS

Track 73

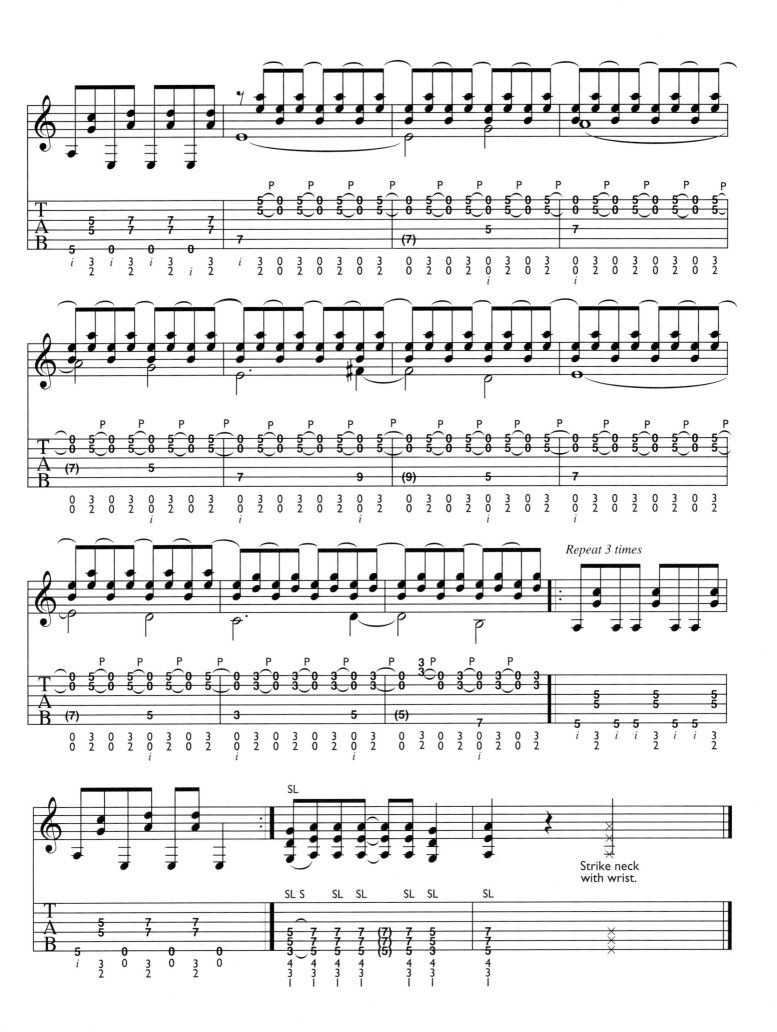

A *motive* (also called a motif) is a short phrase used in the development of an arrangement or composition. Motifs that portray a defining character are good choices for development. The identification of these motifs is the prerogative of the arranger. In the following example, three motifs have been labeled with brackets.

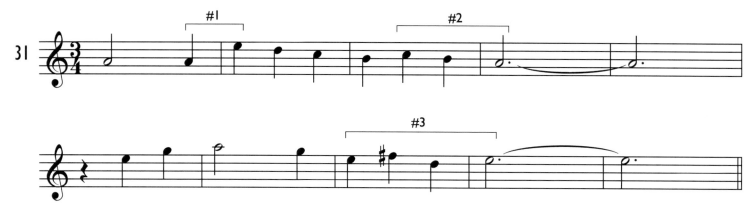

In Scarborough Fair: Motivic Variations, these motifs are presented on different levels of the scale (transposed). In measures 13 and 14 there are "fill" notes in between the notes of the motive. Subtle variations on the repeated motives create interest while still contributing to thematic unity. In the second to the last measure, bracket #1a presents motive #1 in reverse. This is referred to as retrograde.

Play freely and with expression.

SCARBOROUGH FAIR: MOTIVIC VARIATIONS

Track 74

In the following arrangement, the circled notes represent the melody of *Scarborough Fair*. The melodic rhythm has been stretched out in order to insert other material. The (*8va*) above certain notes indicates that the melody has been transposed up an octave.

Notice the repeated use of the interval of a 4th. This helps define a character in the musical drama. Notice the use of non-diatonic tones (notes from outside the key) three measures from the end which creates surprise and helps to hold the listener's interest.

Play very expressively. Notice the many arpeggiated chords. Experiment with varying your arpeggiated chords, especially at the end of the arrangement. For instance, try reversing the direction—"roll" the chord from the 1st string down to the 6th.

SCARBOROUGH FAIR: MELODIC ELASTICITY

Track 75

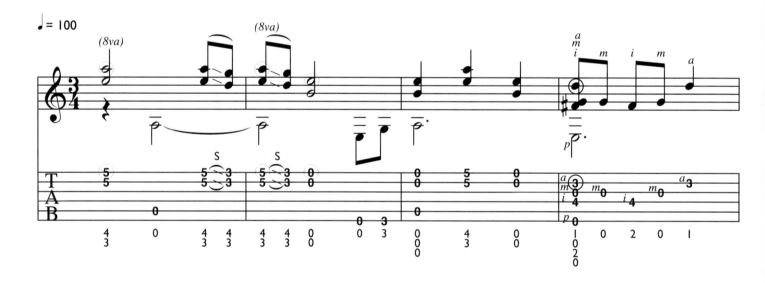

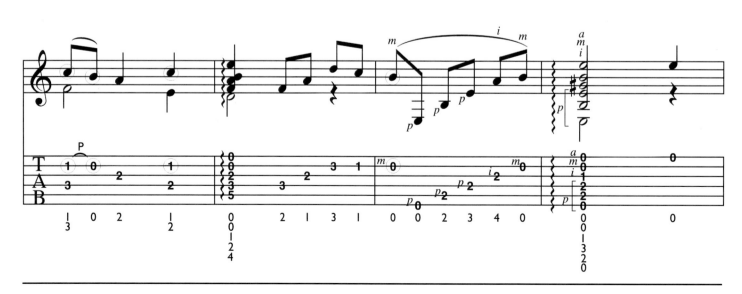

In developing variations on a folk song such as *Scarborough Fair*, the original rhythm may be retained while the melody is completely changed. The rhythm will still be recognizable to the listener, while the new melody creates variety.

For additional practice:
1) Write a variation using fragments of the original melody, but using completely different rhythms.
2) Extend the following arrangement, continuing to create new melodies and harmonies using the original rhythm of Scarborough Fair. Leave out the last three measures of this arrangement, perhaps put them at the end of your extended arrangement.

Focus on the rhythm of *Scarborough Fair* as you play this piece. Although the melody is quite different from *Scarborough Fair*, you want it to <u>move</u> as *Scarborough Fair* <u>moves</u>.

SCARBOROUGH FAIR: SAME RHYTHM, DIFFERENT MELODY

Track 76

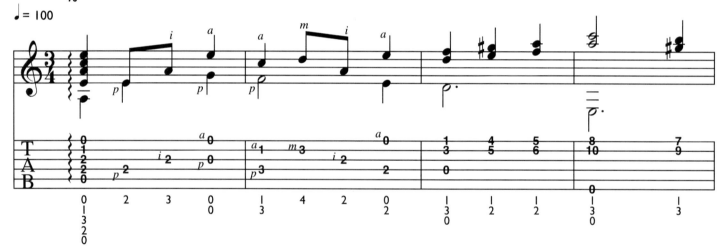

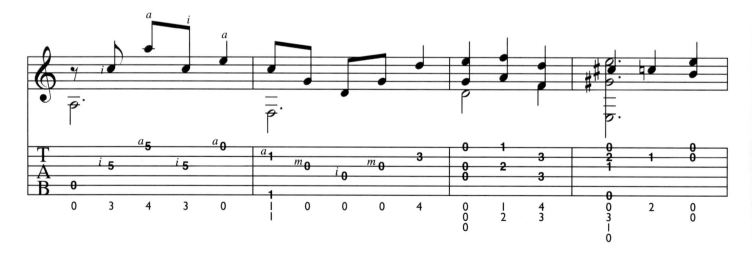

Harmonizing a diatonic melody with non-diatonic tones helps to build energy, momentum and interest. Intervals of minor 9ths, minor 2nds, major 7ths, augmented 4ths and 2nds are useful tools for this purpose.

Measures 2 & 3:   Major triads moving in strict parallel motion underneath the melody.

Measures 4-7:   Voicings in 4ths moving in half steps and whole steps underneath the melody.

Measures 10-12:   A single line moving in chromatic motion underneath the melody.

Measure 13:   The G melody note is harmonized with a non-diatonic triad.

Measures 14-17:   Dominant 7th (13th) chords moving in half-steps underneath the melody.

Measures 18-21:   Each measure is harmonized with a surprise chord. In this case, the "numerical" value of the melody note is changed to our guitaristic advantage. For example, in measure 19 the melody note E originally would be the 5th of A Minor. Here it is changed to the 6th of G Minor. This technique, which is discussed more in the next section on modulation (page 284) is called *interpolation*.

Measures 22 & 23:   The melody is harmonized with ♯11 chords moving in strict parallel motion.

Measure 24:   The melody is harmonized with diatonic and non-diatonic triads, superimposed over non-diatonic and diatonic bass tones.

Last measure: Take any melody note and hang a surprising guitaristic chord underneath it.

For the very last chord, use the *waterfall technique*: (1) strum the chord normally with the thumb (2) play a three-finger tremolo (*a, m, i*) on the highest string (3) while the tremolo motion continues, drag the fingers across the strings from the highest to lowest in pitch (4) end with the index finger playing the lowest note of the chord.

♩ = 100

Rubato

SCARBOROUGH FAIR: HARMONIC VARIATIONS

Track 77

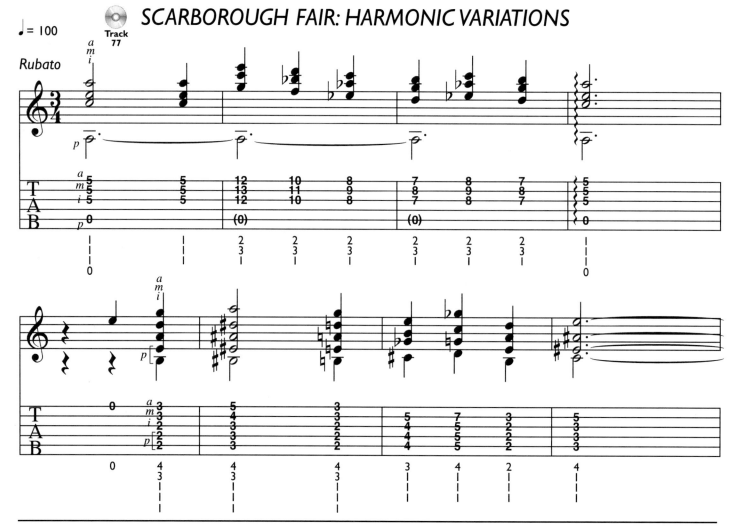

Musical *modulation* is the change from one key to another.

The following arrangement demonstrates several of the most common modulation techniques. Choices were made with guitaristic and musical considerations is mind.

1. *Interpolation*—Interpolation involves changing the numerical function of any note. The numerical function of A in the key of A Minor is "1." In this case the function has been interpolated to the numerical value of being the "9" of a G Minor chord. The G Minor chord then takes us in a new harmonic direction.

2. *Interchange*—Quality characteristics of one chord can be interchanged with that of another quality. In this case the D Major is interchanged with D Minor. Although major/minor interchange is common, any quality can be interchanged with another quality at the arranger's discretion. This also called *mutation*.

3. *Interpolation*—The E, which is the 2 of D Minor, becomes the 9 of C♯ Minor.

4. *Deceptive Resolution*— The listener expects a resolution to the tonic of the key of C♯ Minor. For the purpose of surprise, and to extend the piece, the chord movement avoids the tonic and lands on A Major, the diatonic ♭6 chord in the key of C♯ Minor.

5. *Leading-Tone Modulation*—Any tone of a chord can resolve by half-step up or down to any tone of another chord. In this case, the 5th of the A Major chord, E in measure 20, resolves down by a half-step to the 5th of A♭ Major. The concept of leading-tone modulation can be expanded so that any tone can lead to another tone in another chord using larger intervals. For example, the last C♯ in measure 20 could have led up a 4th to F♯ Minor.

This arrangement has a *homophonic* (melody and accompaniment) texture. Be sure the melody is clearly heard above the accompaniment.

SCARBOROUGH FAIR: MODULATION

Track 78

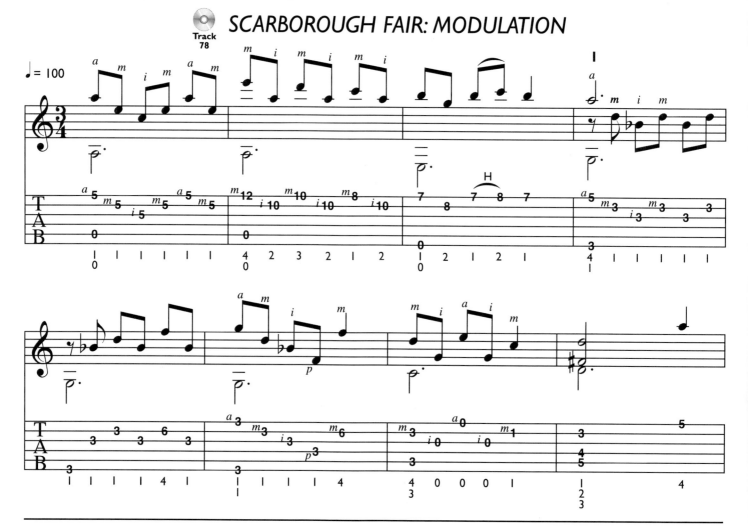

As a creative artist, you do not have to re-invent the wheel every time you begin a new piece. Following the examples of composers ranging from Bach to Duke Ellington, you should carefully study models to imitate, personalize and improve on. One way to remember this is with the slogan, "with every new project there should be a concurrent new study." Your structural map can be as simple or detailed as necessary. A detailed analysis would include the use of staff paper. A simple outline could look this:

STRUCTURAL CHARACTERISTICS	GUITAR TECHNIQUES	DURATIONS
slow, A Minor	block chords	:15
groove starts	muted bass pattern	:15
theme stated, A section	melody over picking pattern	:45
second theme, B section, C Mixolydian	higher range on neck	:45
interlude repose pattern	muted bass pattern	:15
improvisational section	tapped treble, bass melody	1:30
codetta, solo climax	strummed block chords/non diatonic tones	:15
soft, original groove resumes	muted bass pattern	:15
theme repeated with phrase extensions	melody over picking pattern	:45
original groove-meter change-fade	muted bass pattern	:30

Total Duration: 5:30

In addition to studying the structure of an individual piece as shown above, you can make a template of an entire album. Choose your favorite fingerstyle album and use a template like the one shown below.

SONG TITLE	TEMPO	METER	GROOVE	KEY/MODE

PLAYFUL MELODIC VARIATION

Starting with minimum amount of musical material and developing it increases the potential for compositional unity. Think of this concept as musical economy—we are doing a lot with a little. The following example demonstrates ways of developing the opening motif of *Scarborough Fair*.

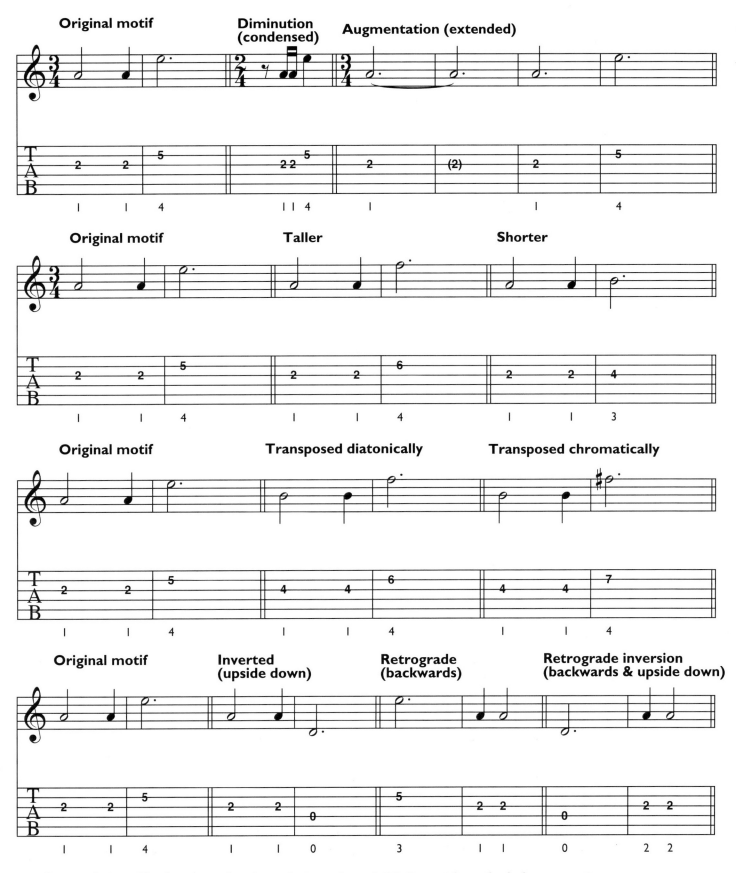

Congratulations. You have completed your journey through this fingerstyle method. As you continue on your musical travels, keep your mind and ears open to new ideas and keep learning. Happy trails!

alfred.com